Sir Thomas Browne

Twayne's English Authors Series

Arthur F. Kinney, Editor

University of Massachusetts, Amherst

TEAS 448

Sir Thomas Browne with his wife, Dorothy
Attributed to Joan Carlile, ca. 1641–50
Reproduced courtesy of the National Portrait Gallery, London

Sir Thomas Browne

By Jonathan F. S. Post

University of California, Los Angeles

Twayne Publishers
A Division of G. K. Hall & Co. • *Boston*

Sir Thomas Browne

Jonathan F. S. Post

Copyright © 1987 by G.K. Hall & Co.
All Rights Reserved
Published by Twayne Publishers
A Division of G.K. Hall & Co.
70 Lincoln Street
Boston, Massachusetts 02111

Copyediting supervised by Lewis DeSimone
Book production by Janet Zietowski
Book design by Barbara Anderson

Typeset in 11 pt. Garamond
by Modern Graphics, Inc., Weymouth, Massachusetts

Printed on permanent/durable acid-free paper
and bound in the United States of America

Library of Congress Cataloging-in-Publication Data

Post, Jonathan F. S., 1947
  Sir Thomas Browne.

  (Twayne's English authors series ; TEAS 448)
  Bibliography: p. 178
  Includes index.
  1. Browne, Thomas, Sir, 1605–1682—Criticism and
Interpretation.   I. Title.   II. Series.
PR3327.P67   1987   828'.409   86–29537
ISBN 0–8057–6948–X (alk. paper)

F. W. P. (1910–77)

Tabesne cadavera solvat
An rogus haud refert.

Contents

Editor's Note
About the Author
Preface
Chronology

Chapter One
Browne's Life: A "Cabinet of Rarities"   1

Chapter Two
The Magus and the Man of Science   24

Chapter Three
Browne's Religion: Playing Down Differences   40

Chapter Four
Elements of Style   56

Chapter Five
The Politics of Laughter: Comic Autobiography in
Religio Medici   76

Chapter Six
Pseudodoxia Epidemica, or Global Inquiries   95

Chapter Seven
Motives for Metaphor: *Urne-Buriall* and
The Garden of Cyrus   120

Chapter Eight
Christian Morals and After   147

Notes and References   159
Selected Bibliography   178
Index   185

Editor's Note

"Sir Thomas Browne," writes Jonathan F. S. Post, "discovered a flexible style that was sufficiently rarefied to reveal the odd twists and paradoxes of his profoundly inquisitive imagination." In a wide-ranging study of his own, Post not only shows but demonstrates how Browne's mind, grounded in the "collateral truths" of religion and science, combined a rich play of language with a serious commitment to pursuing knowledge in a world perceived as possessing various shades of meaning and a few elemental realities. Post examines, in considerably fresh detail, all of Browne's major resources—his life, his interest in science, his religion, his style—before analyzing each of the major works in turn. The extraordinary precision and clarity of these analyses add much to our understanding of both the author and his individual works, showing us in new and provocative ways how Browne could speak, in varying tones, to his immediate contemporaries and to later generations of readers and writers. From the acute analysis of particular samples of Browne's much-heralded style to larger concerns with Browne's place as an Interregnum author, Post's study will stand as corrective and contributor to a deeper, fuller, and more immediate understanding of one of the most haunting writers of the English Renaissance. This is a book beginning students and seasoned scholars will return to again and again: while sophisticated and subtle, it is also richly clear and illuminating.

—Arthur F. Kinney

About the Author

Jonathan F. S. Post is associate professor of English literature at UCLA and a specialist in seventeenth-century literature. He received his A.B. from Amherst College in 1970, his Ph.D. from the University of Rochester in 1976, and from 1975 to 1979 he was assistant professor of English at Yale University. A recipient of fellowships from the Folger Shakespeare Library, the National Endowment for the Humanities, and the John Simon Guggenheim Memorial Foundation, he is the author of *Henry Vaughan: The Unfolding Vision* (Princeton, 1982) as well as a number of scholarly articles and reviews in the field of Renaissance and seventeenth-century English literature. His interest in Browne began as an undergraduate.

Preface

"That masse of flesh that circumscribes me, limits not my mind."
Browne's is no idle boast. He is one of the most self-consciously
elusive and, partly because of his elusiveness, one of the most cap-
tivating authors in the history of English prose, an example of his
own description of how the wise and prudent man "so contrives
[his] affairs that although [his] actions be manifest, his designes are
not discoverable." The following study does not attempt to circum-
scribe Browne's mind; nor does it propose a single thesis that will
make the design of his work suddenly visible to all. It attempts,
rather, to introduce new readers to some of the major features of
the man and his writings, and to risk doing so without offering any
easy labels to identify this "great and true Amphibium": Browne
the skeptic, Browne the virtuoso, Browne the good or bad physician,
Browne the prose poet, the scientist, Neoplatonist, or Christian
humanist. To a degree unusual in literary studies, each possesses a
piece of the truth, a situation that would undoubtedly have pleased
the author himself, but none seems either sufficiently precise as a
descriptive category or sufficiently inclusive of Browne to win the
day. The better part of wisdom in this case might simply be to
honor Browne with a hyphen and then to be "soft and flexible" in
what we attach to it.[1]

The first four chapters are thus given to presenting different
dimensions of the author. Chapter 1 offers a general overview of
Browne's life, with a brief summary of his writings and their immediate reception. The next three then attempt to deepen these
perceptions by singling out for further discussion salient features of
the author: his place in the emerging world of "science" in the
seventeenth century, as reflected in his important works (chapter
2); his religion, seen in its immediate historical context (chapter 3);
and some of the distinguishing elements of his style (chapter 4).
These are by no means the only dimensions of Browne deserving
individual treatment, but they are ones that continually recur in
the critical heritage and should be of general interest to the reader.

The subsequent three chapters then offer close readings of the
major works, a turn anticipated at the end of chapter 4 by the

detailed discussion of the stylistic revisions of *A Letter to a Friend*. Chapters 5 *(Religio Medici)*, 6 *(Pseudodoxia Epidemica)*, and 7 *(Urne-Buriall* and *The Garden of Cyrus)* are meant to dovetail with, not depend upon, material presented in the earlier portion of the book. They can thus be read either in isolation (for the benefit of the student who wishes a quick perspective on a single work) or, for those wishing a fuller view of the author, in conjunction with the other chapters. The book then concludes with a necessarily brief glance at *Christian Morals* and an even more compressed attempt to see Browne in a continuing tradition of imaginative prose writers. The bibliography at the end, besides registering in part my considerable debts to other scholars, is intended to indicate possible directions for further study.

If the principal aim of the book is to honor the diversity of Browne's accomplishments, it also seeks to make central the broadly comic perspective of the author's vision: not just the wit involved in a work like *Religio Medici* but Browne's more comprehensive role as a sustainer of traditions, as someone deeply committed to living and to the living even if, or rather especially when, he meditated on human mortality. This is a role, moreover, that was undoubtedly heightened, not diminished, by the English Civil War and the Interregnum, the period from 1642 to 1660 when all of Browne's works that were published during his lifetime appeared. And in his evident concern with continuity—with "revolutions" in the older scientific, not the more recent, political sense of the word—he also serves as a valuable counterpoint to other Interregnum authors like Milton, Marvell, Cowley, and Vaughan, authors who responded powerfully during these years to a radical, even apocalyptic, view of history, and did so regardless of their particular political loyalties. Although much has been said of late about this aspect of the mid-seventeenth century, less has been said of the other. By recording a different kind of response to contemporary events, one that, like the urns of *Hydriotaphia,* acquires a peculiar energy by virtue of its apparent indifference to the drums and tramplings of human conquest, the following study attempts in part to redress this situation.

Some obvious apologies need to be made. The first is perhaps for my decision to reexamine the major texts from a variety of perspectives and the possible repetition this method invites. *Religio Medici,* for instance, figures continually into the four chapters preceding the single one devoted to it. My excuse is the rich complexity of attitudes embodied in it, a point borne out in part by its having been edited over one hundred times since its first appearance and by the various critical approaches it has inspired. The second involves the largely descriptive nature of the chapter on *Pseudodoxia Epidemica.* After spending nearly a year with this book as my constant companion—and occasional antagonist—I became convinced that the best way to represent a work now read only by specialists but still unpredictably fascinating in its particulars is simply to give the general reader some idea of its contents. The last involves my choice of editions. Although Geoffrey Keynes's four-volume *Works of Sir Thomas Browne* (1964) remains in some sense the "standard" text, it is no longer in print, difficult to find outside of university or research libraries, and in some ways it has been superseded by the Clarendon Press editions of *Religio Medici and Other Works* by L. C. Martin (1964) and *Pseudodoxia Epidemica* by Robin Robbins (1981). I have therefore elected the more cumbersome but perhaps finally more helpful route of using a combination of Keynes, Martin, and Robbins: Keynes for the minor works and letters (designated *K*); Martin for *Religio Medici (RM)*, *Hydriotaphia* or *Urne-Buriall (UB)*, *The Garden of Cyrus (GC)*, *A Letter to a Friend (LF)*, and *Christian Morals (CM);* and Robbins for *Pseudodoxia Epidemica (PE)*. Page references are to the respective editions in which a work appears. Because other editions might be used by the reader, I have also cited book and chapter or section, whichever is relevant, according to the following format: *RM, 1.5, p. 5 (Religio Medici,* book 1, chapter or section 5, page 5).

Portions of this book have appeared elsewhere. A slightly different version of chapter 1 was published in *English Language Notes* 19 (1982): 313–35, while some of the ideas in chapters 3 and 5 are drawn from my "Browne's Revisions of *Religio Medici*," *SEL* 25 (1985): 145–63. An invitation from the graduate Renaissance seminar at the University of Reading to speak on Browne provided a delightful opportunity to rethink some of my views of *Religio Medici.* The work has also benefited greatly from the help of specific individuals: professors Michael Allen, Cedric Brown, Susan Gallick, Christopher Grose, George Guffey, Arthur Kinney, Louis Martz, Annabel Patterson, C. A. Patrides, Joseph Summers, Stanley Stewart, and Stephen Yenser. Despite acquiring a new last name, Esther Gilman Richey remains the most intrepid of proofreaders. For responding to specific queries, I wish also to thank Elizabeth Wrigley,

Director of the Francis Bacon Library, and Sir Nicholas Bacon of Raveningham, Norfolk. For several years now, my debts have been mounting to the undergraduates and graduates at UCLA who risked enrolling with me in English 153, 180 and 248. Those to the secretarial staff at UCLA, Nora Elias, Gail Fuhrman, and Jeanette Gilkison, are past reckoning.

The following institutions have aided significantly in the research and completion of this book: UCLA for continuing to assist in funding portions of my research; and the John Simon Guggenheim Memorial Foundation for allowing me the luxury of a year's leave from teaching in 1984–85, during which time much of the writing was accomplished. I wish also to express my appreciation to the staffs of the Bodleian Library, the British Library, Cambridge University Library, the Henry E. Huntington Library, the Norwich Public Library and Record Office, and the University Research Library at UCLA. As a peace offering, this book ought to be dedicated to those who found Churchgate Cottage, Haslingfield, dangerously close at times, but I hope they will continue to forgive me if I look, momentarily at least, in another direction.

Jonathan F. S. Post

University of California, Los Angeles

Chronology

1605   Thomas Browne born on 19 October or 19 November. Gunpowder Plot; Bacon's *Advancement of Learning.*

1613   Father dies; mother marries Sir Thomas Dutton.

1616   Admitted to Winchester College.

1623   Matriculates at Broadgates Hall (now Pembroke College), Oxford.

1625   Death of James I; accession of his son, Charles I.

1626   Admitted to the degree of Bachelor of Arts at Oxford.

1629   Admitted to the degree of Master of Arts at Oxford. Probably spends summer in Ireland.

1630   Travels to the Continent to study medicine at Montpellier, Padua, and Leiden.

1633   Receives M.D. from Leiden in December; begins medical apprenticeship somewhere in Oxfordshire.

1634–1635   *Religio Medici* reportedly composed.

1637   Incorporated M.D. at Oxford. Moves to Norwich.

1641   Marries Dorothy Mileham.

1642   First and second unauthorized editions of *Religio Medici.* Civil War begins.

1643   Authorized version of *Religio Medici.*

1644   Edward Browne born.

1645   Laud executed; Book of Common Prayer is abolished.

1646   *Pseudodoxia Epidemica.*

1649   Charles I executed on 30 January; Commonwealth proclaimed.

1653   Protectorate established under Cromwell.

1658   *Urne-Buriall* and *The Garden of Cyrus;* registered with the Stationer on 9 March. 3 September, Cromwell dies after a brief illness.

1660   Charles II restored.

1671   Knighted by Charles II.

1672   "Sixth and Last Edition" of *Pseudodoxia Epidemica*, constituting Browne's final version.

1682   Browne dies on 19 October.

1683   *Certain Miscellany Tracts*, edited by Thomas Tenison.

1686   Tenison supervises the publication of the first collected edition of Browne's *Works*.

1690   *A Letter to a Friend, upon Occasion of the Death of his Intimate Friend* is published posthumously by Browne's son, Edward.

1711   Browne's library dissolved; *Sale Catalogue* published.

1712   *Posthumous Works* brought out; includes *Repertorium* and *Brampton Urns*.

1716   *Christian Morals*.

Chapter One
Browne's Life:
A "Cabinet of Rarities"

Early Years

"I went to see Sir Thomas Browne, with whom I had sometime corresponded by letter, though I had never seen him before," records the Royalist virtuoso John Evelyn in his diary of 17 October 1671. "His whole house and garden [were] a paradise and cabinet of rarities, and that of the best collection, especially medals, books, plants, and natural things."[1] Evelyn's survey does not compass Browne's interests altogether, but his glance hints at the extraordinary learning and lore for which the Norwich physician was famous in his day. Author of one of the most celebrated religious "confessions" of the century, natural philosopher or scientist of considerable distinction, Honorary Fellow of the Royal College of Physicians, and noted antiquary—to say nothing of his being the father of twelve children—he was the first citizen of Norwich, a city second only in size to London in the seventeenth century. He had been duly knighted by Charles II a month earlier.

Browne was just two days short of sixty-six when he received Evelyn. If he could write with pleasing diffidence of the first half of his life as "a miracle of thirty yeares" (RM, 2.11, p. 69), there is little on the surface to prevent extending this happy judgment over the whole. In a century notable for producing durable authors— Donne, Jonson, and Milton lived into their sixties, Vaughan into his seventies, and Herrick into his eighties—Browne's seventy-seven years stand him in good company, and his increasing fame in his own day as well as the autobiographical nature of much of his writing allows us to picture his life in considerable detail.[2] At a glance, it reads like an extended gloss on his comment in *Religio Medici* that "Wisedome is [God's] most beauteous attribute, no man can attaine unto it, yet *Solomon* pleased God when hee desired it" (1.13, p. 12).

Browne was born in London in the Parish of St. Michaels, Cheap-

side, on either 19 October or 19 November 1605.[3] Biographers
have generally favored the earlier date, which descends from information supplied by Browne's daughter, Elizabeth; but in a letter
to John Aubrey the author himself gives the latter (*K*, 4, p. 374).
Drawing his horoscope in *Religio Medici,* which can be used to
support either birth date, Browne attributed to the time of his
nativity his slightly melancholic temperament: "I was borne in the
Planetary houre of *Saturne,* and I think I have a peece of that Leaden
Planet in me" (2.11, p. 71). Melancholy, we should remember,
was frequently associated in the Renaissance not just with moroseness
but also with speculation, as Shakespeare's Hamlet and Milton's "Il
Penseroso" readily tell us.

The child of Thomas Browne, a successful mercer or clothes
merchant, and Anne Garroway, originally of Herefordshire, Browne
was the second youngest of five and their only boy. We know little
about his siblings except that they all married, and almost nothing
of his relationship to them, either early or later in life, except that
he was apparently friendly with one group of in-laws—the Cradocks.
We know only slightly more of his parents. Neither was of noble
lineage although "Browne's paternal grandmother could trace her
ancestry back to Norman knights."[4] His father's family had just
recently received their lands outright late in Elizabeth's reign, and
the single surviving memory Sir Thomas had of his mother's house,
which he conveyed in the final year of his life to his own son Edward,
is remarkable rather for its plainness: "I remember when I was very
yong & I thinck butt in coates, my mother carryed mee to my
Grandfather Garrawayes howse in Lewys. I retaine only in my mind
the idea of some roomes of the howse and of the church" (*K* 4, p.
203). A single reminiscence of his, preserved by his daughter, Elizabeth, does tell us, however, that the young child was nurtured in
domestic security: "His father used to open his breast when he was
asleep, and kiss it in prayers over him, as 'tis said of Origen's father,
that the Holy Ghost would take possession there."[5]

The Holy Ghost did take possession of Browne, as his later writings amply indicate, but the one incident from his early years that
does survive in the records is of a decidedly worldly nature. In the
autumn of 1613, when Thomas was eight, his father became ill.
He died before the year was out, whereupon he left an estate valued
at some £5,000 to be divided equally in thirds between his wife,
Anne, his children, and certain other legacies. Anne and her brother-

in-law, Edward, were named executors. Shortly thereafter, Anne married Sir Thomas Dutton, a notorious spendthrift and suitor to royal favor, whose most memorable action was to kill in a duel his superior officer, Sir Hatton Cheke. Young Thomas himself composed some verses on the "heedlesse villainy of duell," which most scholars have assumed to be an allusion to the affair; but it was Samuel Johnson who amplified a note left by Browne's longtime friend and first biographer, John Whitefoot, into a grim lament that the orphan "was left to the rapacity of his guardian, deprived now of both his parents, and therefore helpless and unprotected."[6]

It should be noted, however, that there is nothing in Browne's writings to suggest that he viewed himself as a hapless victim of an evil stepfather; indeed, there is indication that the two traveled amicably around Ireland together.[7] But as the painstaking researches of Norman Endicott show,[8] Dr. Johnson's account does have an element of truth to it beyond his exaggerated pity for the boy. In the year following her husband's death, Anne had apparently altered some of the debts owed to the deceased. As Endicott phrases it, quoting the Court of Alderman then acting as a special Court of Orphans, she " 'wasted & consumed' some part of the estate so that 'it is likely & very much to be feared that unless somme speedy Course be taken . . . very great losse will fall to the five orphans' " (p. 185). The speedy course involved delegating to Edward the sole responsibility of executor, while Anne (now married to Sir Thomas Dutton) was to receive her share of the estate, amounting to approximately £1,500, providing she relinquish her role of executrix. Edward, in turn, administered the remaining sum to the children over a period of years, of which the total amount of money accruing to Sir Thomas was probably in the neighborhood of £600, his fair portion of the estate. He was thus not swindled by his guardians as is suggested by Andrew Kippis's account of Browne in the *Biographica Britannica* (1730), repeated in a brief life of him prefixed to Torbuck's edition of *Religio Medici* (1736), and reported again by Johnson in the life he attached to his edition of *Christian Morals* in 1756, but there is no question that his mother and stepfather played a little loose with their charge. Possessed of a finely tuned equanimity toward worldly fortune throughout his life and nearly always charitable to others, young Thomas seems not to have been tainted by the incident. He did write later in *Religio,* however, that "to me avarice seemes not so much a vice, as a deplorable piece of madnesse"

(2.13, p. 73), and in another section he commended "their reso-
lutions who never marry twice" (2.9, p. 66).

Education

Of "a moderate and peaceable discretion" (*RM*, 1.19, p. 19),
sometimes melancholic, and not born to riches, young Thomas was
nonetheless hardly wanting, and the lion's share of both his inheritance and his imagination was undoubtedly used to develop, in
Whitefoot's phrase, "the Horizon of his Understanding [which] was
much larger than the *Hemisphere* of the World."[9] Browne's schooling
covered some twenty-one years. It also came near to testing the
limits of his immediate hemisphere by including study at five institutions in four different countries—Winchester College, Oxford,
Montpellier, Padua, and Leiden, with a return to Oxford to be
incorporated M.D. in 1637. Along the way, he received his B.A.
from Oxford in 1626 and his M.A. in 1629; he probably then spent
the summer in Ireland before going to the Continent to begin four
years of medical studies.[10] In December 1633, Browne returned to
England for another four years of medical apprenticeship during
which time he also composed *Religio Medici*. His service performed
most likely in Oxfordshire as Anthony à Wood initially suggested
and not in Halifax as proposed by Wilkin, the apprenticeship allowed Thomas the opportunity to practice physic while fulfilling
the time requirement necessary for the Oxford M.D.[11] As someone
who thought of a man as a little world made cunningly, as a microcosm of the universe, Browne was himself a sharp reflection of
the institutions he attended and the places he visited.

Education in the early seventeenth century was invariably influenced, if not determined, by the great humanist reform movement
of the previous century. Its aim, in the oft-quoted phrase by Milton,
was "to repair the ruins of our first parents by regaining to know
God aright, and out of that knowledge to love him, to imitate him,
to be like him."[12] Its ideal, in short, was something like complete
knowledge, a goal Browne gestures at in *Pseudodoxia Epidemica* and
which is readily apparent in the encyclopedia of allusions that forms
the intellectual nerve center of his writings. If the ideal seems grand,
its pedagogical methods were, paradoxically, limited and covered a
narrow terrain cultivated with thoroughness and rigor but narrow
nonetheless. As John Mulder observes, "ancient history, classical

languages, and the pursuit of eloquence remained the foundation of the curriculum."[13] To be sure, the first two books of Bacon's *Advancement of Learning* advocating a significant place for the sciences in education had been published in 1605, more than ten years before Browne matriculated at Winchester College, but its effects were not to be felt until nearly mid-century when Puritan reformers like Comenius, Hartlib, and to some degree Milton pushed for a more "practical" curriculum. Indeed, it is even questionable whether Browne was familiar with the *Advancement* much before 1640.[14]

Founded by William of Wykeham in 1387, Winchester was the oldest grammar school in England. It was thus an unlikely place for scholastic renovation when Browne entered on 20 August 1616 at the age of ten. Its reputation lay rather in another direction— as "a place of strict discipline and order,"[15] writes Izaak Walton, where Sir Henry Wotton, later ambassador to Venice and provost of Eton, had been sent "so that he might in his youth be moulded into a method of living by rule." Browne, too, was not immune from its discipline: "my common conversation I do acknowledge austere, my behaviour full of rigour, sometimes not without morosity," he remarked in *Religio* (1.3, p. 4) in a phrase that reflects perhaps as much on his early schooling as on his saturnine disposition.

He also absorbed the instruction there. Browne's "grammar learning"—to borrow Whitefoot's description—was spent on Latin and Greek, two of the (at least) six languages of which he boasted mastery in *Religio* (2.8, p. 65). These together allowed him access in the original to the classics and to the New Testament with their Latin commentaries. (The study of Hebrew was reserved usually for the university.) The first three of his six years would have been devoted to Lily's *Grammar* for Latin. The young student undoubtedly worked on syntax, figures of speech, and prosody, and composed simple and complex sentences while learning to vary his diction. He probably read also in the original from Cato, Erasmus, and the eclogues of Mantuan, and in Latin translations from Aesop and the New Testament. In the fourth form, Browne would have graduated to the study of poetry and probably begun concentrating on Greek. Ovid's *Metamorphoses* was the major literary text at this stage, portions of which were to be memorized and then analyzed for their grammatical and rhetorical content, with the etymology of words determined, and then the passages elegantly "Englished" before being turned back into Latin. Finally, the upper two forms included expanded readings in history, concentration on the Greek and Latin orators (Demosthenes, Isocrates, and Cicero), and, of course, a knowledge of Virgil, "The Prince and purest of all Latine Poets."[16] Browne's memory, wrote Whitefoot years later, "though not so eminent as that of Seneca or Scaliger, was capacious and tenacious, insomuch as he remembered all that was remarkable in any book that he had."[17]

If the meticulous attention to history, to the importance of stylistic detail, and to the acts of memory and imitation seem imposing to the modern imagination, such was not the usual view of Renaissance schoolmasters, and it was certainly not Browne's. Sixty years after matriculating at Winchester, he wrote to his son Edward about the value of reading and writing in Latin "upon any subject morall or phylosophicall or rhetoricall": "you shall excitate your invention & many things will returne into your head by reminiscence wch otherwise lye dormant & uselesse" (K, 4, p. 69). Antiquity as well as devotion to "antique" methods of learning, with their special focus on languages, was clearly liberating, rather than crippling, to Browne's intelligence. They were also central to his later interests and excellence as a writer. He not only went on to compose a respectable essay "Of Languages and particularly of the Saxon Tongue" and to coin many words, of which a good number have stuck ("electricity," "hallucination," and "antediluvian," for instance), but he wrote what has come to be viewed as the quintessence of elegant prose in its Latinized English form. Browne's legendary proximity to the past began at Winchester; he remembered the debt at age seventy-four when he gave twelve pounds toward building a new school at the College.

Although awarded a scholarship at Winchester, Thomas matriculated at Broadgates Hall—soon to be called Pembroke College—Oxford as a Gentleman Commoner on 5 December 1623. Browne would normally have progressed to New College rather than to Broadgates, as Jeremiah Finch has observed,[18] since New College owed its foundation to William of Wykeham, but the young scholar's uncharacteristically average performance before his examiners prevented him from succeeding to a vacancy, should he have wished one in the first place. He thus joined a growing list of eminent Winchester graduates who failed in their election to New College.[19] The incident perhaps also caused him later to copy down a squib in one of his commonplace books: "William Oldis / silly dimme owl / John Smith / shyt on him" (*K,* 3, p. 274). In all probability, Oldys had been one of his examiners, while Smith was another unpopular proctor at Oxford. Never "rusticated" like Milton for ruffling his tutor's feathers, the less controversial Browne still quietly kept score, which he evened on a more public front when, at the ceremony commemorating the "transmutation" of Broadgates Hall to Pembroke College, he was one of three students and the only undergraduate chosen to formalize the event by giving a Latin address. It was the first of Browne's many distinctions.

Oxford both continued and extended the currriculum at Winchester. Still structured around the medieval trivium (grammar, logic, and rhetoric), quadrivium (arithmetic, geometry, astronomy, and music), and three philosophies (moral, natural, and metaphysical), it valued Aristotle's authority above all, and the method of instruction continued to rely heavily on public lectures and disputations by the students, an arrangement attacked by Bacon and that later formed the volatile center of the mid-century controversy between the "ancients" and the "moderns." Thus, for instance, the lecture in grammar would be supplemented by readings from Virgil, Horace, or Cicero, authors encountered in grammar school but now read with greater thoroughness. The study of rhetoric followed a similar scheme; but it would be a mistake to suppose that the entire curriculum represented only a refinement of previous reading. Although Winchester numbered among its graduates men of medical eminence, it was left to the universities to begin formal instruction in natural philosophy, the discipline most appropriate to an undergraduate's training for a future in medicine. Furthermore, during the years in which Browne attended Oxford, the sciences were undergoing some significant, even if by modern standards rudimentary, reforms.[20] In addition to the Regius professorships of divinity, law, medicine, Hebrew, and Greek established by Henry VIII, Oxford witnessed the creation of two chairs by Sir Henry Savile in 1619, one in geometry, the other in astronomy; and five years later in 1624 Richard Tomlins established a readership in anatomy that included an annual dissection every spring of "a Sounde body of one of the Executed persons" found within twenty-one miles around Oxford."[21]

The creation of these positions reflects the growing interest in science at the universities in the 1620s and 1630s; indeed, many scholars eventually involved in the foundation of the Royal Society in 1660 were undergraduates at Oxford and Cambridge during these years. But anyone wishing a career in medicine still had to master the full liberal arts curriculum, which involved four years for a B.A., another three for an M.A., and then another seven years for the doctorate in medicine, performed either in England or abroad.[22] Browne's schooling at the undergraduate and graduate levels followed just such a course. His Latin poem honoring Camden—the first of his published works (1623)—reveals Thomas as a witty student of history and poetry, perhaps even under the influence of Ben Jonson; and two undated Latin compositions, obviously inspired by Horace, may come from the same period: "Amico Opus Arduum Meditanti" (To a friend contemplating a difficult work) and "Amico Clarissimo, De Enecante Garrulo Suo" (To an illustrious friend on his wearisome chatterer). Pembroke College, furthermore, had a tradition of witty if not always distinguished poets in John Heywood, Edward Dyer, Fulke Greville, George Peele, Francis Beaumont, and Richard Corbett; and Browne, without ever striving to become a university don, must have absorbed much of the college's literary flavor. He would also have read deeply in moral philosophy and theology in these years, and it is likely, as Frank Huntley suggests[23] that the heresies stemming from his "greener studies," described in *Religio* 1.7, come from this period of his life. As for his study of science, Browne would have encountered John Bainbridge, first Savile Professor of Astronomy, and Henry Briggs, who held a comparable post in geometry. Both figure into *Pseudodoxia* (4.13, p. 356, and 2.2, p. 93, respectively). But Browne's warmest recollection of a former teacher belongs to Robert Hues, the aging cartographer from Thomas Cavendish's expedition that sailed around the world from 1586 to late 1588: "Hee was [a] very good & playne dealing man, & had read Euclide & Ptolomie very accurately, and also Aristotle, whereof wee should often discourse" (*K,* 4, p. 84).[24]

In contrast to the grammar school, whose curriculum reflected the biases of the headmaster, public instruction at the university was supplemented by the private teaching that passed between tutor and student. Dr. Thomas Clayton, the first Tomlins Lecturer in Anatomy and Regius Professor of Physic, must certainly be credited with stimulating Browne's interest in medicine and perhaps too with his decision to study at Montpellier. But Browne's tutor, Thomas Lushington, played an equally significant role in his life by alerting his pupil firsthand to the outer limits of religious polemic. Lushington was a witty student of theology, "a very learned and ingeniose man," with an M.A. from Lincoln College in 1616 and later "a high churchman of the Laudian school."[25] As an Anglican divine, moreover, he subsequently helped to persuade Browne to practice medicine in Norwich. The two men also shared an interest in Neoplatonism, with Browne citing Lushington's work on Proclus in a 1673 letter to John Aubrey about his former tutor (*K,* 4.175–76).

At Pembroke, though, Lushington was best known for two sermons, "The Resurrection Rescued from the Soldier's Calumnies," delivered on Easter Monday, 1624, and a recantation of it the following week. Lushington's Easter Sermon is bold and dramatic, in both its celebration of the resurrection and its criticisms of the current anti-Spanish mood in Parliament, where, in the wake of the failed match between Prince Charles and the Spanish Infanta, the Protestant cause was assuming new militancy. "Nothing now contents the *Commonalty* but *Warre* and *Contention,*"[26] he pointedly remarked, but his ardent "pacifism" also brought him under censure by the vice-chancellor, Dr. Piers, and he was forced to retract his views. More than a decade later when Browne was writing *Religio Medici,* he quietly asserted, in a remark that has become ineluctably linked with his character, "I have no Genius to disputes in Religion" (1.6, p. 6). We need not ascribe his calculated diffidence here solely to a memory of Lushington's misfortunes, but we ought to observe that as an apology intended to disarm would-be critics, Browne's naive admission of incompetence suggests that he understood, in fact, many of the rules of religious disputes. He never had to recant a single word of *Religio.*

Browne chose to go to the Continent to further his medical education. Despite recent improvements made in the curricula, Oxford and Cambridge, in the sciences, still lagged considerably behind the great European universities at Paris, Montpellier, Basil, Padua, and Leiden. The majority of medical students, therefore, continued to follow the trail abroad roughed out at the end of the fifteenth century by Thomas Linacre, founder of the Royal College of Physicians and the first English translator of Galen into Latin, and smoothed by more recent luminaries like John Caius and William Harvey. All studied at Padua. Whether or not by design, the order of Browne's scholarly itinerary reflected the historical order of medical developments in Europe. Montpellier was probably his first stop and the least prestigious of the three institutions he attended. The main repository of Arabic learning, then in decline, its strength lay principally in botany and in the lectures on surgery by Lazare Riviere, whose *Praxis Medica* (1640) was in all likelihood the text that Browne recommended to his friend and medical aspirant, Henry Power, in 1646. Next was Padua, the place of Andreas Vesalius, the great anatomist. His work, *De Humani Corporis Fabrica* (On the fabric of the human body), was published in 1543, the same year in which Copernicus's *De Revolutionibus* appeared; it challenged the authority of Galen and Aristotle by reexamining and, in effect, discovering the structure of human anatomy. Although Browne does not figure in the records of either Montpellier or Padua—thus making it impossible to determine the precise dates of his attendance—he probably spent the greatest portion of his time at Padua. It was one of the leading centers of science in Europe. Along with housing the first permanent anatomy theater in Europe (it was founded in 1594–95 by the person whom Harvey credited as his guide to discovering the circulation of the blood, Fabricius of Acquapendente, and can still be visited today), Padua was also the academic residence of Galileo from 1592 to 1610. Browne, who at thirteen witnessed a comet beginning "in Libra [and which] moved northward, ending about the tayle of ursa major" (*K,* 4, p. 19), and studied astronomy at Oxford, was in good company here. Just when he left Padua and arrived at Leiden remains uncertain, but on 21 December 1633 he was certified M.D. With several distinguished graduates from Padua on the faculty, Leiden was prominent in anatomy; it was also in the process of becoming preeminent in the field of chemistry, the major medical innovation of the seventeenth century.

The full sweep of Browne's studies abroad is at least partially indicated in the letter he sent to Henry Power in which he cites some twenty-seven works, ancient and modern, for the young scholar to absorb. "Galen and Hippocrates must be had as fathers and fountains of the faculty," Browne admonishes his pupil. Recollecting a school of Paduan authorities, he continues: "Lay your foundation in Anatomy. . . . And be sure you make yourself master of Dr. Harvey's piece *De Circul. Sang.;* which discovery I prefer to that of Columbus." He then lists a variety of botanists, perhaps picked up partially at Montpellier, ranging from Theophrastus to "our English Herbalists," to which he recommends should be added a knowledge of pharmacology and chemistry acquired by studying the works of Wecker, Renodaeus, Morelli, and Crollius, among others. "Surgery and Chymistry, may be your diversions and recreations," we learn, but "Physic is your business." By "Physic" Browne goes on to say he means the study of diseases and their cures, and he insists that Power read "two or three times over" until he becomes "a perfect master" of the *Institutes* (1611) of Daniel Sennertus, Professor of Medicine at Wittenberg from 1602 to 1637 and an amalgamator of various theories held by Aristotle, Galen, and Paracelsus (*K,* 4, pp. 255–56). Although Browne apologized that the list was brief and contained "but few books," the substance of it has certainly convinced most scholars that he had mastered the medical authorities of his day.

Browne's four years abroad were significant in other ways as well. The outward purpose of travel, Bacon wrote in a letter to Lord Rutland in 1596, was "to see the beauty of many cities, know the manners of many countries, and learn the language of many nations"; the inner goal was to achieve "that which in moral philosophy we call *cultum animi,* the tilling and manuring of your own mind."[27] If we can judge by his later writings and habits, Browne succeeded in both these goals and even made the experience available to his sons as well. Indeed, *Religio Medici* is designed to reveal a young man's cosmopolitan response to the world. The frequent allusions to foreign incidents ("I remember a Doctor in Physick of Italy," or "With another I was familiarly acquainted in France, a Divine"), the casual remembrance of Rabelais (whose ghost Browne encountered at Montpellier), and certainly the quiet boast that "besides the *Jargon* and *Patois* of severall Provinces, I understand no lesse then six Languages":[28] all of these recollections assure us that the youthful author viewed travel as a significant extension to his studies, while the very presence of the references in a work devoted to describing a physician's religion affirms that the experiences helped in the "tilling and manuring" of his mind.

Private and Professional Life

Browne never went back to the Continent. Upon his return, he pursued his medical apprenticeship in Oxfordshire during which time he composed *Religio Medici,* probably in 1634, although the work was not published until seven or eight years later (1642) and then first in a pirated edition. By this time he had settled in Norwich, a city of some thirty thousand people. Apparently lured there by Oxford friends including Nicholas Bacon, Justinian Lewyn, Charles Le Gros, and Lushington, Browne arrived sometime around 1637. We know almost nothing of the early years of his practice, but we can say that despite the medical erudition shown by someone of Browne's caliber, the actual practice of physic in the mid-seventeenth century was still a primitive affair. Keith Thomas's litany of grim statistics reminds us of how powerless most doctors were in attempting to treat serious illness. The physician "focused on what we should regard as the symptoms of disease—fever or dysentery—rather than the disease itself."[29] Depending upon the patient's condition, determined usually through urine analysis, a doctor might order bloodletting, purges, or an emetic followed by prescriptions of plasters, ointments, and potions. One contemporary of Browne remarked that "we shall find more who have died within thirty or thirty-five years of age than passed it," to which Keith Thomas adds that "even those who survived could anticipate a lifetime of intermittent physical pain."[30] Browne suffered himself from a frequent ache in his feet, the occasional cold, and a chronic "payne in my loynes wch makes mee unable to go or stand" and which lasted for several days at a time (K, 4, p. 77). With good reason he wrote in *Religio* that "I cannot goe to cure the body of my Patient, but I forget my profession, and call unto God for his soule" (2.6, p. 63).

The best record of Browne's medical practice is contained in his correspondence with other doctors, including those with his eldest son Edward, who followed his father in his choice of profession. They reveal a compassionate man, diligent in his duties, who never lost sight of the bizarre. He was conscientious about patient referral and forgiving of hypochondriacs. His opinion of "a woeman or mayd in Suffolk, who had a julking and fluctuation in her chest" was quoted in the *Philosophical Transactions* of the Royal Society in 1667. With bemused wonder, he reported, too, of amazing recoveries: "I remember also a woeman who being thirstie in a quartan ague, called for a bottle of beere in the windowe, butt the servant in hast brought her a bottle of Inck wch stood in the windowe, & shee dranck a good draught & vomitted much and black, and the ague left her." And then there was the patient who, taking liberties with Browne's modest prescription of eating six or seven peaches for a urinary discomfort, consumed twenty-five in a single morning "and found extraordinary releif & his payne ceased" (*K,* 4, pp. 146, 138–39, 145).

Elsewhere, Browne took more pride in his remedies. Many were borrowed from the *Pharmacopoei Londinensis,* the standard guide for apothecaries authorized by the Royal College of Physicians in 1618, but he improvised freely and, on occasion, happily passed along to Edward the ones that had some claim to being restorative: "I contrived a pickle out of oysters, anchoves, pickled cowcumbers, onyons, Rhenish wine &c," he writes, "which I caused your mother to make, & I gave it to a patient whose weake & vomiting stomack was helped thereby." And then he adds, "I intend when Colchester oysters are good, to send you a litle glasse for you to tast" (*K,* 4, p. 161). All in all, Browne's medical practice was a mixture of science and folklore. He experimented with prescriptions in order to find cures, but he was not reluctant to send patients to the king to be touched; and though we can certainly sympathize with Browne's complaint that "the ignorance of chirurgeons . . . creates so many mountebanck & stage quacksalvers" (*K,* 4, p. 113), it is not always easy to know exactly where someone in the seventeenth century might draw the line between a healing and a hazardous treatment.

Browne was a busy and respected physician whose medical opinions were sought until his death. He even applied for and was granted the lease of a meadow in the Norwich Cathedral Precincts in 1669–70 in order to find grazing room for the horses that carried him on his rounds.[31] But he was not only a successful doctor. His marriage in 1641 to Dorothy Mileham, fourth daughter of Edward Mileham from the parish of Burlingham St. Peter, near Norwich, was starting to bear fruit. Their first child, Edward, was born in 1644 and for each year thereafter, with the annual birth of a daughter or son until 1650, the couple made a half-truth out of Browne's whimsical wish in *Religio* that people "might procreate like trees" (2.9, p. 67). Six more children were born to them in the 1650s, bringing the total to twelve, but of this number five died before their sixth birthday and two more by their twenty-fourth. Only Edward, Anne, Elizabeth, Frances, and another daughter whose name has not come down to us lived to adulthood, a doleful percentage that was nevertheless about average for the time.[32]

According to Whitefoot, Dorothy Browne was "A Lady of such a Symmetrical Proportion to her worthy Husband, both in the

Graces of her Body and Mind, that they seemed to come together by a kind of Natural Magnetism."[33] A half-length portrait of her with her husband survives in the National Portrait Gallery in London (see frontispiece). Painted shortly after their marriage and attributed to Joan Carlile (1606?–79)—a familiar figure at the Stuart court and one of the first women to paint professionally in England[34]— it testifies to the truth of Whitefoot's observations. Dorothy appears with quiet simplicity, dressed modestly in white lace and a pale blue gown, and she reveals only the slightest upward turn of the lips to balance the more somber presence of her husband. Intelligent but not highly educated (judging from the postscripts she added to Sir Thomas's letters), Dorothy was a stabilizing presence in what must have been at times a chaotic household. Because of her husband's constant experimenting—to say nothing about the irregular hours he must have kept as a physician—there was more than the usual amount of domestic turmoil: the "chickens and mice [that needed to be] weighed before and after strangulation to see whether their weight increased when the vital spirits left them; [or] the toad 'in a glass included with many spiders' [that required observation in order] to test the belief that there is a natural antipathy between them."[35] Their home also served on at least one occasion as an ark for some forty creatures of undetermined species when the plague was afflicting a neighbor. And then there was a rare pelican, perhaps belonging to the king, that hung in the house from 1668 onward. Even Mrs. Browne's domestic talents (and perhaps patience) could be tested when she was called upon to prepare the day's cuisine from the remains of a dissected dolphin: "Your mother hath an art to dress & cooke the flesh so as to make an excellent savory dish of it," writes Browne with a note of pride to Edward, and in the next breath adds, "the King being at Newmarket I sent collars thereof to his table, which were well liked of" (K, 4, p. 61). Dorothy must have been long suffering, as Joan Bennett observes,[36] but her affection for her husband and their children is evident everywhere in her letters, and their marriage of forty-one years was the longest of any involving a major seventeenth-century author. It might be only a coincidence—yet one worth noting—that among the household curiosities was also a portrait of Philemon and Baucus, the legendary favorite couple of Jupiter and Mercury (K, 3, p. 281), hanging in the parlor.

Browne's children, at least the ones we know much about—

Edward, Thomas, and to a lesser degree, Elizabeth—all reflect different elements of their father without any child equaling his wide range of interests. Edward, the eldest, followed his father in having a distinguished medical career of his own. Born in 1644, he was educated at Norwich Grammar School and Trinity College, Cambridge, where he took his B.A. in 1661 and his M.B. (Bachelor of Medicine) in 1663. After a brief period working with his father and a short stay in London, he toured the Continent in the company of William Trumbull, Samuel Tuke, and Christopher Wren, and then returned to study for his M.D. which he received from Merton College, Oxford, in 1667, the same year as his admission into the Royal Society. He rose quickly to a position of eminence in the scientific community. He became Breed Lecturer in Chirurgeons Hall in 1675 and a Fellow of the Royal College of Physicians where he was eventually chosen Censor of the college in 1678, 1685, and 1686: among his distinguished patients, he ministered to the ailing Restoration rake, John Wilmot, Earl of Rochester. But the resemblance between father and son stops here. Edward wrote no works of lasting significance, although he did participate in a 1682 translation of Plutarch's *Lives,* and, judging from the voluminous correspondence that survives between father and son from 1665 to 1682 as well as from his own journals, Edward lacked Sir Thomas's delicate inquisitiveness into either nature or human nature. As Simon Wilkin observed, in a remark that could be extended to Edward's character, "he was, in short, a *conscientious* traveller, not supplying from imagination what was wanting in reality."[37]

Browne bequeathed the major portion of his fancy and literary flair to his namesake, who died at age twenty-one. Young Tom, the second son, followed a career not in medicine but in the navy, a choice that immediately signals the romantic bent of a character revealed in more detail in his letters and journals. Although written at an earlier age than Edward's, these reflect an altogether different sensibility. Thomas, like his father, was interested in both painting and prose, and his good-humored account of his journey through Derbyshire stands in sharp contrast to the dogged lists of observations his brother frequently made. Together with his sympathy for his fellow seamen, he demonstrated strong intellectual potential: "You are like to prove not only a noble navigator butt a great schollar," his father wrote to him in the last year of his son's life, "which will bee much more to your honour and my satisfaction and content" (*K*, 4, p. 24). Such was not to be the case, however, and it remained for Edward to bring to his father in his later years the pleasures of a professional companion in the family.

We know less about Elizabeth, Browne's fifth child and third daughter, since only four of his letters to her have survived, but she was obviously a keen source of domestic comfort to him. Born probably in 1648, she remained at home until 1680, the year of her marriage to George Lyttleton. Among her pleasures were drawing and reading to her father at night. Indeed, in her commonplace book, she has left an impressive record of the many histories and books of travel literature that absorbed their attention in the evenings (*K*, 3, pp. 331–32). Elizabeth continued in her literary duties after her father's death, moreover, when she gathered together the manuscript of Browne's *Christian Morals* and authorized its publication in 1716, the year of her own death. Perhaps because of their special relationship, Browne's few letters to her contain some rare moments of personal reminiscence almost entirely absent from his correspondence with others. It is here we learn that Browne "came once from Dublin to Chester at Michaelmas and was so tossed, that nothing but milk and Possets would goe down with me 2 or 3 days after" (*K*, 4, p. 200). We also find here the only surviving references Browne made to young Thomas. And on at least one occasion he was inspired to transform his usually commonplace epistolary reports into a moving meditation on human frailty:

Tho it were noe wonder this very Tempestious and stormy winter, yet I am sorry you had such an uncomfortable sight, as to behold a ship cast away, so neer you; this is noe strang tho unwelcom sight at Yarmouth, Cromer, Winterton and sea Towns; tho you Could not save them I hope they were the better for yr Prayers, both those that Perishd and those that scapd. Some wear away in Calmes, some are Caried away in storms: we Come into the World one way, there are many gates to goe out of it. God give us grace to fit and prepare our selves for that Necessity, and to be ready to leave all when and how so ever he shall call; the Prayers of health are most like to be acceptable; sickness may Choak our devotions, and we are accepted rather by our life then our death; we have a rule how to lead the one, the other is uncertain and may Come in a Moment. (*K*, 4, p. 200).

The only biographically related incident involving Browne that has caused some embarrassment for his later readers stems from an opinion the doctor gave in a 1664 trial in which two women, Amy Duny and Rose Cullender, were accused of witchcraft. Browne never mentioned the event in his writings, and had it not been for Francis Hutchinson's *Historical Essay Concerning Witchcraft* (1718), the trial itself as well as Browne's role in it might have gone unnoticed. To the "enlightened" Hutchinson, Browne is a credulous villain: the learned doctor's bookish view of witches existing in Denmark was sufficient authority to convince a jury of "Country People . . . wonderfully bent to make the most of all Stories of Witchcraft"[38] to bring in a negative verdict, and the women were subsequently hanged. Hutchinson's version quickly made its way into the Browne legend and, by the early nineteenth century, it had received easy endorsements from Hazlitt, Scott, and Godwin. Although Simon Wilkin attempted a spirited apology shortly thereafter, he nonetheless failed to persuade notable twentieth-century scholars such as Edmund Gosse and William Osler of the doctor's innocence. Browne, after all, had confessed in *Religio* that "for my part, I have ever beleeved, and doe now know, that there are Witches" (1.30, p. 29).

But Hutchinson was a better dramatist than court reporter. As Malcolm Letts showed in the early part of this century, there might be little doubt about the substance of Browne's testimony, but there is considerable question about Hutchinson's placement of it in the trial proceedings and his subsequent interpretation of its effect on the jury.[39] Comparing the essayist's description of the trial with a copy of the single authentic account of the trial report of 1682, Letts, seconded by Dorothy Tyler, demonstrated how Hutchinson clearly doctored the account. First of all, Browne's testimony was not the only one given (indeed, he was but one of twelve witnesses called); and, second, his opinion, stated after those of eight others, was not pivotal but preceded, instead, a practical experiment designed to discover whether the women were, in fact, bewitched. The doctor's authority, in other words, hardly went uncontested; and if his opinion coincided, regrettably, with the jury's, his testimony did not provide the dramatic turning point that Hutchinson assigned to it.

Browne's conscience seems to have been untroubled by the incident; or at least he did not interpret the ball of fire that fell upon his house the following year as an act of divine retribution. "The noyse & lightening," he exclaims, "were so terrible that they putt

the whole citty into an Amazement, & most unto their prayers."
The side of his house facing the marketplace suffered damage to the
windows and flueboards, while another fire ball fell into the court-
yard apparently independent of a "freestone" that bore "an hole as
big as a footeball . . . through the wall which is above a foot thick"
(*K*, 3, p. 239). The meteorological event was also one of the few
recorded disruptions of Browne's later years. His hours were otherwise spent still vigorously pursuing experiments in zoology, biology, and botany, practicing medicine, receiving eminent naturalists
like Evelyn and John Ray (the latter of whom came to observe, with
Browne's help, the "shrub-stonecrop" at Norwich),[40] and attempting, through the aid of Edward living in London, to keep up with
the latest transactions of the Royal Society.

Yet during these years, Browne was not immune from personal
sorrow. In the ten years from 1652 to 1662, he lost five children,
including twins on 17–18 October 1656, the approximate time
when he was composing *Urne-Buriall;* and it is possible that the
deepening note of pathos in that work—its haunting evocation of
the forgotten dead who "must be content to be as though they had
not been" (*UB*, 121) and its description of our ignorance of the
next world as "a Dialogue between two Infants in the womb concerning the state of this world" (*UB*, p. 116)—owes something to
these experiences. Young Thomas also died in 1667, followed by a
daughter, Mary, at age twenty-four in 1675, and Elizabeth departed
for Guernsey in 1680. But as the voluminous correspondence with
Edward attests, Browne's life was full until the end. His last letter,
written probably four months before his death, is busy with in-
structions about a patient referral.

Browne died 19 October 1682, either exactly on or one month
shy of his seventy-seventh birthday. "The witt of Astrologie" (*K*, 3,
p. 285), at least, commends the former since Browne loved nothing
better than to meditate on the higher mysteries suggested by coincidence, especially those involving birth and death when, to borrow his metaphor, the tail of the snake might return to the mouth
and describe the circle of eternity (*LF*, p. 182). Years earlier in
Religio Medici, Browne had also written that "I am not so much
afraid of death, as ashamed thereof" (1.40, p. 38); and "in his last
sickness," observed Whitefoot, "he continued about a week's time,
enduring great pain of cholick, besides a continual fever, with as
much patience as hath been seen in any man, without any pretence

of Stoical apathy, animosity, or vanity of not being concerned there-at, or suffering no impeachment of happiness."[41] According to Whitefoot, Browne's last words were "that he did freely submit to the will of God, being without fear." It is hard to imagine how it could have been otherwise.

Writings and Reputation

Browne's family life and medical profession were sources of obvious comfort and stimulation to him. Equally so was the public reception of his works and the scholarly affiliations they brought him. Partly because of the publishing circumstances, *Religio Medici,* an extraordinarily witty apology for a doctor's faith, won almost immediate recognition for its author.[42] Having circulated in manuscript for a number of years—so far eight copies, none in the author's hand, have surfaced—the text was surreptitiously brought out twice in 1642 in anonymous editions by Andrew Crooke, an enterprising publisher with a flair for controversy. (The number of manuscript copies lends support to Browne's sometimes questioned claim, made in the 1643 preface, that the work *"was set downe many yeares past."*) In its unauthorized form, the printed work was then quickly commended by the Earl of Dorset to "that noble and absolutely complete gentleman, Sir Kenelm Digby,"[43] who, as a staunch supporter of Charles I, had been captured by Parliamentary soldiers in the early days of the Civil War and was being held prisoner in Winchester House, London. Digby began writing a commentary on it (he had just published with Daniel Frere a twenty-five-page letter analyzing the Pythagoreanism of *The Faerie Queene,* 2.9.22) when Browne somehow got wind of the project. Browne wrote directly to Digby to ask him to withhold publishing his "Animadversions" until the younger man could supply Digby with a true copy of the text for him to "discourse thereon." Digby responded, admitting only that he had set down some hasty notes, not animadversions, and further equivocated about whether he ever planned to have them published. He apparently did. His *Observations Upon Religio Medici* were published shortly thereafter, though not by Crooke or for the authorized *Religio* but by Frere, who was simply reprinting one of the 1642 versions. Crooke then brought out the revised, authorized *Religio* in the same year, 1643, replete with Browne's preface. Advertising it now as "a true and full copy of that which was most imperfectly and surreptitiously printed before," Crooke published, along with the revised text, the correspondence between Browne and Digby as well as a note of his own, signed A. B., ridiculing the fatuous nature of Digby's *Observations* (See *RM*, pp. 76–79).

Such were some of the hazards and rewards that accompanied the breakdown of press censorship in the late 1630s and early 1640s; but it would be wrong to assign the immediate popularity of *Religio* simply to publication circumstances and the generally favorable commentary of one of the country's leading wits. England had a strong taste for devotional literature, especially for anything that smacked of controversy, and the style of *Religio*, variously referred to by Digby as "witty," "handsome," and "sweet," made the work quickly palatable to a wide audience. It was reissued twice in 1645. In a fourth edition of 1656, the text received further annotations, this time by Thomas Keck, who initiated the practice of associating Browne with Montaigne, before Crooke acquired the rights to Digby's *Observations* in 1659, which he bound to Browne's work in a fifth edition published in that year. By the time of Browne's death in 1682, *Religio* was into its eighth edition. It had also been translated into Latin for publication in Leiden in 1644 and into Dutch and French in 1668.

Meanwhile, during this period, the author and his work became a minor cause célèbre. Although Browne was to prove remarkably reticent about *Religio* (after he wrote the preface, only one comment by him about his work survives), others were not. The rough-and-tumble James Howell reported in a published letter of 1645 that Browne's whimsical desire "to propagat[e] the world without conjunction with women" was "most unmanly,"[44] while the indefatigable Alexander Ross, in *Medicus Medicatus* (1645), fiercely attacked the work for being Popish in the same year that, as luck would have it, *Religio* was both included in the Vatican's *Index Expurgatorius* (Index of prohibited books) and was perhaps being read sympathetically by the Norwich Quaker Samuel Duncon.[45] In the midst of controversy, *Religio*, too, began to inspire a host of imitators and redactors of whom the most famous was to be Dryden in *Religio Laici* (1682). Recognizing the growing need to differentiate Browne from a field of pretenders, Alexander Brome quipped in 1661, "Physick and Preaching ill agree, / There is but one *Religio Medici*." Shortly thereafter, Samuel Pepys summed up the effect of Browne's work on a generation of readers when he wrote in his *Diary* in 1664 that Sir William Petty, "one of the most rational men that ever I heard speak," said "that in all his life these three books were the most esteemed and generally cried up for wit in the world—Religio Medici, [Francis] Osborne's Advice to a Son, and [Samuel Butler's] Hudibras."[46]

The publication of *Pseudodoxia Epidemica* (1646) was a more sober affair, not least of all because of the work's formidable length and content. Subtitled "Enquiries into Very many received Tenants and commonly presumed Truths," *Pseudodoxia*, or as it is often called, "Vulgar Errors," was the great scholarly and "scientific" effort of Browne's middle years and in many ways a natural extension of interests initially explored in *Religio*. Composed "during snatches of time, as medical vacations, and the fruitless importunity of Uroscopy would permit," "Vulgar Errors" and *Religio* overlap in a number of areas, such as Browne's consideration of the annual flooding of the Nile or of whether Eve was formed out of Adam's left side.[47] But *Religio Medici* is a personal inquiry into the paradoxical nature of one man as a microcosm of all men: it is skeptical, idiosyncratic, and above all devotional, while *Pseudodoxia* is a more objective catalog of human errors, encyclopedic in its scope and, to some degree, systematic in its treatment of ideas. Never a popular work in the same sense as *Religio*, it nonetheless confirmed Browne's place in the learned community of his day. Consulted by serious thinkers and hack experimenters alike, by students and gentleman scholars, its mixture of fable and fact appealed strongly to a generation of readers whose imaginations were stirred by the "New Philosophy" but who had not yet been persuaded to accept the wholesale existence of a mechanistic universe. A second edition of 1650 appeared quickly after the first, followed by another in 1658, and finally by a sixth, replete with the author's corrections, revisions, and additions in 1672. Despite being attacked, again by the quarrelsome Alexander Ross, the text appeared on at least one schoolmaster's list of "standard" works to be read by those who had "come to the university not with intention to make scholarship their profession, but only to get such learning as may serve for delight and ornament and such as the want whereof would speak a defect in breeding rather than scholarship."[48] Sir Thomas could be praised by the eminent chemist Robert Boyle as "the learned Dr. *Brown*,"[49] but even his most difficult work offered enough pleasure to escape a charge of being called simply learned lumber.

Twelve years later, Browne published his last work, or rather pair of works, those astonishingly curious and elegant prose treatises, *Hydriotaphia (Urne-Buriall)* and *The Garden of Cyrus* (1658). Dedicated respectively to his close friends, Thomas Le Gros of neighboring Crostwick and Nicholas Bacon in Gillingham near the Suffolk border, the essays show Browne narrowing his sights to a single object of contemplation—urns or gardens—while bringing to each all the antiquarian and natural lore he was gathering during the Interregnum. The works have since come to be viewed as Browne's most exquisite productions, with the fifth chapter of *Urne-Buriall* often regarded as without rival as a meditation on human vanity. But in Browne's day the two essays were read principally as scientific or quasi-scientific texts, and they helped to extend his reputation for erudition. In the year of their publication, the author was brought into correspondence with Sir William Dugdale, the leading antiquarian of his day, in order to aid him with his *History of Imbanking and Drayning* (1662). For his efforts, "the learned Dr. *Tho. Browne*," along with *Urne-Buriall,* received acknowledgment. Several years later, at the instigation of Sir Robert Paston of the ancient Paston family in Norfolk, Browne also began corresponding with John Evelyn. Evelyn was hoping "to engage [Sir Thomas's] assistance in suppliing my omissions" for an ambitious, though never completed, project entitled *Elysium Britannicum,* or *Plan of a Royal Garden (K,* 4, p. 276). Browne readily cooperated, sending him, among other things, a brief tract, "Of Garlands and Coronary or Garland-plants" (*K,* 3, 49–52), some observations on grafting (*K,* 3, 374–78), and a note on Norfolk oak trees (*K,* 4, 280–81), cited by Evelyn in his famous work on forestry, *Sylva* (1664). This generous action was repeated with Christopher Merrett, Fellow of the Royal College of Physicians, when Browne contributed some lengthy remarks on the natural history of Norfolk for an enlarged edition of that author's *Pinax Rerum Naturalium Britannicarum.* As early as *Religio Medici,* Browne had asserted that "I intend no Monopoly, but a Community, in learning; I study not for my owne sake onely, but for theirs that study not for themselves" (2.3, p. 58). Living in Norwich but communicating with other scholars as far away as Iceland, he never abandoned this ideal.

Browne died an eminent author. Although many of his writings remained still in manuscript—some of significant literary merit—the principal works by which he is known today were published during his lifetime. The major exceptions include *A Letter to a Friend*, printed by Edward in 1690 but begun probably in the 1650s, and *Christian Morals*, which Elizabeth saw to the press in 1716. Otherwise, the material collected in the 1683/84 edition of his *Miscellany Tracts*, like those added to the Browne canon with the first collected edition of his writings in 1686 and the publication of his *Posthumous Works* in 1712, increase our knowledge about the range of his interests without adding significantly to his literary reputation. The most valuable of these certainly include his notes from commonplace books, his tract "Of Languages and particularly of the Saxon Tongue," and the brief essay "On Dreams." In contrast to many of his contemporaries, moreover, Browne did not have to wait until the twentieth century to be "discovered." He has always attracted considerable attention from some of the best critical minds and most resourceful stylists in the history of English and American letters: Samuel Johnson in the eighteenth century; Coleridge, Hazlitt, Lamb, Melville, and Pater in the nineteenth; and a host of authors, critics and editors in our time. Without ever having composed a novel, written a play, or produced much poetry worth preserving, Browne remains one of the preeminent literary figures of his day.

Chapter Two

The Magus and the Man of Science

In his celebrated letter to Sara Hutchinson about Sir Thomas Browne, Coleridge remarked, "he is a quiet and sublime Enthusiast with a strong tinge of the Fantast, the Humorist constantly mingling with & flashing across the Philosopher, as the darting colours in shot silk play upon the main dye."[1] Coleridge's rich description of the texture of Browne's mind happily combines what is often easy to sunder: the complex fusion in Browne of the humorist and the philosopher, of the witty trickster of conceits and the serious scholar ploughing through tome after tome in search of a forgotten truth. Indeed, this potential sundering is written large in the split between the present and the previous century's estimation of the author. Valuing the eccentric at the expense of the scientist, Coleridge's immediate nineteenth-century heirs delivered a continuous encomium to the author's quaint and fantastic turns of thought. The twentieth century, on the other hand, has diligently sought to restore Browne to the more respected place he once occupied in the intellectual world of the seventeenth century. Published almost one hundred years after Walter Pater's "appreciation" (1886), Robin Robbins's monumental two-volume edition of *Pseudodoxia Epidemica* (1981) represents the culmination of an unacknowledged campaign to take Browne "seriously."[2]

As in so many instances, Coleridge's critical perceptions possess a telling truth; but however difficult it is to keep *his* Browne in full view, we cannot hope to understand how "the darting colours in shot silk play upon the main dye" if we skip over the dye itself and the vat from which it comes. Browne was, in some respects, very much a man of his age. Responsive to the religious controversies that riddled England in the 1640s and 1650s, he also participated in the Baconian program for the advancement of knowledge, which in so many ways helped to shape the intellectual contours of the seventeenth century. He was thus deeply—even if in the first case reluctantly—involved in what might be termed the two great events or movements of the period: the wars of truth that erupted in the actual fighting that pitted Anglican against Puritan, Royalist against Parliamentarian, and the rise of "science" or what in contemporary usage was called "natural" or "experimental" philosophy, the first word denoting the province of inquiry (nature rather than man) and the second suggesting the method of study (inductive rather than deductive).[3]

Given the potentially competing claims of religion and science, especially as they can appear to a modern, post-Darwinian audience, Browne's double involvement might seem another instance of his love of paradox, but such is not the case. Although religion and science have rarely accommodated each other with ease, they were also not necessarily viewed as irreconcilable opposites in the seventeenth century. From certain perspectives, in fact, they could be perceived as mutually enhancing activities. The "Book of Nature" had always been revered by both Catholics and Protestants as the manifestation of God and hence a legitimate ground of pious scrutiny so long as one did not, in George Herbert's words, "rest in Nature [but in] the God of Nature."[4] Indeed, upon reading *Pseudodoxia Epidemica,* Christopher Wren, the ejected dean of Windsor and father of the famous architect and scientist, wrote in the margin opposite Browne's allusion to St. Paul's injunction to beware of vain philosophy: "the worde (vaine) is a sufficient Commentarye to a Christian that by forbidding that which is indeed vaine, Hee advanceth true Philosophye: Such is that of the Hexameron or 6 Dayes creation: Whereon many of the Auncient Christians, have left admirable Treatises setting forth in those workes the incomprehensible Wisdom, and Majesty, and Omnipotency of the Creator."[5] On a more modern note, sociologists and historians have sought to underscore the connections between Protestantism and the rise of a technologically informed culture. "The sharp division in Protestant theology between natural and supernatural knowledge helped to establish the independence of the former," writes Christopher Hill, whose research into the practical discoveries made by sixteenth-and-seventeenth-century English merchants and sailors proceeds in a context emphasizing the general demystification of the Catholic church that began with Luther.[6] With its strong worldliness, Protestantism encouraged rather than discouraged inquiry into its immediate surroundings.

The individual who did the most to make natural philosophy respectable as a branch of learning in the seventeenth century was, of course, Francis Bacon. In William Harvey's measured phrase, he wrote of science *"like a Lord Chancellor."*[7] First in *The Advancement of Learning* (books 1–2, 1605) and then in *The Great Instauration* and its companion, *The New Organon* (1620), Bacon lent his persuasive voice to a new investigation of nature by attempting to free the field of inquiry from church authority and a crippling allegiance to the ancients, particularly Aristotle. In the first case, Bacon brought his superior skills of argumentation to bear on the problem of separating qualitative from quantitative knowledge, knowledge of God (metaphysics) from knowledge of second causes (physics): discriminating between "the proud knowledge of good and evil" and the "pure knowledge of nature and universality," he accommodated the conservative and antipathetic view of knowledge traditionally held by the divines but then transcended their criticisms by emphasizing how in the study of nature "man passeth on farther, and seeth the dependence of causes and the works of Providence; then, according to the allegory of the poets, he will easily believe that the highest link of Nature's chain must needs be tied to the foot of Jupiter's chair."[8] In the case of the ancients, Bacon's repudiation of their authority was part and parcel of his belief in progress. Since scholastic philosophy, the principal legacy of the ancients, had discovered nothing since the days of Aristotle, it was only a hindrance to the gradual revelation of truth Bacon sought in the study of nature.

Bacon's desire to redirect the course of learning, however optimistically presented, was nonetheless shaped by a careful recognition of human limitation. Strongly influenced by skeptical attacks on certainty, Bacon absorbed part of their criticisms of sensory knowledge—enough to demolish the methods of scholastic science—but then begged off taking the Pyrrhonian plunge into complete uncertainty in favor of an attitude approaching a "constructive" or "mitigated" skepticism.[9] Although human reasoning was scarcely infallible, Bacon assumed that errors could be anticipated and, with the aid of instruments, corrected. It was thus possible to create an environment in which an unimpeded empirical mode of inquiry into the laws of nature could proceed. Redefining the various "distempers of learning" mentioned in *The Advancement, The New Organon* gives memorable shape to what Bacon identified as four causes of error: "Idols of the Tribe" (the mistaken perception by man that he is the measure of all things when in fact "the human understanding is like a false mirror, which, receiving rays irregularly, distorts and discolours the nature of things by mingling its own nature with it"); "Idols of the Cave" (the particular limitations of an individual owing to his education and nature); "Idols of the Market Place" (the vagaries of language); and the "Idols of the Theater" (the received systems of thought that, without any claim to truth, still play upon the individual judgment).[10]

For Bacon the four idols were the necessary starting point for an intellectual reformation with practical consequences. In attempting to discover the basic laws of nature, the lord chancellor sought to inaugurate a systematic program of observation and experimentation in which the various branches of knowledge would be purged of error and brought to perfection. Natural, civil, ecclesiastical, and literary histories were to be written, the physical sciences explored and purified, the art of medicine remedied, investigation into light performed, the logical arts reformed, a recodification of language attempted, and so on. Bacon's program was nothing if not ambitious. It was a vision of communal inquiry worth, at the very least, the utopian expression it received in his depiction of the House of Solomon in *The New Atlantis* (1627).

In actual fact, the program's progressive note took on an eschatological ring through Bacon's own allusion to Daniel that in these latter times "many shall pass to an fro, and science shall be increased"; it is this millenarian call, repeated by various mid-century divines, that has led Charles Webster to remark that "Bacon became the most important philosophical and scientific authority of the Puritan Revolution."[11] After the Interregnum, of course, Bacon became the patron saint of the Royal Society. Although recent scholars have underscored the theoretical limitations of Baconian empiricism in connection with the mathematically founded discoveries of the seventeenth century (especially those associated with Galileo and Newton), there can be little doubting Bacon's general significance in contributing to the concept of a scientific revolution.[12] Enshrined on the frontispiece of the Royal Society's first history, he is identified by its author, Thomas Sprat, as the ideal modern experimenter "in whose Books there are every where scattered the best Arguments that can be produc'd for the Defence of experimental Philosophy."[13]

In helping to free natural philosophy from the burdens of the past, Bacon's signal accomplishment, according to Paolo Rossi, was to transform the image of science from that of the Renaissance magus writing in secrecy to a community of researchers working collectively. Partial though he was to alchemy, astrology, and natural magic, Bacon thoroughly opposed "the conception of scientific collaboration as a meeting of *illuminati* jealousy guarding their precious mysterious discoveries."[14] Paracelsus, Agrippa, Cardano, and Della Porta—great Renaissance practitioners of the occult—all sought to keep knowledge from the uninitiated. Relying upon riddles and obfuscating terminology, they privileged the quest for knowledge at the expense of enhancing the field of learning, while, to Bacon's mind, their methods of experimentation were so idiosyncratic as to be useless. "The derivations and prosecutions [of astrology, alchemy, and natural magic], both in the theories and the practices, are full of error and vanity," wrote Bacon in *The Advancement of Learning,* "which the great professors themselves have sought to veil over and conceal by enigmatical writings, and referring themselves to auricular traditions, and such other devices to save the credit of impostures."[15] In contrast to this elitist view, Bacon envisioned a more systematic and humble method of interpretation. The quest was to include the much despised mechanical arts and to proceed through a patient inquiry by many, not just a select few, of the laws of nature: "For the strongest and swiftest runners are perhaps not the best fitted to keep their torch alight since it may be put out by going too fast as well as too slow."[16]

The Quasi-Baconian

Browne was neither the swiftest nor the slowest in the pack of seventeenth-century scientists. He formally enrolled in the Baconian movement with *Pseudodoxia Epidemica,* a response to the call in *The Advancement* for a calendar of popular errors; but even before he directly encountered Bacon, the younger man, who had studied botany, anatomy, and chemistry on the Continent, revealed a decidedly sympathetic attitude toward science in his first published work, *Religio Medici.* As a defense of a physician's faith, that work sought in part to extricate the author from "the generall scandall of [his] profession," the charge "ubi tres medici duo Athei" (of every three physicians, two are atheists), by showing how neatly the scientist and the Christian united in the single figure of the inspired reader of God's two books, nature and Scripture. Browne's alternately bold and bashful persona is, in many respects, a later-day Solomon. Alluded to more often than any other figure in *Religio,* he is the type of the pious inquisitor whose investigations into nature bring glory to God (1.11, p. 11). "The wisedome of God," writes Browne, "receives small honour from those vulgar heads, that rudely stare about, and with a grosse rusticity admire his workes; those highly magnifie him whose judicious enquiry into his acts, and deliberate research into his creatures, returne the duty of a devout and learned admiration" (1.13, p. 13). Indeed, the bond between the two is further strengthened when Browne remarks how he "could with patience behold the urne and ashes of the *Vatican* [library], could I with a few others recover the perished leaves of *Solomon"* (1.24, p. 24). The "perished leaves" reputedly included a book of natural philosophy; its loss was several times lamented by Bacon and once by Marlowe's Faustus, who asks for "one booke more . . . wherein I might see al plants, hearbes and trees that grow upon the earth."[17]

As a pious inquirer into God's works, Browne did not need to have read Marlowe to recognize the potential Faustian dimensions of his quest. In a lengthy portion added to the 1643 text, made presumably when Browne was deep in his study preparing *Pseudodoxia* (1646), the speaker suddenly discovers that he has entered into combat with the devil: "the villany of that spirit takes a hint of infidelity from our Studies, and by demonstrating a naturality in one way, makes us mistrust a miracle in another" (1.19, p. 20). And in the ensuing struggle, in which his alter-ego-as-devil has been reading Paracelsus's *Archidoxis* and observing "some experiments of *Bitumen,"* Browne describes how Satan has attempted to subvert his faith by attributing biblical miracles to secondary causes: "Thus the Devill playd at Chesse with mee, and yeelding a pawne, thought to gaine a Queen of me, taking advantage of my honest endeavours; and whilst I labour'd to raise the structure of my reason, hee striv'd to undermine the edifice of my faith."

These Faustian interludes in *Religio,* however, are only flickering moments of temptation that otherwise help to prove the general rule of the physician's faith. If the scientist is occasionally cornered by Satan, the fideist continually eludes the devil's grasp. Like Herbert, Browne does not "so forget God, as to adore the name of Nature" (*RM,* 1.16, p. 15). His world, or rather his view of God's world in *Religio,* remains vitalistic throughout, animated from above, a place of continual wonder and bemusement: "those strange and mysticall transmigrations that I have observed in Silkewormes, turn'd my Philosophy into Divinity" (1.39, p. 38). God is the cause he gropes after; Copernicus is relegated to a jesting parenthetical inclusion in the final section.

Browne's fideistic reading of nature parallels, in a finer tone, Bacon's assertion in *The Advancement* that "the highest link of nature's chain must needs be tied to the foot of Jupiter's chair," but the later author's desire to graft theology to natural philosophy ultimately leads him to value a whole mode of Platonically inspired thought that was anathema to Bacon's empirical bent.[18] In *Religio,* Browne possesses something of the mystic whom Bacon so roundly repudiates. Rather than attempting to drive a wedge between natural philosophy and magic, the author of *Religio* asserts the points of continuity between them: "Thus I thinke at first a great part of Philosophy was Witchcraft, which being afterward derived to one another, proved but Philosophy, and was indeed no more but the honest effects of Nature" (1.31, p. 30). To Browne, only a small step separates the magus from the natural philosopher, the sorcerer's incantation from the holy man's investigation. His reading of God's second book thus assumes a mysterious, self-initiating function. Not only is the author careful to distinguish vulgar interpretations of nature that admire with a "gross rusticity" from judicious inquiries and deliberate research, but these careful measurements are further refined through allusions to Pythagoras, Hermes Trismegistus, and Paracelsus. "I have often admired the mysticall ways of *Pythagoras,* and the secret Magicke of numbers," Browne writes in one of several famous excursions into numerology in *Religio:*

Beware of Philosophy, is a precept not to be received in too large a sense; for in this masse of nature there is a set of things that carry in their front, though not in capitall letters, yet in stenography, and short Characters, something of Divinitie, which to wiser reasons serve as Luminaries in the abysse of knowledge, and to judicious beliefes, as scales and roundles to mount the pinnacles and highest pieces of Divinity. The severe Schooles shall never laugh me out of the Philosophy of *Hermes,* that this visible world is but a picture of the invisible, wherein as in a pourtract, things are not truely, but in equivocall shapes; and as they counterfeit some more reall substance in that invisible fabrick. (1.12, p. 12)

If the allusion to the ladder of ascent is a Neoplatonic common-place in the Renaissance, Browne nonetheless sets out to persuade us that he is one of the masterful readers of God's fine print. Others might behold the divine "but asquint upon reflex or shadow" (1.13, p. 12), but Browne's ocular inquiries frequently verge on the luminous. They do so, however, not because the author describes what others have not seen, but because he surrounds the operation of his sight with a discourse that privileges the attempt:

Now there are besides these Characters in our faces, certaine mysticall figures in our hands, which I dare not call meere dashes, strokes, *a la volee,* or at randome, because delineated by a pencill, that never workes in vaine; and hereof I take more particular notice, because I carry that in mine owne hand, which I could never read of, nor discover in another. *Aristotle,* I confesse, in his acute, and singular booke of Physiognomy, hath made no mention of Chiromancy, yet I beleeve the *Egyptians,* who were neerer addicted to those abstruse and mysticall sciences, had a knowledge therein, to which those vagabond and counterfeit *Egyptians* did after pretend, and perhaps retained a few corrupted principles, which sometimes might verifie their prognostickes. (2.2, p. 57).

"I dare not call," "I take more particular notice," "I could never read," "I confesse," "yet I beleeve": this is a conditional grammar of assent that honors its own perceptions, a practice of verbal individuation that parallels the special signature in his hand, "which I could never read of, nor discover in another." But Browne never actually reads his palm. The speaker's mysterious character—that is, the character written on his hand—is not disclosed by the author; we discover it instead only as the author first distinguishes himself from Aristotle, who is silent on the issue of chiromancy, and then as he allies himself with the Egyptians, whose "abstruse and mysticall sciences" are not to be identified with "those vagabond and counterfeit *Egyptians,*" the gypsies. The full sweep of Browne's thought, in short, tells us little about *what* he sees but much about *how* he sees, and the process is not to be confused with the methods of vulgar pretenders.

When Browne turned to writing *Pseudodoxia Epidemica,* he swapped an epistemology that sought to tease reason out of thought for one that attempted to establish a standard of reliability in the philosophical inquiry into nature. If the heart of *Religio* is Tertullian's paradox "certum est quia impossible est" (it is certain because it is impossible), the central concern of *Pseudodoxia* is to distinguish the improbable from the probable, the fabulous from the admissible, by invoking "the three determinators of truth, Authority, Sense, and Reason" (3.5, p. 176). Browne's focus is not an individual's belief in God but the general credulity of common opinion in its attempt to understand God's world. In addressing the topic of popular error, he was thus abandoning the subject of moral certitude in favor of examining what a recent scholar of the period has described as the "lower reaches" of knowledge, "mere opinion" and "conjecture,"[19] a subject that Bacon saw worthy of address if the study of natural philosophy were to be liberated from superstition and error: "The registering and proposing of doubts has a double use: first it guards philosophy against errors, when upon a point not clearly proved no decision or assertion is made (for so error might beget error), but judgment is suspended and not made positive; secondly, doubts once registered are so many suckers or sponges which continually draw and attract increase of knowledge; whence it comes that things which, if doubts had not preceded, would have been passed by lightly without observation, are through the suggestion of doubts attentively and carefully observed."[20]

Bacon's call for a "Calendar of Dubitations," to which should be annexed a "*Calendar* of Falshoods and of popular Errors, now passing unargued in Naturall History, and in Opinions," provided the occasion, and much of the shaping strategy if not all of the inspiration, for *Pseudodoxia*. In the preface "To The Reader," Browne hopes that his work will not be "unwelcome unto those honoured Worthies, who endeavour the advancement of Learning" (p. 4). He assumes, moreover, the posture of the patient Baconian researcher working "in the slow and sober wheele" of the world (p. 1). And though he does not participate in a community of researchers working collectively, he is careful to apologize for his audacity in addressing such a large and difficult topic when it "did well deserve the conjunction of many heads" (p. 1). Browne even echoes Bacon's sentiments in *The Advancement* that "overmuch credit . . . hath been given unto authors in science in making them dictators" when he reassures the reader that "wee are not Magisteriall in opinions, nor have wee Dictator-like obtruded our conceptions, but in the humility of Enquiries or disquisitions, have only proposed them unto more ocular discerners" (p. 4).

As for the many causes of human error, Bacon and Browne assign some of the most important to the same sources. Both men struck out against what Browne called "a resolved prostration unto Antiquity" (1.7, p. 40). Both were equally critical of human credulity: Bacon's third distemper of learning in *The Advancement* and Browne's third cause of common error dovetail in their focus on man's habitual willingness to accept things weakly authorized. Each writer also identified language—what Browne referred to as "the fallacie of Æquivocation and Amphibologie" (1.4, p. 22)—as the most persistent source of confusion. Bacon argued that the Idols of the Market Place, a variation on his second distemper of learning, are the most troublesome of all since "words stand in the way and resist change. Whence it comes to pass that the high and formal discussions of learned men end oftentimes in disputes about words and names." Browne officially recognized six causes of verbal error, but he was most concerned with two categories that merge into a single one: ambiguities inherent in words themselves stemming from the Fall and the vulgar misapprehension of a literal for a metaphoric sense. As an example of the latter instance (which in fact embraces the former), he describes how Pythagoras's injunction for his disciples to abstain from eating beans was not a dietary prohibition, as many suppose, but a political pronouncement, "for by beanes were the Magistrates elected in some parts of Greece" (p. 23).

Pseudodoxia, however, is too huge to owe its existence to any single source of inspiration, even one as magisterial as Bacon. If Browne repeatedly echoes Baconian phrases and ideas in book 1 and perhaps even derives his seven-book structure from *The Advancement,*[21] his encyclopedic study of human error naturally leads him to wander off in the company of others as he attempts to traverse the labyrinth of truth. James Primerose's *De Vulgi in Medicina Erroribus* (1638) and Laurent Joubert's *De Vulgi Erroribus* serve as Browne's acknowledged ports of embarkation ("To the Reader"); George Hakewill's *An Apologie . . . Consisting in an Examination and Censure of the Common Error Touching Nature's Perpetuelle and Universall Decay* (1627)—dubbed by R. F. Jones as "the first significant defence of modernity in England"[22]—remains Browne's unacknowledged guide to particular places. Browne then produces a nearly bewildering number of ancient and modern authorities in his progress through his seven categories of error: (1) general, (2) mineral and vegetable, (3) animals, (4) man, (5) pictures, (6) geography and history, and (7) the Bible and history.

Browne's is very much a grand tour for the educated. Despite its

popular subtitle of "Vulgar Errors," *Pseudodoxia* is not written for
a popular audience. The author who played the Neoplatonic *illuminatus* in *Religio* now serves as one of the leading pedagogues of
the country opening up his vast library to the gentry. Allowing
them full access to his texts, he consciously defines the exclusive
nature of the venture: "Nor have wee addressed our penne or stile
unto the people, (whom Bookes doe not redresse, and are this way
incapable of reduction) but unto the knowing and leading part of
Learning." Although Browne does choose to write *Pseudodoxia* in
the vulgar tongue rather than Latin, he is prompted by patriotic
rather than egalitarian concerns; and though he remarks jestingly
that "wee shall within few yeares bee faine to learne Latine to
understand English" in order to meet a supposed increase in the
number of works written in Latin, he is not opting for a back-to-
the-basics native style. "I confesse, the quality of the Subject will
sometimes carry us into expressions beyond meere English apprehensions," he rhapsodizes on his way to remarking how his understanding must be watered from higher regions (pp. 2–3).

Nonetheless, under the pressure of Browne's skeptical intelligence
and occasional experiments, the world of sympathetic insinuations,
signatures, chiromancy, and astrology so valued in *Religio* loses much
of its luster in *Pseudodoxia*. When Browne writes of Egyptian hieroglyphics now, he does so not to celebrate the abstruse mysteries
they might contain but to criticize them for continually misrepre-
senting the physical world. Hieroglyphs are described as simply
"the best evasion" of a linguistic confusion that originated with the
tower of Babel; they are not a solution to a problem caused by the
Fall involving the gap between language and nature, sign and signified, since they are also the product of human invention (5.20,
pp. 419–20). Likewise, among the many authors whom Browne
urges to be read with caution are Cardano and Della Porta. Although
both can be of "singular use unto a prudent Reader," the former is
described as "a great enquirer of truth, but too greedy a receiver of
it"; the latter is included, in Baconian fashion, among those "who
pretend to write of secrets" (1.8, pp. 52–53).

But if there is a rule to Browne's "assimilating phancy" (*PE*, 2.6,
p. 141)—to borrow his own description—it follows the river Ar-
ethusa. Ideas, "though they lose their currents in one place, they
rise up againe in another" (*RM*, 1.6, p. 7). The Neoplatonist takes
a back seat to the Baconian in *Pseudodoxia*, the magus gives way to

the empiricist, but the author who seeks to "maintaine a naturall and proper course, in the slow and sober wheele" of this world never really forgets the swing and rapture of the other (*PE,* "To The Reader," p. 1). In Browne's final two authorized publications, *Urne-Buriall* and *The Garden of Cyrus* (1658), the Neoplatonist gets the upper hand, although not without a few odd twists.

In the case of *Urne-Buriall,* Browne is very much the Baconian scientist trudging about a burial site with an imaginary team of researchers. Usually adopting the passive voice, he rarely speaks in the first person. This is to be an objective recording of the "facts," a report about urns that includes particular descriptions and plausible datings. Many of Browne's sentences are simply elaborately punctuated lists devoid of a speaking subject; others occasionally include the first-person plural to give the effect of a consensus view: "These upon view were judged to be wood, but sinking in water and tried by fire, we found them to be bone or Ivory" (p. 103). An initial opinion is corrected by an experiment, a more authoritative understanding of the material emerges, and it receives the endorsement of the community in the introduction of "we" into the sentence. And yet in the closing meditation on the vanity of human wishes, these empirically formed judgments come to assume the appearance of "nothing in the Metaphysics of true belief" (p. 125), a point Dr. Johnson somberly recognized long ago when he spoke "of the uselessness of all these enquiries."[23] Browne's Baconian researcher seems to sink in the muck of oblivion, only to be recovered in a very different form at the end of *The Garden of Cyrus.*

The Garden of Cyrus is written in another key altogether, as Frank Huntley observed in his valuable study of the contrasting and complimentary dimensions of these two works.[24] Browne has exchanged an epistemology stressing human ignorance for one emphasizing individual illumination, and there is surely in the author's dedication of the work to Nicholas Bacon, the kinsman of Francis, a witty play on the idea of a new advancement of learning. But this is also no longer the Baconian empiricist employing a team of researchers, as in *Urne-Buriall.* Browne is, with some apology, a Pythagorean *illuminatus* who has found in the number 5 a possible answer to the workings of the universe. His earlier attempt in *Religio* to privilege the Neoplatonic vision is now written large in the vision itself, which discovers a mathematical scheme for the universe in the quincunx originally found in the garden of Cyrus. But the quincunx is not simply an order that Browne discovers in nature; it is also an instrument through which he divines all reality, a mystical figuration that does just what Bacon criticized Gilbert for doing with the lodestone: attempting to construct a philosophy out of a single discovery.[25] In his methods, his subject matter, his wry, somewhat grandiose pretensions, his trafficking with Della Porta (whose encyclopedic treatise on gardening is quietly appropriated into the first book), and his acknowledged love of cryptography, Browne could not be less Baconian. And yet at the very end of this essay, Browne comes down a step to assume perhaps the most Baconian posture in all his writings.[26] I say "perhaps" because his magniloquent invitation for others to join him in tracing the labyrinth of truth seems tinged with just enough wit and humor to keep the matter in doubt:

Flat and flexible truths are beat out by every hammer; But *Vulcan* and his whole forge sweat to work out *Achilles* his armour. A large field is yet left unto sharper discerners to enlarge upon this order, to search out the *quaternio's* and figured draughts of this nature, and moderating the study of names and meer nomenclature of plants, to erect generalities, disclose unobserved proprieties, not only in the vegetable shop, but the whole volume of nature; affording delightful Truths, confirmable by sense and ocular Observation, which seems to me the surest path, to trace the Labyrinth of Truth. (*GC,* p. 174)

This is Browne's signal call for a communal inquiry into nature, his miniature *Advancement of Learning,* his House of Solomon. But the preceding queries whose answers are to be hammered out in Browne's forge make the whole enterprise liable for a smile: "Why *Proteus* in *Homer* the *Symbole* of the first matter, before he setled himself in the midst of his Seamonsters, doth place them out by fives? Why the fifth years Oxe was acceptable Sacrifice unto *Jupiter?* Or why the Noble *Antoninus* in some sence doth call the soul it self a Rhombus?" (*GC,* p. 173). Browne's House of Solomon remains a cabinet of curiosities; this Vulcan seeks "delightful Truths," as the sweat mentioned at the outset seems to evaporate under the witty pressure of the author attempting to transform his garden into "a vegetable shop." The quincuncial-minded Pythagorean does not split with but humorously assimilates the Baconian empiricist.[27]

Summary Overview

Browne's excursions into the world of seventeenth-century science were significant enough to earn him an honored place among his contemporaries. They were also sufficiently varied to make easy generalizations by later scholars difficult. Like Bacon, his interests were primarily, though not exclusively, those of a "naturalist," a term that Marie Boas Hall usefully invokes in order to distinguish Browne both from "virtuosi" (with their dilettantish habits of inquiry) and from scientists like Robert Boyle and Robert Hooke, who valued experimentation over mere observation and produced significant discoveries in the fields of chemistry and optics.[28] Browne's breakthroughs were modest, to say the least. In *Urne-Buriall,* he reported observing what was later formally identified as *adipocere,* a strange fatty substance that clings to certain corpses, while his experiments with chicken eggs have earned him at least the claim to be considered one of "the first to experiment in the field of chemical embryology."[29] In general, however, his investigations of nature were essentially attempts to judge what was probable; they did not issue from "a search for the absolute,"[30] at least insofar as the laws of nature were concerned.

And yet, however small Browne's achievements might seem today, his attitude toward advancing learning was finally not simply whimsical. In a celebrated section of *Christian Morals,* he urges, "Let thy Studies be free as thy Thoughts and Contemplations: but fly not only upon the wings of Imagination; Joyn Sense unto Reason, and Experiment unto Speculation, and so give life unto Embryon Truths, and Verities yet in their Chaos. There is nothing more acceptable unto the Ingenious World, than this noble Eluctation of Truth; wherein, against the tenacity of Prejudice and prescription, this Century now prevaileth" (221). Whether these remarks constitute a genuine recognition of the importance of hypothesis in experimentation—a point later seventeenth-century scientists viewed as a deficiency in Bacon's heavily inductive approach—remains questionable, as does the larger issue of whether Browne was a "true Scientist."[31] But the passage, buttressed by an additional sentence, reveals Browne's commitment to the whole investigative enterprise—"this noble Eluctation of Truth"—and the special place he saw being reserved for "this Century" in the eyes of posterity: "What Libraries of new Volumes aftertimes will behold, and in what a new

World of Knowledge the eyes of our Posterity may be happy, a few
Ages may joyfully declare; and is but a cold thought unto those,
who cannot hope to behold this Exantlation of Truth, or that obscured Virgin half out of the Pit" (2.5, p. 221). Admitting in
Religio Medici that "the world growes near its end" (1.45, p. 43),
counting the clock more exactly in *Urne-Buriall,* Browne's response
was finally not to sit down and contemplate darkness but to attempt
to contribute to the increasing light.

In doing so, Browne's scientific pursuits were shaped by geography, profession, and a humanist's respect for antiquity and the
written word, secular and sacred alike. He possessed an Englishman's
characteristic regard for empirical inquiry over theory,[32] and a physician's preference for the microscope rather than the telescope.
Although he owned most of Descartes's works, he showed little
inclination to model his reasoning after the tight logic of mathematics. His was the old math of Euclidean geometry, given special
sanction by Plato, not the new math of physics, which led Galileo
and Newton to discover the laws of motion. The moons of Jupiter
and the Ptolomaic-Copernican controversy (*PE,* 2.2, p. 87; 4.6, p.
468) remain largely peripheral to his more immediate interests in
biology, botany, and the desire to erase the "tenacity of Prejudice
and prescription." Not surprisingly, Browne's two great champions
of modern science were both English physicians. William Gilbert,
whose *De Magnete* (1600) laid the foundation for the study of terrestrial magnetism, is hailed as the "Father Philosopher" (*PE,* 2.2,
p. 96) who found more than "Columbus or Americus," and William
Harvey receives a similar salutation for his discovery of the circulation of the blood. Browne's special admiration for these two men
cannot be simply chalked up to a residual scientific chauvinism since
their works were among the most celebrated of the first half of the
century; but his high estimation of them does indicate that for all
his wide reading and travels, Browne was scientifically most at home
in his own country, and even there he seemed most comfortable
observing small things, like plants, bees, and chicken eggs. In this
regard, it is worth noting that while he was a Neoplatonist in many
things, he did not join his Neoplatonic contemporaries, Henry More
or John Milton, in one of the favorite intellectual pastimes of the
period: speculating about life on other planets.

In the year in which Browne died, the botanist Nehemiah Grew
wrote, "All Nature is one Great Engine, made by, and held in

[God's] hand."[33] Browne would certainly have endorsed Grew's protective image of the world being cradled in God's hand, but he would have resisted the mechanistic view of the universe suggested by the metaphor of nature as one great engine. Without explicitly doing so, Browne opposed this interpretation made fashionable by Hobbes at mid-century and increasingly favored by scientists like Grew. The physician's loyalties were to an older, though hardly outdated, notion of the deity, not to an incipient deism. His universe is one of generation and change, growth and decay, animated by spirits that signaled a God very much concerned with a world in which man was its only, still much privileged, interpreter. For Browne, as for many of his contemporaries, there was no vast incongruity in considering the function of tutelary angels on one page of notes and the sex life of frogs on another. Both had their origins in the final cause. Both therefore belonged in the same book.

Chapter Three

Browne's Religion: Playing Down Differences

Browne's was very much an Englishman's science that radiated outward to include Continental thinkers. So, too, his religion was very much of the Church of England forged out of the Elizabethan compromise between Rome and Geneva. "There is no Church," he observed in *Religio Medici,*

whose every part so squares unto my conscience, whose articles, constitutions, and customes seeme so consonant unto reason, and as it were framed to my particular devotion, as this whereof I hold my beliefe, the Church of *England,* to whose faith I am a sworne subject, and therefore in a double obligation, subscribe unto her Articles, and endeavour to observe her Constitutions: whatsoever is beyond, as points indifferent, I observe according to the rules of my private reason, or the humor and fashion of my devotion, neither believing this, because *Luther* affirmed it, or disproving that, because *Calvin* hath disavouched it. I condemne not all things in the Councell of *Trent,* nor approve all in the Synod of *Dort.* In briefe, where the Scripture is silent, the Church is my Text; where that speakes, 'tis but my Comment; where there is a joynt silence of both, I borrow not the rules of my Religion from *Rome* or *Geneva,* but the dictates of my owne reason. (1.5, pp. 5–6)

It would be difficult to find in the whole of the seventeenth century a more succinctly phrased pledge of allegiance to the Church of England. In syntax, tone, and argument, Browne's judiciously flexible definition of the via media recollects in miniature Richard Hooker's much vaster *Ecclesiastical Polity* (1593, 1597), the *summa* of sixteenth-century apologies on behalf of the English church. The triple use of "reason," the careful allusion to points indifferent, and the concluding hierarchy of Scripture, church, and reason: these were among the celebrated catchphrases of Anglican apologists from Jewel to Chillingworth as they sought to guide the church they inherited from Henry VIII's split with Rome through the rough seas of the Protestant Reformation.

For Browne, as for Hooker, neither Papal infallibility nor scriptural authority could serve as the single determiner of truth—the necessary rock upon which a religion could be built. As Protestants, both steered away from Rome and naturally elevated the Bible to a position of supreme authority in their religion, recognizing that the things absolutely necessary for salvation were "plainly set down in Scripture, so that he which heareth or readeth may without any great difficulty understand."[1] But neither assumed, in contrast to strict Calvinists, that the converse was true: that everything in Scripture was essential for salvation. Nor did either assume, again as Calvin had done, that biblical silence on a subject indifferent to salvation, like forms of worship, necessarily indicated divine disapproval: there was much that could be done in the name of goodness that was still not dictated by Scripture.

In place of what was interpreted as too rigid an adherence either to Scripture or tradition, Geneva or Rome, religious moderates like Hooker sought to construct a more flexible and rational relationship between Church liturgy and biblical truth. This was a church, writes John Booty, that condemned "the falsities of the extremists while accepting and affirming the truths that the extremists hold."[2] Such a potentially comprehensive strategy was, to be sure, vulnerable to criticism since it could be readily charged that the church was hedging its bets when only those most ardently committed to the truth would receive St. Peter's blessings. To certain zealous individuals, wrote the coolly observant Bacon, "all speech of pacification is odious." And yet Bacon also recognized that it was not easy to expound upon the virtues of quietism—to "accommodate points of religion by middle ways"—without simply delivering "witty reconcilements" that betray a lukewarm faith.[3] Hooker's strategy, an elaborate version of Bacon's and in turn further and more comically elaborated upon by Browne in *Religio Medici,* was to distinguish between the fundamental points of faith and those of custom and opinion, and then to argue for their judicious and witty assimilation in a *reasonable* worship of God that imitated the rational order of God's universe.

In practical terms, obedience to the English church in the early seventeenth century meant observing both the Thirty-Nine Articles and its liturgy. The former, with its Calvinistic cast, emphasized, among other things, that salvation was by faith alone, that good works done without the inspiration of Christ "have the nature of sin," and that God had predestined an elect community of the saved.[4] The latter, with its vestigial Catholicism, valued the rituals and ceremonies prescribed in the Book of Common Prayer produced first in the reign of Edward VI, banned under Queen Mary, and then reinstituted with minor modifications early in Elizabeth's time, where it remained intact during Stuart England until the Civil War when it was temporarily supplanted in 1645 by the plainer Westminster Directory of Public Worship. This preservation of ancient rites also included honoring feast days; it could even involve maypoling, morris dancing, or drinking on Sundays after church service, in keeping with James I's statutes in *The Book of Sports,* issued first in 1618 and then reissued by Charles I in 1633.

Since from its early days under Henry VIII the English church was a "reformed" church superimposed upon a people who worshipped an older faith, it was constantly subject to internal pressures, frequently aided by rival powers from the Continent, especially in Spain. These struggles are amply illustrated in the considerable amount of controversial literature produced during the sixteenth and seventeenth centuries. Such struggles were also more spectacularly and hideously exhibited in the many victims persecuted for their faith. The execution of Sir Thomas More for refusing to subscribe to the Oath of Supremacy is legendary (though his own persecution of Protestants is less well known). So, too, are the many acts of reprisals perpetrated by Mary Tudor on Protestants during the five years of her reign (1553–58). The biblical translator John Rogers was the first to be burned for heresy, and he was joined shortly thereafter by some 280 others, the majority taken from the working class, while the leading clerical martyrs included Nicholas Ridley and Hugh Latimer. These and the lives of other Protestant martyrs fill the pages of John Foxe's enormously popular *Actes and Monuments* (first published in 1563), a work that served to remind later reformists of the atrocities committed by the Catholic queen, someone whom a recent historian, A. G. Dickens, has charged with doing more than anyone "to create that unreasoning Protestant bigotry which for a century and a half after her death was to prove England's most evil inheritance from the Reformation. As usual, one extremism enhanced its opposite extremism; the noisome smoke inevitably followed the horrors of the fire."[5]

Dickens has in mind, of course, the anti-Catholic legislation enacted under Elizabeth that made it high treason for any Jesuit or seminary priest to be within the queen's dominion. The number of executions during her reign—around 153—did not quite even the score, though it was to be helped in the early years of James's rule by the public disembowelment of Guy Fawkes and his associates for the role they supposedly played in a Catholic "conspiracy" to blow up Parliament on 5 November 1605. The event was known as the "Gunpowder Plot," and its "discovery" was viewed by contemporaries, Browne included, as an act of God; the event is still celebrated today, though usually without the providential overtones. When Archbishop Laud (1573–1645), with the encouragement of Charles I and his Catholic wife and "Romish" court, sought to reinstitute a highly ceremonial form of worship in the 1630s that de-emphasized the historic role of Puritanism in the church and supposedly subscribed to an "Arminian" view of salvation (in which predestination was downplayed in favor of a saving grace that might be distributed at large), and then, in order to enforce this program for a uniform religion, insisted upon strengthening the ecclesiastical hierarchy, there was bound to be trouble.

Or so it seems in retrospect. The first obvious sign of strain surely occurred with the infamous trial in 1637 of Henry Burton, John Bastwick, and William "Marginal" Prynne for sedition and libel. It succeeded largely in making them martyrs to the Puritan cause, though the punishment only involved imprisonment, fines, and ears being clipped. Laud's attempt to impose the Prayer Book upon a traditionally recalcitrant and strongly Calvinistic sector of Scotland brought embarrassment on a larger scale: the defeat of the Royalist army in the First Bishops's War in 1639. The following year witnessed further attempts to defend Laudian episcopacy in the face of increasing attacks on its claim that the bishop received his authority from God (*jure divino*) and not from the king (*jure humano*). But these, too, proved ultimately unsuccessful. By 1641, Laud was in prison. By 1643, episcopacy was abolished by Parliament; and in 1645, with the Parliamentary forces largely in control of the nation and the king in no position to offer support, the former archbishop was executed. The beheading of Charles I followed some four years later.

Laud, of course, cannot be asked to shoulder the full weight of the Civil War, the causes of which are multiple and deeply embedded in social, economic, and constitutional issues as well. But his role in bringing about the temporary demise of the English church as a functioning "middle way" seems unquestionable. When in 1625 he handed the newly crowned Charles a list of divines labeled *O* for Orthodox and *P* for Puritans to be used in appointing ecclesiastical officials, a list, moreover, that "inverted what the religious majority believed to be the true order of things,"[6] he set the church spinning, slowly at first, and then more precipitously, in a divisive direction that culminated in war. As Bacon recognized, it is never easy to give a persuasively embracing reading of Matthew 12:30, "He that is not with us is against us," except perhaps to offer the converse in Luke: "He that is not against us is with us" (9:50).[7] The church emerging from the Elizabethan settlement and visible in the first quarter of the seventeenth century under James's peaceful rule did its best and perhaps temporarily succeeded in embodying the tolerance implied in Luke's statement. Under Laud, the potential paranoia contained in Matthew's remark took over.

Religio Medici: A Moderate Proposal

Browne was the great proponent of Luke's reading and of a spacious pre-Laudian high church. Having left for medical studies on the Continent in 1629, the year in which Laud was extending his bid for ecclesiastical supremacy as bishop of London, he returned to England at the end of 1633, the year in which Laud was made archbishop. Browne's sympathies, however, were more for the church he left than the one that was emerging under Laud; and, after four years of living abroad he attempted to reincarnate it in his "soft and flexible" discourse: hierarchical but not authoritarian, ceremonial but not insistently so, and favoring uniformity of worship but not necessarily at the expense of extirpating sects.

Begun shortly after his return, *Religio Medici* articulates the devotional perspective of a moderate. Browne shifts constantly and happily between Rome and Geneva, France and Holland, defining and refining his religious temper in relation to doctrines, attitudes, and stances borrowed from each—all the while underscoring the central place in his worship of God of a tolerance bordering on pacifism. The irenic persona identifies himself with "that reformed new-cast Religion, wherein I dislike nothing but the name [Protestantism] (1.2, p. 3). He disavows any skill at religious controversy, preferring the buckler to the sword of faith, shrinks from pulpit invective, and reproves the violence associated with martyrdom. Although as an English Protestant Browne could hardly escape reading Foxe's *Acts and Monuments* (K, 3:321), *Religio Medici* nonetheless seeks to carve out a place in which the proving ground of faith is separate from the pyre. "'Tis not in the power of every honest faith to proceed thus farre, or passe to Heaven through the flames; every one hath it not in that full measure, nor in so audacious and resolute a temper, as to endure those terrible tests and trialls, who notwithstanding in a peaceable way doe truely adore their Saviour, and have (no doubt) a faith acceptable in the eyes of God" (1.25, p. 26).

As a spokesman for, or rather the embodiment of, the via media (it is impossible fully to separate the two attitudes), Browne favors proportion and balance—an attitude mirrored in the many doublets in the work—as much as he does a tactful subscription to a few fundamental rules of faith. If he underscores the general Protestant creed that "there is no salvation to those that beleeve not in Christ" (1.54, p. 50), he guards cautiously against the reduction of beliefs into slogans. Reflecting upon the semantics of religious controversy, he reminds us that "martyr" and "heretick" are relative terms whose meaning will be fixed only at the end of time and only by God: "There are many (questionlesse) canonized on earth, that shall never be Saints in Heaven; and have their names in Histories and Martyrologies, who in the eyes of God, are not so perfect Martyrs as was that wise Heathen *Socrates,* that suffered on a fundamentall point of Religion, the Unity of God" (1.26, pp. 26–27). Protestant theology cannot be twisted into saving the "wise Heathen" or even expanded sufficiently in a Catholic direction to create a limbo for him, but in the narrow lexicon of religious disputes Socrates' presence warns us that our vocabulary is not necessarily God's. In a similarly skeptical vein, Browne subscribes to the Calvinist doctrine of predestination (1.11, p. 11), but not rigidly. He is more concerned with the mysterious nature of the Last Judgment, in which "many [will be] saved who to man seeme reprobated" (1.57, p. 53), than he is with the particular requirements involving the relation of faith to works necessary for admission into heaven. "I doe not deny, but that true faith, and such as God requires, is not onely a marke or token, but also a meanes of our Salvation, but where to finde this, is as obscure to me, as my last end" (1.60, p. 54).

Browne will always be remembered for his modest wish "to be but the last man, and bring up the Rere in Heaven" (1.58, p. 53).[8]

From a doctrinaire Calvinistic perspective, if there is a potential danger in Browne's theology, it is the temptation of too generous a view of God's charity, an attitude that runs throughout *Religio* but appears in its most concentrated form in the author's discussion of his heretical "greener studies." One of these heresies was Origen's (the other two involved denying the immortality of the soul and praying for the dead). With Origen, Browne thought "that God would not persist in his vengeance for ever, but after a definite time of his wrath hee would release the damned soules from torture" (1.7, p. 8). As D. P. Walker has argued, Origen's heresy is intimately connected with the decline of the idea of Hell in Western thought; it was assumed that "if the fear of eternal punishment were removed, most people would behave without any moral restraint whatever and that society would collapse into an anarchical orgy."[8] The radical nature of this belief, moreover, had particular currency among seventeenth-century Arminians and Neoplatonists who were reacting "sharply against Calvinist predestinationism."[9] Browne's endorsement of it was thus not idle reportage nor was his retraction, for if his initial temptation into sympathy with Origen proceeds out of a need for "a ready weight to sway me from the other extream of despaire," his recognition of his error surely returns him to the mainstream of Calvinistic thought. Furthermore, despite his continued dilations on the infinite power of God's mercy in *Religio,* Browne does not attempt to cut corners on this issue, as did later latitudinarians like Archbishop Tillotson.[10] At the end of section 54, with its moving consideration of the virtuous heathens, the author's sympathy for them falls like gentle rain until it lands on the bedrock of doctrine where it coolly evaporates in the light of ultimate truth: "It will therefore, and must at last appeare, that all salvation is through Christ; which verity I feare these great examples of vertue must confirme, and make it good, how the perfectest actions of earth have no title or claime unto Heaven."

In the hieroglyphics of Browne's religion, *P's* and *O's* do not exist as separate categories of being; they lose their discrete outlines in the general alphabet of the author's faith. This is not to suggest that there are not distinctly Calvinistic or Catholic strands to Browne's religion, nor is it to say that his faith could not be attacked for appearing heretical to either Calvinists or Catholics. It is to argue, along with Leonard Nathanson,[11] that Browne's Neoplatonic cast of mind blended with his moderate attachment to a few shared fundamentals of faith, and together they encourage a broad, inclusive view of the church. "I am sure there is a common Spirit that playes within us, yet makes no part of us, and that is the Spirit of God" (1.32, p. 31), he observes. "It is the common wonder of all men," he notes elsewhere, "how among so many millions of faces, there should be none alike; Now, contrary, I wonder as much how there should be any" (2.2, p. 57). Browne's is a perspective that simultaneously narrows and expands, that particularizes only to show the folly of over particularization: "I doe desire with God, that all, but yet affirme with men, that few shall know salvation, that the bridge is narrow, the passage straite unto life; yet those who doe confine the Church of God, either to particular Nations, Churches, or Families, have made it farre narrower than our Saviour ever meant it" (1.55, p. 52). His persona, too, can seem at times that of both a precisian and a high church man: "my common conversation I do acknowledge austere, my behaviour full of rigour, sometimes not without morosity; yet at my devotion I love to use the civility of my knee, my hat, and hand, with all those outward and sensible motions, which may expresse, or promote my invisible devotion" (1.3, p. 4).

As a moderate Protestant who emphasized that "we have reformed from [Rome], not against [it]" (1.3, p. 4), Browne's patience was severely tested on only two related issues: excommunication and religious schism. Both threatened the universal order and harmony he sought in religious experience; both issues are also addressed in sections added in 1643 when the idea of a via media was collapsing under the weight of political and religious pressures. In section 56, Browne rejected out of hand the power of one church to exclude another from heaven, regardless of whether the excommunicating agent was Rome or the Church of England or other subreformists like the Atomists or Familists. At the same time, he also revealed a decided distaste for separatists and sectarians: "for heads that are disposed unto Schisme and complexionally propense to innovation, are naturally indisposed for a community, nor will ever be confined unto the order or economy of one body; and therefore when they separate from others they knit but loosely among themselves; nor contented with a generall breach or dichotomie with their Church, do subdivide and mince themselves almost into Atomes" (1.8, p.

9). As was true with his own involvement with Origen, however, Browne interpreted the line between "heresy" and "singularity" as being often a very thin one; rather than etching it deeper, he sought to diminish it, and in the process of doing so perhaps to reclaim an errant soul for the Church of England. The sentence that follows this (for Browne) unusually harsh image of mincing atoms is a masterful attempt to reknit the fabric of the church by having it seemingly expand until it can incorporate heresy itself:

'Tis true, that men of singular parts and humors have not been free from singular opinions and conceits in all ages; retaining something not onely beside the opinion of his own Church or any other, but also any particular Author: which notwithstanding a sober judgement may doe without offence or heresie; for there is yet after all the decrees of counsells and the niceties of the Schooles, many things untouch'd, unimagin'd, wherein the libertie of an honest reason may play and expatiate with security and farre without the circle of an heresie.

Browne's strategy of flexibility not only denies easy categorical distinctions between who is in and who is out, who is saved and who is not; it also presents a persona whose response to religious extremes seems the very incarnation of Christ in Luke: speaking to his disciple worried about a pretender, Jesus remarks, "Forbid him not: for he that is not against us is for us" (9:50). Browne's whole approach in *Religio* is to minimize the possibility of conflict by minimizing the concept of opposition. If he does not defend sectarians, he also does not attempt to forbid them their gatherings, and in this act of toleration, Browne distinguishes himself most clearly from Laud. Both are conservative; both wish to preserve the notion of a national church, but Browne wishes to preserve it in its ideal form: as a via media, as a place where at least some heads that might be otherwise disposed to schism can discover sufficient room to "play and expatiate with security and farre without the circle of an heresie."

Civil War, Interregnum, and Restoration Responses

While *Religio Medici* was being cried up for wit—and occasionally attacked—its author had to face the hardships of Civil War and the realization that it was no longer a simple task to "follow the great wheele of the Church" (*RM,* 1.6, p. 7), particularly in East Anglia. Since Elizabethan times, Norwich had been a Puritan stronghold, even something of a harbor for separatists like Robert Browne, and in the late 1630s it had become the special target of Laudian reform. When the easygoing Bishop Corbett died in 1635, he was replaced by Matthew Wren, Laud's most efficient and (to many Puritans) his most hated disciple. Something of Wren's role as an enforcer is indicated by Thomas Fuller's measured remark, made in another context, that the bishop "noted the Prerogative of the *kings Hounds,* by vertue whereof they could lawfully do *that* for which other Dogs were beaten."[12] In Norfolk, Wren's zeal for his task was immediately revealed in the twenty-eight articles he issued in 1636, all with the purpose of prescribing high church discipline and conformity. He was also responsible—or so he was later charged—with "excom-municat[ing], suspend[ing] or depriv[ing] and otherwise cen-sur[ing] and silenc[ing]" some fifty "godly, faithful preaching ministers."[13] Wren was bishop of Norwich for only two and one half years before moving on to Ely, but his deeds were remembered well into the next decade when his name became synonymous with prelacy and oppression.

By early 1642, in fact, strong reactions were already stirring. *True News from Norwich* delivers a satirical account, written from a Puritan perspective, of how some "Cathedral Blades" sought to defend the structure of the church from an attack that did not actually happen: "Oh how loath they are to part with their Dianas, their Altars, Images, Crucifixes, Copes, Surplices and Romish Vest-ments; no (as some of them said) they would rather lose their lives than their Organs, so fast they are glued to their Pipes and Popish trinkets."[14] A year and a half later, derision turned into destruction. The Parliamentary ordinance of September 1643 urging the removal or demolition of superstitious and idolatrous monuments in churches was effectively enforced by the sheriff of Norwich shortly thereafter. "What clattering of Glasses, what beating down of Walls, what tearing up of Monuments, what pulling down of Seats," begins Joseph Hall in a litany of complaint that details the particular acts of violence done to the cathedral, which lay unused as a place of worship until the Restoration.[15] Hall, too, was one of the casualties. As bishop of Norwich he was deprived of his office and sequestered in a "little cottage" in the village of Heigham where he occasionally preached in the parish church.

Browne's "position" amid this and the ensuing confusion of Civil War and the Interregnum is nearly impossible to pin down with any precision. Apart from his own published writings, which respond with characteristic obliquity to historical circumstance (see chapters 5–7 below), there is almost nothing that survives from his private correspondence that helps to illuminate his nonmedical activities during this period. The few relevant historical documents also need to be read with greater care than is usually given them. Browne's name appears among those who refused to give money to aid the Parliamentary forces in their attempt to regain Newcastle in 1643.[16] But whether this (again characteristically) negative response constitutes a firmly Royalist action can only be a matter of conjecture. It might express a neutralist sentiment or even simply his antipathy to violence.

The second document is even more problematic. The name "Thomas Browne" appears on a printed pamphlet entitled *Vox Norwici, or The Cry of Norwich, vindicating their ministers . . . from the lying Libell intitled Vox Populi.* The pamphlet is the last of four published in 1646 when the agitation in Norwich between Independents and Presbyterians was particularly acute. Notwithstanding the difficulty of placing *Vox Norwici* in the shifting sands of religious disputes (Frank Huntley's characterization of it as "moderate" seems unquestionably true only for its rhetorical strategy),[17] there is the further and more elementary problem of determining whether this Browne is ours. As of 1643–44, there were at least four other persons with the same name living in Norwich. All are mentioned in the Norwich Subscription for Regaining Newcastle where our Browne simply bears the designation of "Dr," with no first name given. Since only the printed version of *Vox Norwici* survives and does not designate the professions of the signatories, we have no way of knowing which Browne it might be. Furthermore, the suggestion that it must be Dr. Browne because one of the ministers defended is John Carter, the minister of Peter Mancroft, is hardly persuasive since one of the few things that we do know for sure about Browne during the Civil War is that he did not assume permanent residence in this parish until 1650, four years after the petition appeared.[18]

Much can be and has been surmised about Browne's political and religious activities during this period: from early depictions of him by romantics and Victorians as a blithe spirit transcending the turmoil of the times to recent attempts to present him as a Royalist secret agent taking advantage of his professional license to move to and fro.[19] The truth probably lies somewhere in between and is less glamorous. As someone with Royalist sympathies but opposed to violence, Browne had little choice but to accept Parliamentary rule, which was quickly, though not uncontestably, established in Norwich. And as a physician of note, he had a wide cross-section of patients, not just those of Royalist persuasion. But if with many he sought a peaceful settlement with the new powers and accepted a plainer church—indeed, John Carter was the most vocal reformist minister in Norwich—he also continued to number among his closest friends persons conscious of their repressed status during the 1640s and 1650s: John Whitefoot, Justinian Lewyn, and Thomas Le Gros.[20] Without directly confronting the reigning authorities, Browne's deepest sympathies were clearly with those now on the outskirts of power.

There can be no question, however, that Browne welcomed the Restoration of Charles II in the spring of 1660. He is perhaps the "Tho. Browne" who, with many, signed the Declaration from the Gentry of Norfolk and City of Norwich, a petition given to General Monck in the waning days of the Commonwealth listing the hardships and grievances suffered under Parliament and urging that excluded members of Parliament be restored without "the obligation of taking the Engagement or any other oath."[21] (The hurried nature of the signature makes it difficult to be certain whether it is Browne's hand, though its appearance in a column beginning with the name of Sir Edmund Bacon, whom Browne had warmly commended fewer than two years earlier in the preface to *The Garden of Cyrus* [1658], makes it probable.) There can be also no question that he continued to think of himself as an English Protestant, perhaps slightly chastened by recent events, who belonged to a broadly reformed church. Writing to his son, Tom, who was traveling in France in 1661, Browne several times enjoins him to "hold firm to the Protestant Religion and be diligent in goeing to Church when you have any Litle Knowledge of the Language. God will accept of yr desires to serve him in his Publick worship, tho you cannot make it out to yr desires" (*K,* 4, p. 4). In another letter, he continues to hope that his son will attend "the Protestant Church, to which you must not be backward, for tho there Church order and discipline be different from ours, yet they agree with us in doctrine and the main of Religion" (*K,* 4, pp. 8–9). And in a third, he voices concern over the severe treatment of Protestants by Louis XIV: "we hear the Protestants in France are but hardly [harshly] used, noe doubt the King will be carefull to keep them low haveing had experience of their strength; however serve God faythfully and be constant to yr Religion" (K, 4, p. 14).

As for events at home, Browne writes with evident but restrained relief about the turn in political fortune. He notes "some riseings there have been in London of the Anabaptists, fift Monarchie men and others, but soon suppresed and 13 Executed." In the same sentence he adds: "upon the Kings letter 5 of our Aldermen were put out wch had got in in the usurpers time in other mens places" (p. 5). Elsewhere he reports that "it is thought by degrees most will come to Conformitie," and then describes the preparations being made for the king's coronation, which includes burning effigies of Cromwell, "whose head is now upon Westminster hall, together with Ireton and Bradshaws" (p. 9). Written so that Tom "might not be totally ignorant [of] how affairs goe at home" (p. 10), these accounts are set down for the most part in a dispassionate prose that avoids the heady wine of a Cavalier celebration—the party in England that most enthusiastically supported Charles's return. Browne's rare moments of fervor are reserved for describing the restoration of the visible church:

our Bishop Dr. Reynolds my loveing friend hath been in Norwich these 3 months, he preacheth often and Comes Constantly to Christ church [Norwich Cathedral] on Sunday Mornings at the beginning of Prayers, about wch time the Aldermen also Come, he sittith in his seat against the pulpit, handsomly built up and in his Episcopall vestments, and pronounceth the Blessing or the Peace of God etc at the end, where there is Commonly a very numerous Congregation and an Excellent sermon by some Preacher of the Combination, apointed out of Norfolk and Suffolk, the one for Winter the other for sommer. (K, 4, 14)

It might be tempting to say that in his enthusiasm for priestly vestments Browne is finally unveiling his Laudian sympathies, but such is not the case. Browne's "loveing friend," Bishop Edward Reynolds, provides a valuable gloss on the Norwich physician's leanings during the early months of the Restoration. A moderate Presbyterian under Cromwell, Reynolds had a long and distinguished career as a tolerationist. During the early days of the Civil War he accepted the accommodation with Parliament and became a member of the Westminster Assembly of Divines in 1643 (the Presbyterians who displaced the bishops), and then during the Protectorate he advocated a broad interpretation of the church. In a sermon preached before Parliament in 1657, notably entitled *Brotherly Reconciliation,* he readily accepted that "there will be *variety of Judgments* in the church," but emphasized the "main *Fundamental* Doctrines" that unite all, "the Truths wherein we agree *in Love,* Unity and Constancy." Like Browne, Reynolds believed that there will always be heresies and sects, but he sought "to restore those that are overtaken with any Error, *with the Spirit of Meekness.*"[22]

In the ecclesiastical complexities confronting Charles upon his return, the three parties negotiating for the king's favor included those, like Peter Heylyn, who supported a return to Laudian uniformity in which the bishops would once again assume a powerful position in the state; the Presbyterian Covenanters who opposed any restoration of the bishops; and a moderate group made up of both Presbyterians and Episcopalians, who favored a limited episcopacy, which meant some form of cooperation between the bishop and the parish clergy.[23] This last group, termed "Reconcilers" by Richard Baxter, included Reynolds; and when he was appointed bishop of Norwich, he set out to spread the gospel of limited episcopacy. Preaching at Browne's church of St. Peter Mancroft on 22 September 1661, he chose as his text 2 Corinthians 4.5: "For we preach not ourselves, but Christ Jesus the Lord; and ourselves your servants for Jesus' sake."[24] Admittedly apologetic, the sermon sets out to vindicate the dignity of the apostolic office from slander as well as from the abuses it had suffered at the hands of both ignorant "mechanick" preachers and ambitious prelates. "The ministry of Reconciliation," as Reynold's defines it, finds its calling in the recognition of its *limited* power over the people: "we have not dominion over your Faith, but are helpers of your Joy" he underscores by way of quoting 2 Corinthians 1.24.[25] And near the end of the sermon, he describes the responsibility of the clergy by defining carefully the relationship between church authority and Scripture, between things circumstantial and things fundamental: "Though it belong to the Duty, Authority, and Wisdom of the Church to direct meer Circumstantials in the Service of God, so as may most conduce unto that order and decency which God requireth, so as may best become the Seriousness, Simplicity, and Sanctity of so Heavenly and Spiritual Worship: Yet She may not impose as *Doctrines her Commandments,*

Matt 15. 19. She may not add *any* *thing* to the alsufficiency and plenitude of the Holy Scriptures."[26]

Browne was very likely in the audience for this sermon preached at his church. His letter to his son in which he refers to Reynolds was dated only slightly more than a month later, and it is easy to see why the dignified yet conciliatory nature of his "loveing friend" so appealed to him. The flexible arrangement between church and Scripture put forward in a "mild" tone, in which ceremony is admired but not worshipped, corresponds exactly with the sentiments Browne expressed in *Religio Medici* in the days immediately preceding the Civil War. We cannot say for sure whether Browne was acquainted with Reynolds before the bishop came to Norwich (the expression "loveing friend" suggests that he was), but we can be certain about the depth and duration of his admiration afterward. Amid the dusty catalog of the dead in *Repertorium,* Browne reserves space to recollect the names of the bishops whose bones were not buried in the cathedral proper. The largest "plot" goes to Reynolds who receives some thirteen lines; he is followed by the better-known Joseph Hall with eleven, while Matthew Wren, on the other hand, gets an inglorious single line of remembrance (*K,* 3, pp. 133–34).

Reynolds's limited episcopacy and Browne's latitude in matters of faith look forward to the gradual emancipation of religious worship in England, but it would be a mistake to represent Browne as finally a great champion of religious toleration in the positive sense endorsed by W. K. Jordan when he speaks of *Religio Medici* as "a noble defence of the right of individual criticism and the sanctity of freedom of belief."[27] This is, rhetorically at least, to turn Browne into Milton, *Religio Medici* into *Areopagitica.* Browne nowhere argues for religious freedom as the inalienable right of the Godly, nor does he ever defend the right of individual criticism as a basic principle for all to enjoy. Had he felt this strong a calling, he might have practiced medicine in the New World rather than Norwich, or at the very least written of Bermuda in the modestly zealous spirit of Andrew Marvell. He did neither of course. In divinity, Browne loved "to keepe the road" (*RM,* 1.6, p. 7), and in *Religio Medici* he accepts the existence of sectarians as the lesser of two evils—the other being a single repressive view of the church as basically an instrument of excommunication instead of a place of worship. In the shifting semantics of *Religio,* separatism, which is the logical extension of freedom of religion, is endured, not embraced, in the hope that tolerance would induce conformity; but if it did not, Browne saw only further trouble in insisting upon a single normative code involving all aspects of religious behavior.

As for defending the freedom of individual criticism, Browne seems equally wary of it as an unrestricted right to be exercised according to personal whim. In the epistle to the reader prefacing *Religio Medici,* he does assert the need to come forward and publish an authorized version of *"that Peece which was most imperfectly and surreptitously published before,"* but this justification is made only after he has declaimed against the tyranny of a too-liberal press that has already defamed the name of both king and parliament. It is a personal reaction rather than a principled defense, although the reaction itself does not necessarily argue that he favored censorship,[28] at least in the crude ways it had been enacted in the Star Chamber under Laud in 1637 and was being renewed by Parliament in 1643. Browne is defending something more like the right to have private opinions, but that privilege is also inseparable from a code of genteel modesty in which the good and the godly man are conditioned by the same richly textured respect for hierarchy: *"Lastly all that is contained therein is in submission unto maturer discernments, and as I have declared shall no further father them then the best and learned judgements shall authorize them; under favour of which considerations I have made its secrecie publike and committed the truth thereof to every ingenuous Reader"* (*RM*, p. 2). For Browne, the right to speak is never a cherished ideal. How to say something is.

Chapter Four
Elements of Style

Whatever Browne's achievements were as a scientist and an Anglican apologist, he is best known today as a stylist who created one of the most distinctive and recognizable voices in the history of English prose. The "stylist," Austin Warren reminds us in his valuable essay on Browne, is someone "whose originality lies not in his big ideas (his major concepts, often philosophically derivative and 'eclectic') but in his little ideas, his discriminations and nuances, his intellectual sensibility."[1] Warren is not arguing that ideas are unimportant to Browne or that the author's style can be understood apart from its intellectual context; he is making the simple but valuable observation that in reading Browne's published and some of his unpublished work (not his domestic correspondences) we are always very conscious of the author's "attire." Coleridge said as much when he remarked that *Religio Medici* "is a fine Portrait of a handsome man in his *best* Cloathes."[2]

What is true of fashions in clothes, though, is also true of style: not everybody equally appreciates the dress, and among his many admirers Browne has had some conspicuous detractors. In his own day, Alexander Ross was the most vigilant in adopting a plain-style attack on the "Rhetoricall flourishes" of *Religio*. "*Where is most painting, there is least beauty,*" Ross admonishes the reader with proverbial zest, and then adds: "as I suspect that friendship, which is set out in too many *Verball Complements;* so doe I that Religion, which is trimmed up with too many *Tropicall pigments,* and *Rhetoricall dresses.*"[3] In our day, Stanley Fish has played Abdiel to a Satanic Browne by ringing a more sophisticated change on Ross's anti-Papist remarks when he criticizes the author's art for failing to self-consume: "Browne's prose betrays no such modesty. It repeatedly calls attention to what it *is* doing, and what it is doing is displaying Browne to advantage, even when the content is, on its face, prejudicial to him."[4] Neither Ross nor Fish, like Warren or Coleridge, misreads this fundamental feature of the witty opacity of Browne's prose; they simply value its effects very differently. They do not like what they see: an art that is too playful, too self-conscious, too "proud" of its own being.

On the basis of sheer numbers, Browne's detractors have been heavily outvoted, but the considerable distance between his admirers and his antagonists is probably impossible to bridge in any but a flimsy way. As Lytton Strachey remarked in defending Browne's verbal eccentricities against the strictures of Edmund Gosse at the turn of this century, "there is a great gulf fixed between those who naturally dislike the ornate, and those who naturally love it. There is no remedy; and to attempt to ignore this fact only emphasizes it the more."[5] We might wish to expand Strachey's innocent "naturally" to include political, psychological, moral, and religious assumptions, and we might also want to add, as Warren has demonstrated, that Browne wrote in more than one style, but we cannot escape observing that his is, above all, a literary person's prose—that is, a prose that happily indulges itself in what Roland Barthes includes more generally in "the pleasures of the text": its own joyful linguistic operations.

Emerson, who was a careful reader of Browne, once remarked that "all good conversation, manners and action come from a spontaneity which forgets usages and makes the moment great."[6] Although he need not have had Browne in mind when making his pronouncement or its sequel—that "Nature hates Calculators"— the remark nonetheless captures in distilled form the essence of Browne's prose: its spontaneous, well-mannered grandeur. Browne's prose is almost always polite, usually unpredictable, and occasionally lofty. At its very best, it makes "the moment great." Whether through the effects of diction or syntax, the brief utterance of a simple sentence or the gradual revelation of a thought over the course of several paragraphs, Browne discovered a flexible style that was sufficiently rarefied to reveal the odd twists and paradoxes of his profoundly inquisitive imagination. In reading him, we are always aware of witnessing not just a recorder of detail but a connoisseur in the process of studying himself and his surroundings.

Diction

One of the most remarkable features of Browne's style is certainly his language or, as Dr. Johnson said, his "many languages."[7] An omnivorous reader of ancient and modern texts as well as the author of a general tract "Of languages, and particularly of the Saxon tongue," Browne was something of a literary cormorant who hatched an exotic species of Latinate English. *Pseudodoxia,* particularly, delivers a brood of verbal oddities nearly unequaled in the seventeenth century. "Reminiscential," "paradoxologie," "ampliate," "empuzzle," "decollation," "immoderancy," "farraginous," "indigitate," "augurial," "tripudary," "fabulosities," "sententiosity," "desume," "extispicious," "mundification," and "consectory" are just some of the "expressions beyond meere English apprehensions" alluded to by the author in the preface and which appear in the first book. All are derived from Latin and cited by the *Oxford English Dictionary;* most are now obsolete, and some, like "empuzzle" and "immoderancy," are the only examples given of the variant form. These are joined by the myriad of phrases, taken in this case from a few pages, which, without employing any neologisms, reveal their exoticism in pairs: Adam "infringed the omnisciency and essentiall ubiquity of his Maker" (1.2, p. 10); God is the infallible creator "in whose opticks there is no opacity" (p. 11); and at Judgment day, Satan will not "present unto God a bundle of calumnies or confutable accusations, but will discreetly offer up unto his Omnisciencie, a true and undeniable list of our transgressions" (p. 12).

Needless to say, diction as intoxicated as this is open to both praise and ridicule, serious imitation and burlesque, and Joyce knew that he had located a howler when in *Ulysses* he parodically compressed Browne's "forget not how assuefaction unto any thing minorates the passion from it" (*CM,* 3.10, p. 234) into "Assuefaction minorates atrocities," and then added for good measure, "as Tully saith of his darling Stoics."[8] But however pompous certain passages might seem, Coleridge went too far when he accused Browne of corrupting the true classical style, epitomized in Hooker, by introducing "learned words merely because they were learned."[9] Coleridge's version of a linguistic "fall" (like Eliot's "dissociated sensibility") is simply too schematic to be persuasive. We might just as easily argue, as Bulwer-Lytton did,[10] that Browne enriched the language and cite as evidence some of his coinages that are still with us, like "incontrovertible" and "retrogression," even, happily, "literary" and "medical." But it is also inaccurate in another way, for Browne's use of "learned words" was not just for the sake of appearance. Johnson, who was temperamentally less disposed than Coleridge to liking Browne's style, was closer to the truth when he remarked that "in defence of his uncommon words and expressions, we must consider, that he had uncommon sentiments, and was not content to express in many words that idea for which any language could supply a single term."[11]

If Browne habitually employed Latinate diction in varying degrees, he rarely forgot his native Saxon tongue. The homespun word or phrase served to give ballast to his imagination, anchoring it in the particulars of a reality that both illuminated and defined the iridescence of the abstraction. Perhaps the most spectacular example of this practice occurs in the next to last paragraph of *Urne-Buriall,* a passage sufficiently pleasing to its author that he copied it almost verbatim at the end of *Christian Morals:* "And if any have been so happy as truly to understand Christian annihilation, extasis, exolution, liquefaction, transformation, the kisse of the Spouse, gustation of God, and ingression into the divine shadow, they have already had an handsome anticipation of heaven; the glory of the world is surely over, and the earth in ashes unto them" (*UB,* chap. 5, pp. 124–25). As George Williamson notes, Browne uses here "five Latin abstractions and three metaphorical extensions to adumbrate the mystical experience,"[12] but we should also observe that if the abstractions hint at a future ecstasy (Browne even gives us a sense of an alphabetical scale operating with the abstractions), the biblical plainness of "kisse of the Spouse," in its sensuous immediacy, moves us suddenly a half-step forward in our "handsome anticipation of heaven."

One of the hallmarks of Browne's style is, in fact, the witty conjunction of the plain and the ornate, the mundane and the extravagant. Browne loved, for instance, to place in parallel sequence words with similar meanings but different roots. The repetition of "funambulatory" and "narrow path" in *Christian Morals* is a case in point; so, too, is the earthy variation of "belching" and "eructation" in *Pseudodoxia,* to which we might add nearly at random doublets like "the account of the *Pensill* or *hanging* gardens of Babylon," "one common *name* and *appelation*," "*allurements* and *baits* of superstition," "we are that *bold* and *adventurous* piece of nature," and "these are certainly the *Magisteriall* & *master pieces* of the Creator" (my italics). Whole phrases could also turn gracefully on the repetition of meaning in a different key, as Douglas Bush points out in a passage like "Every man is not a proper Champion for Truth, nor fit to take up the Gantlet in the cause of Veritie."[13] Browne could even orchestrate a symphony of simple and Latinate diction to help produce a sense of the ineluctable and unwieldy march of error which is so much the subject of *Pseudodoxia:* "And as simple mistakes commonly beget fallacies, so men rest not in false apprehensions, without absurd and inconsequent diductions, from fallacious foundations, and misapprehended mediums, erecting conclusions no way inferrible from their premises" (1.4, p. 22). The key to the verbal wit here is how "simple mistakes" generates a Latin lexicon of error ("fallacies," "false apprehensions," "fallacious foundations," etc.), which, like the reasoning process it criticizes, sinks deeper in a linguistic mire the further along it goes.

The most exotic of Browne's bilingual effects belong, of course, to the fifth chapter of *Urne-Buriall* and to *The Garden of Cyrus.* Much of the strangeness of *Urne-Buriall* is due to the oscillating tide of Latin and Saxon phrases in which the splendid pomp of ambition is played off against the blunt reality of gravestones, while *The Garden of Cyrus* delivers an extraordinary mélange of simply sown and ripe diction. In the latter work, pine trees do not remain pine trees for long; closer inspection reveals "the Rhomboidall protuberances in Pineapples maintaining this Quincuncial order unto each other" (chap. 3, p. 145). Elsewhere, this antiquarian-turned-Adam muses on "favagonious Sockets" and the "exiguity and smallnesse of some seeds"; he also names and exults his surrounding with a language as richly varied as the local botanical setting will allow: "Thus hath nature ranged the flowers of Santfoyne, and French honey suckle; and somewhat after this manner hath ordered the bush in *Jupiters* beard, or houseleek; which old superstition set on the tops of houses, as a defensative against lightening, and thunder. The like in Fenny Sengreen or the water Souldier; which, though a militarie name from Greece, makes out the Roman order" (chap. 3, p. 144).

It is a cliché but an accurate one to say that Browne's unusual linguistic feats reflect the wit and fecundity of God's creation. Like Donne and a host of authors in the seventeenth century who subscribed to the theory of correspondences, Browne regarded God as the ultimate artist and the world as an exemplary text, in which, to quote *Religio,* "there was never any thing ugly, or mis-shapen, but the Chaos." This is not to argue that everything should conform to a single rule of order, but to suggest that since all things express the essence of God, Browne saw before him nearly an endless plenitude of imitative possibilities. Even "in monstrosity," Browne writes, "there is a kind of beauty, Nature so ingeniously contriving the irregular parts, as they become sometimes more remarkable than the principall Fabrick." In the case of Browne's prose, there is, by extension, no such thing as a "monstrosity," only the ingenious contrivances of irregular parts, which, viewed in detail, can sometimes seem "more remarkable than the principall Fabrick" (*RM*, 1.16, p. 16).

Formal Structures

Along with the witty conjunction of Latin and Saxon diction, Browne favored certain rhetorical figures. Alliteration is the most obvious, as in the sputtering mouthful of "protuberances in Pineapples" or the lush "flowers of Santfoyne, and French honey suckle." Inevitably relying on this device to highlight some of his more outrageous bilingualisms like "Conigerous animals, which chew the cudd," he also underscored through sound the balancing effect of doublets such as "Magisteriall & master pieces," "in this universe of stairs and manifest scale of creatures," and the memorable "divided and distinguished worlds"; and he frequently used alliteration to achieve moments of graceful symmetry and closure, as in the concluding phrase "came down by *Cancer*, and ascended by *Capricornus*." But however conscious Browne was of the sound of his prose—Strachey reported loving to read him aloud in some hall that smelled of antiquity—he was not a slave to "the sweet falling of the clauses," as Bacon accused the followers of Cicero of being.[14] Alliteration in Browne is nearly always a figure of thought; it helps to signal the odd twists of mind, the slight or sudden change in the argument, or to suggest a fine nuance of meaning. It rarely seems gratuitous and is never used, as it was with Ciceronians, to structure the symmetrical development of an idea.

Browne was especially fond of at least three other rhetorical figures. He exercised frequently a device called "polyptoton," which is the repetition of words from the same root but in different forms or with different endings. "As there were many Reformers, so likewise many reformations" is a simple instance of repetition with variation that strengthens the pat inevitability of the simile. Or again Browne gives us the felicitously wistful, "Gardens were before Gardiners, and but some hours after earth," in which the root echoing reinforces our sense of the primal aspects of paradise. This device can be overused, as occurs in *Christian Morals* ("Pursue Virtue virtuously," or the coinage of "novity" in conjunction with "novellizing"), but it can also lend a note of sublime resonance to a passage, as happens in the last chapter of *Urne-Buriall:* "Time which antiquates Antiquities" and "there is nothing strictly immortall, but immortality." In both cases, the sharp juxtaposition of nearly identical abstractions makes the meaning of each nearly impenetrable and contributes to our sense of the gnomic inscrutability of the human condition. A second device frequently employed is "homoioteleuton," the use of different words with similar endings: "And if any have been so happy as truly to understand Christian annihila*tion*, extasis, exolu*tion*, liquefac*tion*, transforma*tion*", etc. (my italics). Particularly common among his Latinate expressions, the figure could help generate rhythmic grandeur by producing a kind of rhymed prose or, as happens often in *Pseudodoxia,* it could be used to indicate a high-blown irritation with error. The third figure, "catachresis," defines a device for which Browne is perhaps best known—a wildly unlikely metaphor. Sometimes referred to as a "conceit" or more generally as "metaphysical wit," it describes the unusual leaps in Browne's thought and lies partially behind the author's warning in the preface to *Religio* that there are "*many things* [in it] *to be taken in a soft and flexible sense.*" Perhaps the most striking example of this occurs when he is criticizing human arrogance in attributing things to nature that belong to God, "which if with reason we may doe, then let our hammers rise up and boast they have built our houses, and our pens receive the honour of our writings."

On a slightly different plane, Browne's habitual dubiety or skepticism helped to generate a lexicon of genteel uncertainty that has perhaps become his single most identifiable idiom. Since "Some Truths seem almost Falshoods, and some Falshoods almost Truths" (*CM,* 2.3, p. 220), Browne rarely insists on a single absolute point of view. He continually emphasizes shades of meaning, partial perspectives, a desire for precision that admits to the difficulty, if not the impossibility, of the task. If Donne was the great practitioner of "masculine persuasive force," Browne was the afficionado of "Probably" and "Perhaps," words he noted regretfully that "will hardly serve to mollify the Spirit of captious Contradictors" (*CM,* 2.3, p. 220). "I could easily believe," "I am of the opinion," "I am half of the opinion," "I cannot peremptorily deny," "it is a riddle to me" is the malleable idiom of *Religio,* not "it is a truth universally acknowledged." Browne is always attempting "to difference {him} self neerer, & draw into a lesser circle"—to think, like Hamlet, precisely on the event—but the multiple faces of truth keep shifting before his gaze: "That Miracles are ceased, I can neither prove, nor absolutely deny, much lesse define the time and period of their cessation" (1.27, p. 27). "Whether *Eve* was framed out of the left side of *Adam,* I dispute not; because I stand not yet assured which is the right side of a man" (1.21, p. 22). In *Pseudodoxia,* these noun clauses pick up more scholarly heft, but their effect remains largely the same: to reveal a mind holding, in studious fashion, an idea at a distance and turning it around for inspection. Often yielding only further questions, these extended clauses generate in turn an almost limitless number of expressions of uncertainty, beguiling in their variety and, in a work like *Urne-Buriall,* profoundly moving in their cumulative force. I doubt whether any author in English has found half as many ways to keep the door slightly ajar. It seems only right that "precarious" should be among his neologisms.

Syntax

If Browne was a connoisseur of doubt, he achieved this distinction by using a frequently rarefied diction, which lent an elevated tone to his prose, in conjunction with a loose or libertine syntax, especially as exemplified in the recently discovered essay "form."[15] Historically speaking, the personal essay came into being in the Renaissance with Montaigne, who favored the mode because of its provisional, introspective quality; and though Browne was later to disclaim having read more than a smattering of the French author before writing *Religio* (*K,* 3:290), there can be no denying the similar purpose to which each put the essay. Both viewed it as an appropriate vehicle for *trying* out an idea (this is the root meaning of "essayer," as Montaigne made clear). It had no fixed format, no established vocabulary, no predetermined topic. It could be varied according to personal taste and situation, which meant it could embrace both the serious and the whimsical, the grand and the mundane, the contemplation of death as well as the tickle in an ear; and in doing so, it served as an ideal medium to reveal the inner configurations of the author's personality. But in his wish "to be delineated in [his] own genuine, simple, and ordinary fashion," Montaigne also had to seek out a different stylistic strategy from that current Ciceronian model favored by his contemporaries. The Ciceronian period emphasized rhetorical balance, symmetrical sound patterns, graduated sequences of thought, and a copious display of language. As a highly polished and formal prose with its origins in oratory, though, its principal effects were also limited. It generally avoided sudden intellectual turns, which would have been difficult for listeners to follow, and its "finished" style was inhospitable to conveying the motions of thought as they apparently occurred to the author in the process of writing. It denied a sense of the mind working naturally and spontaneously even if that impression was sometimes a carefully contrived effect.

In rejecting Cicero, Montaigne helped to initiate a stylistic change for the seventeenth century whose full effects are still disputed but general outlines are clear. Writers like Bacon, Burton, and Browne, though very different from each other, were nonetheless alike in preferring a style more suited to reflecting the complexities of empirical reality. For Bacon this meant emphasizing a "language of things," an idea that became the rallying cry for a "scientific" prose later in the century. Burton attended more to the hectic motions of the "travelling" intellect:

'Tis not my study or intent to compose neatly, which an orator requires, but to express myself readily and plainly as it happens. So that as a river runs sometimes precipitate and swift, then dull and slow; now direct, then *per ambages* [winding]; now deep, then shallow; now muddy, then clear; now broad, then narrow; doth my style flow; now serious, then light; now comical, then satirical; now more elaborate, then remiss, as the present subject required, or as at that time I was affected. [16]

And Browne, who was both natural philosopher and personal essayist, alternated between something like an attempt at a factual reportage of the bizarre and the idiosyncracies of private narration. Grouped generally together under the broad category of anti-Ciceronians, these authors as well as others adopted a fundamentally asymmetric syntax. Achieved largely by varying concise, seried utterances of differing length with loose, run-on sentences often held together by weak ligatures, it helped to give the effect, in Morris

Croll's well-known formula, of portraying "not a thought, but a mind thinking, or in Pascal's words, *la peinture de la pensée*." The anti-Ciceronians "knew that an idea separated from the act of experiencing it is not the idea that was experienced."[17]

It is impossible to do justice here to the complexities of this historical change, but we can understand at least how Browne assimilated into his own prose some of the syntactic habits of this "movement." Except for rare occasions, Browne eschewed the fully articulated Ciceronian period. He favored a combination of the curt utterance, associated particularly with Seneca, and a loose or libertine syntax made popular by Montaigne, though Browne generally resisted the vigorous aphorisms of the later Bacon and Burton's eccentric prolixity. Almost any passage from *Religio* will serve as an example of his personal "essay" style; for the purpose of illustration, I have chosen one of the shorter sections in order to give a sense of the full sweep of Browne's thought:

I thanke God, and with joy I mention it, I was never afraid of Hell, nor never grew pale at the description of that place; I have so fixed my contemplations on Heaven, that I have almost forgot the Idea of Hell, and am afraid rather to lose the joyes of the one than endure the misery of the other; to be deprived of them is a perfect hell, & needs me thinkes no addition to compleate our afflictions; that terrible terme hath never detained me from sin, nor do I owe any good action to the name thereof: I feare God, yet am not afraid of him, his mercies make me ashamed of my sins, before his judgements afraid thereof: these are the forced and secondary method of his wisedome, which he useth but as the last remedy, and upon provocation, a course rather to deterre the wicked, than incite the vertuous to his worship. I can hardly thinke there was ever any scared into Heaven, they goe the fairest way to Heaven, that would serve God without a Hell, other Mercenaries that crouch unto him in feare of Hell, though they terme themselves the servants, are indeed but the slaves of the Almighty. (1.52, p. 49)

What is most striking about this passage is its unpredictability. In contrast to the Ciceronian period, it does not work toward a single climactic moment but favors instead a series of perceptions held together by a paratactic syntax—that is, a syntax whose clauses are not rigorously subordinated but loosely conjoined either through weak connectors like "and" and "nor" or punctuation that marks a clean break in the author's thought: "I thanke God," "I have so

fixed," "to be deprived," "that terrible terme," etc. Browne's asyndetic style plays down connections and plays up leaps in thought,
not large ones but significant enough to give the impression that
the author is musing rather than arguing, refining his perceptions
about heaven and hell, not advancing a theory about salvation.
Indeed, the degree to which the passage subordinates product to
process can be readily glimpsed by the fact that Browne is describing
a basic dialectic here in heaven and hell, but he refuses any obvious
symmetrical pairing of them: their differences are illuminated only
by the various angles provided by Browne's thought.

An even closer look reveals how Browne muses or "tries out" an
idea. In a very limited sense, the "argument" of this paragraph is
addressed and completed at the outset: Browne is not afraid of hell.
But this "fact" is used only as the point of departure for a series of
spiraling, loosely arranged thoughts. No sooner is the assertion made
than it is repeated, as if the author were trying it on for size, "nor
never grew pale at the description of that place." The now refined
thought comes to an abrupt halt, and the author turns his gaze in
a different direction where the link to the previous clause is only
implied. (Were Browne worried about the "logic" of his argument,
he could easily have subordinated the second to the first clause by
simply reversing the members of the second and adding a connecting
locution like "now the reason. . . .") The second clause then achieves
a moment of symmetry ("and am afraid rather to lose the joyes of
one than endure the misery of the other") only to have its balance
upset by the abrupt entry of a maxim, "to be deprived. . . ." After
another clause, loosely attached to the previous one by the antecedent
pronoun "That," Browne again alters the direction of his gaze by
suddenly announcing the paradox "I feare God, yet am not afraid
of him," a phrase that recollects but from a slightly different angle
the opening pronouncement "I thanke God." Through a series of
partial antitheses, the remaining members of this sentence then
dilate on the difference between being intimidated and wooed into
heaven; these members also help to "explain" his opening expression
of thanks. The entire section is finally concluded by another shift
in gaze, "I can hardly think," which, except for the closing sub-
ordinate clause ("though they terme themselves," etc.), is composed
of a series of short, disconnected utterances.

The obvious effect of Browne's asyndetic style, when used in
conjunction with the personal "essay," is spontaneous fancy, a lyrical

association of perceptions anticipating a Joycean monologue.[18] Indeed, the ending of *The Garden of Cyrus,* with its dreamy evocation of the author drifting off to sleep, has even encouraged at least one critic to speculate on whether Browne, admired by Coleridge and De Quincey, was himself an opium eater. (There is no evidence that he was.) But as whimsical and self-indulgent as he can sometimes be, it is a mistake to think of his style as suitable only for revealing the complexities of the inner life. As Robert Boyle made abundantly clear in 1661,[19] the "essay" ought to serve as the preferred medium for recounting scientific experiments; and though Browne is not held up by Boyle as a specific model for imitation, he could certainly make his prose into a precise instrument for rendering, in an undogmatic idiom, the particularities of the world around him. *Pseudodoxia, Urne-Buriall,* and *The Garden of Cyrus*—all in varying degrees scientific works—possess a number of passages memorable for their sheer descriptive power, for their ability to convey a keen sense of the observing eye in operation. The best instances almost always involve small things, like the celebrated glo-worm passage in *Pseudodoxia* (3.27, pp. 283–84), or the equally scrupulous rendering of the dead-watch beetle, which appears in the same work and is short enough to quote in full:

Few ears have escaped the noise of the Dead-watch, that is, the little clickling sound heard often in many rooms, somewhat resembling that of a Watch; and this is conceived to be of an evil omen or prediction of some persons death: wherein notwithstanding there is nothing of rational presage or just cause of terrour unto melancholy and meticulous heads. For this noise is made by a little sheath-winged gray Insect found often in Wainscot, Benches, and Wood-work, in the Summer. We have taken many thereof, and kept them in thin boxes, wherein I have heard and seen them work and knack with a little *proboscis* or trunk against the side of the box, like a *Picus Martius,* or Woodpecker against a tree. It worketh best in warm weather, and for the most part, giveth not over or under nine or eleven stroaks at a time. He that could extinguish the terrifying apprehensions hereof, might prevent the passions of the heart, and many cold sweats in Grandmothers and Nurses, who in the sickness of children, are so startled with these noises. (2.7, p. 153)

The passage is an exquisite rendering of sensed experience, set down in absolutely limpid but not lifeless prose. Browne is able to take us immediately into the situation with the quietly dramatic and inclusive opening ("Few ears have escaped the noise of the Dead-watch"), after which he reveals the keenness of his own auditory and visual imagination. "Knack" is just the right word (it is of echoic origin) to convey a sense of the insect's sound, while the allusion to the woodpecker as well as to the number of strokes—nine or eleven, not ten—gives the passage a further descriptive precision, a precision underscored by the conscious glossing of technical Latin terminology with native expressions. Finally, the brief "essay" is concluded with a reflexive remark that highlights, through a domestic reference, the modest significance of both the scientist and the essayist, the person who witnesses the fact and the individual capable of reporting it. No passage better reveals the combined qualities of Browne's mind: its human, scientific, and literary bent.

Revisionary Tactics: A Letter to a Friend

Browne was a careful observer of himself and nature; he was also a continual and careful reviser of his prose. His writings, remarked his friend and first biographer, Whitefoot, "were often Transcribed, and Corrected by his own Hand, after the Fashion of Great and Curious Wits."[20] We have ample evidence of the care Browne took in revising the "pirated" Religio, which required both emending "more than six hundred and fifty items" and adding substantially to the pirated text; working from manuscript fragments, Jeremiah Finch has also helped us to appreciate the transmutation of some of the prose in The Garden of Cyrus into art.[21] And, of course, Pseudodoxia was continually being updated with new information. But perhaps the best view afforded of the author in his study occurs with A Letter to a Friend, Upon Occasion of the Death of his Intimate Friend, which exists in both a manuscript version preserved in the British Library (Sloane 1862) and the substantially altered and amplified text as first printed in 1690, eight years after Browne's death. The two versions, when examined together, can tell us much about the fine points of Browne's craft and something about the associative thematics that keep his published writings from coming across as being simply a series of acute but fragmentary observations.

The "occasion" that prompted the letter was in all likelihood the death of Robert Loveday in 1656. Loveday was from an ancient family from East Suffolk, a graduate of Peterhouse, Cambridge, and a translator of some note: suffering from consumption, he was attended by Browne in the final stages of his illness. The person addressed was probably Sir John Pettus. Also of an ancient family, Pettus was from a village just outside of Norwich, a close friend of Loveday, and known to Browne.[22] Whether the manuscript represents a loose copy made of a letter actually sent to Pettus or is itself an intermediary development in the process of revision is difficult to tell. But I doubt that it represents a recension of the manuscript version of the *Letter* as printed in 1690. Frank L. Huntley makes this interesting suggestion, based in part on assumptions involving growing pressures in the seventeenth century for a more "scientific" prose; but it is still hard to imagine why Browne would have spent time bothering to prune a work so evidently unfit for publication in that form, even in the *Philosophical Transactions of the Royal Society*.[23] It is also difficult to assign a precise date for the composition of *A Letter*. Internal evidence points to 1673: Browne alludes to a work published in 1654 as having been written "scarce twenty Years ago" (pp. 184–85); but the reference need only mean that Browne was tidying up a work for publication in that year and then, perhaps for reasons of decorum, decided against sending it.

The manuscipt version is medically informative and sympathetic in tone but hardly a work of art. The finished *Letter,* thought Pater (and he was quickly seconded by Symonds), belonged in the company of *Urne-Buriall* as "the best justification of Browne's literary reputation."[24] The difference between the two versions is clear from the outset. The manuscript begins on a dutiful, earthbound note: "I am sorry you understood so little concerning that worthy gentleman your deare freind & that I must also performe that unwelcome office to tell you Ad portam rigidos calces extendit, hee is dead & buried & by this time no punie in the famous nations of the dead. for though hee left this world not many dayes ago, yet every hower largely addeth unto that Dark societe. & considering the incessant mortallity of mankind you cannot well conceave there dyeth in the whole world fewer then a thousand an hower" (p. 249). The printed text, on the other hand, opens bearing the full regalia of Browne's high style:

Give me leave to wonder that News of this nature should have such heavy Wings, that you should hear so little concerning your dearest Friend, and that I must make that unwilling Repetition to tell you, *Ad portam rigidos calces extendit,* that he is Dead and Buried, and by this time no Puny among the mighty Nations of the Dead; for tho he left this World not very many days past, yet every hour you know largely addeth unto that dark Society; and considering the incessant Mortality of Mankind, you cannot conceive there dieth in the whole Earth so few as a thousand an hour. (p. 179)

The formalized "Give me leave" immediately displaces the informal "I am sorry." "Wonder," suggesting both speculation and grandeur, takes over. News is mythologized (bearing wings like Mercury) and heightened through genteel alliteration (the image also looks ahead to the "Mercurisms" and "Airy Nuncio's" added to the second paragraph in the 1690 text). And the syntax has been made more obviously symmetrical. The cumulative effect of the rhythms now serves both to set off the Latin tag from Persius in the ceremonial manner of a burial service and to solemnize further and ennoble the message of the last clause: "that he is Dead and Buried." Small as it is, the simple substitution of "mighty" for "famous" in referring to the "Nations of the Dead" reveals the touch of an author who values sense as well as sound. It sharpens the contrast with "Puny," suggests more exactly the theme of "the incessant Mortality of Mankind," and continues to orchestrate the grand note. That the revisions should include at the outset at least one doublet (second paragraph) also seems almost inevitable: "the usuall way of knowledge" becomes the less usual and more resonant "common Road, and *Appian* way of Knowledge," a phrase that, besides adding another mortuary echo to the opening, demonstrates how, even when Browne wants to talk about something being ordinary, he is rarely ordinary in doing so.

Elevating his introduction, Browne sought to heighten his role as physician. He considerably expanded the amount of medical lore in the original to include a discussion of Egyptian dentistry (p. 184), a brief history of countries especially hostile to certain illnesses (p. 185), the different ways favored by physicians in predicting consumption—"Cardan eagerly views the Nails" (p. 183)—and the various coughs afflicting animals and man (pp. 185–86). He also amplified sections already containing esoteric speculation. To his discussion in the original noting how the dying man resembled his uncle (grandmother in the manuscript), he added a resonant account of our endings being like our beginnings in which "in our Retreat to Earth, [we] may fall upon such Looks which from community of seminal Originals were before latent in us" (p. 180). And in the fashion of *Pseudodoxia,* he questioned different authorities on general topics of human interest, such as the hour when most are born and die and whether disease is an historically increasing phenomenon: "*Plato* will tell us, that there was no such Disease as a Catarrh in *Homer's* time" (p. 185).

But the gesture that perhaps contributes most to our sense of Browne's expanded "presence" in the 1690 text occurs through the simple redeployment of material already available in the earlier version. In the manuscript, the third paragraph concludes with an ominous acount of the power of medical predictions: "'tis as dangerous to bee condemned by a physician as a Judge" (p. 250). The fourth paragraph then moves on to consider the hopeless condition of the patient. But in the revised text, the passage that intervenes between these two is taken from further along in the manuscript where Browne describes his arrival on the scene: "Upon my first Visit I was bold to tell them who had not let fall all hopes of his Recovery, That in my sad Opinion he was not like to behold a Grashopper, much less to pluck another Fig" (p. 179). In the new version, Browne becomes the judging physician, his earlier "bold" assertion of opinion now more of a final utterance. The strikingly personal allusion to grasshoppers and figs also assumes a further note of remote pathos, an effect Browne was obviously seeking since he changed the earlier phrase, "much lesse to tast another figge" (p. 250) to the more proverbial and delphic "much less to pluck another Fig" (p. 179). Plucking or tasting figs is equally possible in Norfolk, but the finality of the gesture—a fig, like the patient, can only be plucked once—is what Browne is after, and the change is certainly a felicitous one.

It would be nearly impossible to trace the many local changes Browne made to the manuscript in formalizing and amplifying his discourse. But a broader glance at the "structure" of the two works, or rather their "shape" ("structure" is too architechtonic a term for describing the unfolding, organic quality of Browne's "essay"), can alert us to how the author links together his observations to create a text that is discursive and unified, ample yet still possessing a sense of direction. As an essayist, Browne rarely identifies in advance exactly where he is going (*The Garden of Cyrus,* with its areas of concentration spelled out in the subtitle, comes perhaps closest to being "signposted"); but after having gone the route with the author, we rarely sense that the ramble has been altogether random.

The 1690 text, in the light of the earlier version, helps us to understand why this is so.

The manuscript is at best loosely organized. In the first six paragraphs, Browne describes the patient's hopeless condition, after which he moves on to consider a number of separate and discrete phenomena: the victim's emaciated condition, his "soft departure," hour of death, childhood sickness (rickets), the possible significance of the day of his death, his charity, a vague link with Julius Scaliger, and finally his Christian sentiments, the last of which the author extends briefly to the recipient in the form of a few pious warnings about laying up one's treasures while healthy. The beginning remarks have a "logic" to them and the concluding ones move in an obviously eulogistic direction, but the intervening paragraphs possess little continuity. Browne jumps about from topic to topic, without attempting either to forge small links between paragraphs or to suggest larger thematic patterns running through the work as a whole. Not surprisingly, the manuscript has been often described as fragmentary.

The 1690 text, as Norman Endicott points out, "is *in its parallel part,* about two and a half times as long as the manuscript."[25] The part that is not parallel involves some eighteen admonitory paragraphs attached to the end of the printed text; they also reappear in a slightly revised form at the beginning of *Christian Morals.* But with or without the extended ending, the 1690 version possesses a discernible design that both enriches the particular observations and gives a cumulative solemnity to the whole essay.

The later text moves through four large, thematically interrelated stages. The first (pars. 1–8, pp. 179–83), although stylistically heightened and slightly rearranged, remains much the same as in the earlier version: with a graver eye toward immediately consoling his "friend" on the loss of his "intimate friend," Browne gives the general circumstances of the victim's hopeless condition. The signal change here involves retrieving from the manuscript some fragmentary observations on coincidences concerning Charles V and Antipater (they appear also in Browne's commonplace book) and tying them more tightly to the specific occasion of the patient's death. In the manuscript, this material appears arbitrarily after a discussion of the patient's beard. In the 1690 text, it is moved forward so it evolves naturally from Browne's discussion of the specific circumstances surrounding the time of the victim's death.

The material is also more carefully integrated into the structure of "coincidences" running throughout the 1690 version. In the earlier text and repeated in the later one, Browne reports that, in contrast to Charles V and Antipater, who both experience significant events on their birthdays—one being crowned and the other (perhaps like Browne himself) dying—the patient lived fifteen days beyond the anniversary of his nativity to the surprise of some bedside viewers. In the amplified 1690 text, however, Browne adds another, even more compelling, example of coincidence: "Certain it is he died in the dead and deep part of the Night, when Nox might be most apprehensibly said to be the Daughter of Chaos, the Mother of Sleep and Death, according to old Genealogy; and so went out of this World about that hour when our blessed Saviour entred it, and about what time many conceive he will return again unto it" (pp. 181–82). The additional passage serves now not only to link the victim thematically with these other men; it also suggests the deeper comforts of a spiritual bond that will be orchestrated more fully at the end.

The middle portion of the 1690 text has been considerably amplified with new material, but the expansion also leads to a greater clarity of focus. Beginning with his description of how "in this consumptive Condition and remarkable Extenuation he came to be almost half himself" (p. 183), Browne in a second movement descends into the particulars of bodily degeneration, as if giving an anatomy lesson (pars. 9–15, pp. 183–86). His description of the patient's beard, the subject of a single, floating paragraph in the manuscript, is joined to paragraphs on teeth, coughing, and lungs, anatomical fragments now meant to be seen and experienced by the reader as fragments, disconnected from the whole—the patient is "half himself"—and yet, as images of the body, belonging together. In a third movement, Browne then shifts his gaze to questions concerning the head and intellect (pars. 16–21, pp. 186–88). Four paragraphs on interpreting dreams of the fatally ill, absent from the manuscript, are now used to rarefy our perspective on the dying man as he prepares to leave the world, a refinement sustained and continued by the following two paragraphs in which Browne describes the patient's indifference to worldly things. The first, added to the 1690 text, describes the virtuous attitude of the patient about not having children since he could now be "amply satisfied that his Disease should dye with himself" (p. 187). The second passage, contained in the manuscript but unconnected to any larger idea or theme, now evolves out of this transcendent attitude; like Julius Scaliger, he "left the Poetry of his Epitaph unto others" (p. 188).[26]

With the passage on Scaliger in place, Browne then turns in the final movement to eulogize the dead man: to supply, in effect, the poetry of an extended epitaph (pars. 22–30, pp. 188–90). Considerably amplified from the earlier version, these paragraphs further underline the internal, spiritual qualities of the dead man, qualities that insure his status as an exemplary Christian. To a discussion of his good works in the earlier text, Browne contributes some hagiographical touches by comparing the dead man to the ancient martyrs. And by repositioning and refining the phrase in the manuscript about how "to be dissolved, and be with Christ, was his dying ditty" (p. 189; "sick dittie" in the manuscript [p. 255]) so that it appears halfway through the eulogy (not at the outset as in the earlier version), Browne orchestrates a sense of upward movement in the conclusion. The final allusion to the Pauline new man, hinted at earlier in the added material involving the hour of Christ's arrival, now acquires greater point as it brings the descriptive portion of *The Letter* to a sturdy but consoling close: "In brief, he cannot be accounted young who outliveth the old Man. He that hath early arrived unto the measure of a perfect Stature in Christ, hath already fulfilled the prime and longest Intention of his Being: and one day lived after the perfect Rule of Piety, is to be preferred before sinning Immortality" (p. 190).

A reading as schematic as this certainly shears Browne's prose of what Lamb called its "beautiful obliquity."[27] *The Letter* is as full of unusual twists as any of Browne's important works, but attending to the broader rhythmic patterns within a context of stylistic revisions does point to how Browne stitched his various observations together to create a whole greater than the sum of its parts. In the 1690 text, Browne is very much a "medical moralist of the mount," as Endicott emphasizes, but the way the author heightens his style, increases the element of "Airy Nuncio's"—of dreaming—and arranges his text to suggest a loose progress from bodily to intellectual to spiritual concerns leaves room for what Pater impressionistically called Browne's habit in *The Letter* of assisting "at the spiritualizing of the bodily frame by natural process; a wonderful new type of a kind of mortified grace being evolved by the way." Browne's expansions here are done with the intention of both adding and clarifying meaning, and the result is a work that, if not quite of the stature of the ones Browne saw through publication, still bears the unique stamp of his lofty but compassionate intelligence.

The attention Browne gives to expanding the vision of *The Letter* also helps to underscore one further aspect of his art. Browne was an "essayist" through and through. He never seriously attempted to write in any other form; and as an essayist, he recognized and occasionally articulated the particular advantages of the form as residing in part in the "collateral truths" gathered along the way, truths that might be more important than any final truth Browne, as an individual, saw himself capable of reaching. The danger of the essay, of course, is trivialization: the incessant concern with the insignificant or the inability to make the insignificant seem important, a charge Coleridge, rightly or wrongly, leveled against Montaigne when he called him "too often a mere amusing Gossip, a chit-chat [reporter] of Whims & Peculiarities that lead to nothing."[28]

Browne is not altogether exempt from these criticisms. Few readers will be rivetted by every passing detail in *Pseudodoxia,* fewer still by much of the information in, say, his *Miscellany Tracts.* If the essay is in some sense a late Renaissance invention born out of a distrust of the grandiose, the pretentious, and the drive for power, it never entirely escapes the potential for ennui and trivia that presided over its creation. In a very real sense, it is the chosen genre of the unheroic, the natural countervoice to the epic. But in Browne, however—at least in the works usually designated as "major"—the local observation is never allowed full dominion. The grander view lurks in the diction. It is present in the expanding vision of the particular essays, the upward sweep of the Christian moralist conscious of the final claims made on wisdom. And it is heard in the larger unifying rhythms that underlie the individual works. Despite choosing to compose in a form later prized for being "familiar," Browne is never just the person next door. At best, he drops in to remind us that he comes from somewhere else.

Chapter Five

The Politics of Laughter: Comic Autobiography in *Religio Medici*

"So intrinsecal is every Man unto himself, that some doubt may be made, whether any would exchange his Being, or substantially become another Man." Browne's perception of human identity as fundamentally and perhaps inalterably individualized occurs in *A Letter to a Friend* (p. 188), but it might very well serve as at least a partial gloss on *Religio Medici,* the first published of his writings, a work of youthful exuberance, and certainly one of the most singular and beguiling attempts at self-definition in the whole of English literature. To be sure, Browne's "memorial unto himself" is not original for being autobiographical. Augustine's *Confessions* and, if we consider them as autobiographies, Juliana of Norwich's *Showings* and *The Book of Margery Kempe* anticipated *Religio* in the genre of spiritual revelation, as did the spate of personal religious "histories" that began to appear early in the seventeenth century.[1] But *Religio* is without rival when it comes to recording the delicate whimsicalities out of which a person's faith might be spun. Browne's work has no single source or antecedent, only affinities with the essay, the epistle, and the meditation, genres that hardly possess sharp definition,[2] while to read some of the many imitations it inspired is frequently to witness the breaking of the proverbial butterfly over the wheel. The breezy appropriation of *Religio* for crude political purposes is fully evident in the expanded title of a work by H. N., *Religio Bibliopolae* (1691), a work generally attributed to the flamboyant bookseller, John Dunton (1659–1733): *The New Practice of Piety Writ in Imitation of Dr. Browne's Religio Medici: or The Christian Virtuoso: Discovering the Right Way to Heaven between all Extreams: To which is added a Satyr on the House of Lords, for their Throwing out the Bill Against Occasional Conformity* (1704). But the most resolute collapsing in the eighteenth century of Browne's carefully wrought discriminations perhaps belongs to Fielding's Parson Thwackum, who provides a thumping reductio ad absurdum of the first five sections of *Religio:* "When I mention Religion, I mean the Christian Religion; and not only the Christian Religion, but the Protestant Religion; and not only the Protestant Religion, but the Church of *England.*"[3]

Religio Medici is more vulnerable to slogans and paraphrase than almost any other work of seventeenth-century prose because it is preeminently a triumph of texture and mood. Coleridge recognized this fact at once. In objecting to Digby's pedantic criticisms, he identified *Religio* as a dramatic performance rather than a metaphysical argument,[4] and this valuable distinction has since been upheld either implicitly or explicitly by most scholars as a basic rule for interpreting the work. Browne's "soft and flexible" rhetoric has therefore received the kind of New Critical scrutiny usually reserved for the poetry, not the prose, of the period, and the "self" portrayed in *Religio* has been accurately likened to quicksilver in its various shifts in shape.[5] Erasmus's Folly, Rabelais's Pantagruel, and Shakespeare's melancholy Jaques play continually in the shadows of Browne's imagination, while the author further complicates any attempt at a single perception of himself through brief asides like "let us speak like philosophers" or "to speak like a politician" and phrases that recollect at one moment his Pauline heritage and at another his affinity with classical authors like Horace and Lucan. Indeed, in reminding us of yet another of his roles—that of the physician—Browne highlights through pun the theatrical elements traditionally associated with his profession in the paintings and engravings of his day:[6] "Men that looke no further than their outsides thinke health an appertinance unto life, and quarrell with their constitutions for being sick; but I . . . have examined the parts of man, and know upon what tender filaments that Fabrick hangs" (1.44, p. 42). The anatomist and dramatist in *Religio* are surely cut from the same cloth.

In the theater of Browne's imagination, the vision that animates and unites the various modes of action is the author's profoundly comic interpretation of reality. If Burton, the divine-turned-physician, is the great anatomist of melancholy, Browne, the physician-turned-divine, is the great exemplar of amiability. "Forbid him to be humorous," writes Leslie Stephen, "and you might as well forbid him to speak at all."[7] From his frequent perception of God as a witty trickster who keeps us guessing His meanings to his mordant recognition of himself as "wholesome a morsell for the wormes as any" (1.40, p. 39), Browne uncovers a universe in which wit and playfulness are not just pleasant accoutrements but generating principles. "There is a common Spirit that *playes* within us" (my italics), he notes, "yet makes no part of us, and that is the Spirit of God" (1.32, p. 31). "All that is truely amiable is God," he intones near the end of *Religio*, "or as it were a divided piece of him, that retaines a reflex or shadow of himselfe" (2.14, p. 74). From this Neoplatonic outpost, the world could readily appear to him as "but a dreame, or a mockshow, and wee all therein but Pantalones and Antickes to my severer contemplations" (1.41, p. 40). "Pantalones," perhaps cribbed from Jaques's "seven ages of man" speech, were the lean and foolish old men from Italian comedy. Browne even interpreted his saturnalian imagination as evidence that he "was borne in the Planetary houre of *Saturne*": "I am no way facetious, nor disposed for the mirth and galliardize of company, yet in one dreame I can compose a whole Comedy, behold the action, apprehend the jests, and laugh my selfe awake at the conceits thereof" (2.11, p. 71). How seriously we are meant to take the disclaimer "I am no way facetious" seems to be part of the joke, and the wit becomes even more finely tuned if we think of *Religio* as perhaps one instance of his dreaming. After all, Browne readily conceived of his life as the stuff that dreams are made of—"a miracle of thirty years, which to relate, were not a History, but a peece of Poetry" (2.11, p. 69)— and *Religio* is the means of this relation.

If *Religio Medici* places special value on witty improvisation and a comic vertigo in which we continually perceive all the world as a stage, Browne, like Erasmus before him, viewed the New Testament as the ultimate sanction for prizing the improbable. St. Paul's discussion of "the foolishness of God" (1 Corinthians 1:21) underscored the paradox of Christianity in which the low is made high, a "comic" action epitomized in the Incarnation and Resurrection; and when the apostle declaimed against the wisdom of the world for failing to understand the mysteries of Christianity, he established a perceptual mode that favored revelation over reason, the inspired folly of believing in the unbelievable over obeying only that which can be seen and demonstrated. In the Renaissance, moreover, Paul's famous injunction "Eye hath not seen, nor ear heard, neither have entered into the heart of man, the things which God hath prepared for them that love him" (1 Corinthians 2:9) became something of an honored text for fools. Folly quotes it as "her portion" at the end of *The Praise of Folly;* Bottom scrambles its letters but snatches at its spirit in *A Midsummer Night's Dream* (4.1.200–219); and Browne alludes to it in his attempt to describe the indescribable, heaven and hell (1.49, p. 46). In this company of buffoons, Browne is easily the best behaved, but the author of *Religio* still observed "Bottom-like" moments, especially in his perception that "we all are monsters, that is, a composition of man and beast" (1.55, p. 52); and despite getting married in the interim, he retained in the authorized version of *Religio* his witty denunciation, borrowed from Folly, that coition "is the foolishest act a wise man commits in all his life" (2.9, p. 67).

Nonetheless, the comedy of *Religio* differs in degree if not in kind from the spirited ribaldry of Erasmus or the tipsy revelry of Shakespeare. When Browne reports going to a tavern, for instance, he does so in order to describe how his Pythagorean instincts allow him to transform the "vulgar" music heard there into "a profound contemplation of the first Composer" (2.9, p. 67), and it is worth noting that his one scatological reference appears in the form of a literary allusion to Rabelais (1.21, p. 22). Browne's wit is almost always the wit of rarefaction, of the genteel jibe, of the naif who "wonders" at the oddities of God's world and His creations, including man. It invites us, as George Meredith says of the comic spirit in general, to "become a citizen of the selecter world."[8] Browne was therefore careful to dissociate himself altogether from satire and invective, literary modes in which the humor seemed decidedly earthbound and, from Browne's perspective, unbalanced. It was one thing to play at being a Jaques; it was another to endorse as a narrative strategy a melancholy eccentricity that might lead to madness. Democritus, who "thought to laugh the times into goodnesse, seemes to mee as deeply Hypochondriack, as *Heraclitus* that bewailed them" (2.4, p. 60). Like Sidney before him and Meredith afterward, Browne thought true comedy primarily a transcendental and yet socially unifying experience. It refined the sensibilities and asked the reader to see that in the common spirit playing within was a reflex or shadow of the divine.

Browne's Double Comedy

The comedy of *Religio* thus moves on two different but complementary levels, one of which includes something like a comedy of manners, a vision of how to act in this world. The other "higher" level is what Kierkegaard interpreted as "the comedy of faith," a recognition that "there is an endless yawning difference between God and Man," which, the more thoroughly it is explored, the more comical it seems, with the result that "the earnestness of one's faith is tested by one's 'sensitiveness to the comical.' "[9] In the first instance, Browne musters his wit to define a flexible norm for religious behavior—to suggest the sanity of the Church of England. His religion, at the very least, is civilized and "reasonable"; the latter word is a key element in a leitmotif of conservatism that runs throughout the work and reappears conspicuously in the next to last sentence of *Religio* when the author identifies his hopes for happiness in this life as "my most reasonable ambition" (2.5, p. 75). Indeed, in setting a civilized tone for the entire work, the opening section insinuates its moderate posture in the syntax (a marvelous tightrope walk with negative phrases), in the deferential jibe at the public view of his profession, and in the witty way in which, amid a seemingly endless series of qualifications, Browne quietly orchestrates the triumph of his faith by the subtle transformation of "honorable" to "happy" to "glorious":

For my Religion, though there be severall circumstances that might perswade the world I have none at all, as the generall scandall of my profession, the naturall course of my studies, the indifferency of my behaviour, and discourse in matters of Religion, neither violently defending one, nor with that common ardour and contention opposing another; yet in despight hereof I dare, without usurpation, assume the honorable stile of a Christian: not that I meerely owe this title to the Font, my education, or Clime wherein I was borne, as being bred up either to confirme those principles my Parents instilled into my unwary understanding; or by a generall consent proceed in the Religion of my Countrey: But having, in my riper yeares, and confirmed judgement, seene and examined all, I finde my selfe obliged by the principles of Grace, and the law of mine owne reason, to embrace no other name but this; neither doth herein my zeale so farre make me forget the generall charitie I owe unto humanity, as rather to hate then pity Turkes, Infidels, and (what is worse) Jewes, rather contenting my selfe to enjoy that happy stile, then maligning those who refuse so glorious a title.

"Though," "neither-nor," "yet in despight hereof I dare, without usurpation," "not that I," "but having," "I finde my selfe obliged," "neither doth herein my zeale": this is the polite grammar of deference that assures us that even with the boast that he has "seene and examined all," Browne is not going to foist his faith on anyone. The "generall charitie" he owes to humanity readily circumscribes his zeal.

As a citizen of the world, Browne thoroughly suffuses his religion with a verbal playfulness that simultaneously militates against a single reading of theology and works to recover some of the middle ground the author saw eroding through intensifying religious disputes. "His is the rhetoric of 'the happy man,' " writes Anne Drury Hall, "even without the literary prop of a Sabine farm or an English country house."[10] When he identifies himself as "of that reformed new-cast Religion, wherein I dislike nothing but the name" (1.2, p. 3), his coy omission of "Protestantism" raises a smile about the etymology of his faith that slides imperceptibly into a criticism of reformists who seem to be only reactionaries (protesters) against Rome. Three sections later, Browne manages to have a little fun with the inflammatory rhetoric of religious controversy when he establishes a standard of decorum but then immediately flirts with breaking his own rule: "It is as uncharitable a point in us to fall upon those popular scurrilities and opprobrious scoffes of the Bishop of *Rome,* to whom as a temporall Prince, we owe the duty of good language: I confesse there is cause of passion betweene us; by his sentence I stand excommunicated, Heretick is the best language he affords me, yet can no eare witnesse I ever returned to him the name of Antichrist, Man of sin, or whore of *Babylon"* (1.5, p. 6). It might be the method of charity to suffer without reaction, as Browne reminds us (1.5, p. 6), but his ventriloquism here, underscored by the challenge "yet can no eare witnesse" (when we are about to be made witnesses), is a way of entering the arena while claiming to be sitting on the sidelines. Nonetheless, momentarily mimicking an incensed Protestant with witty approval does not make a radical Puritan out of Browne. In the next breath, he distances himself from what he sees as the fulminations of pulpit invective by sputtering, with mocking alliteration, "that a good cause needs not to be patron'd by a passion."

In these instances, Browne seems literally to mediate between Rome and Geneva with something like rambunctious good humor, but his more usual way of undermining the extremities of religious behavior is to subject differences to a genteel, even courteous, laughter of the mind. His quibble over the proper meaning of "martyr," for instance, sets up a logical contradiction which he then adjudicates through irony: "The Councell of *Constance* condemnes *John Husse* for an Heretick, the Stories of his owne party stile him a Martyr; He must needs offend the Divinity of both, that sayes hee was neither the one nor the other" (1.26, p. 26). Rather than attempting the (impossible) task of deciding who is right, Browne simply throws the case out the window and offers a down-home, sympathetic moral about the folly of taking uncertainties for absolutes: "I have often pitied the miserable Bishop that suffered in the cause of *Antipodes,* yet cannot choose but accuse him of as much madnesse, for exposing his living on such a trifle, as those of ignorance and folly that condemned him."

At times, Browne's humor involving religious schism can be so fine as to be altogether transcendent. Following his heated description of the "vulgarity of those judgements" that presume to determine the elect, he remarks with exasperation: "Thus whilst the mercies of God doth promise us heaven, our conceits and opinions exclude us from that place" (1.56, p. 53). But what Browne urges at this moment is not a heavenly flash signaling a community of the saved or a zealous outburst against the presumptuous but a nearly unearthly sense of bemusement generated by the whole scene: "There must be therefore more than one Saint *Peter,* particular Churches and Sects usurpe the gates of heaven, and turne the key against each other, and thus we goe to heaven against each others wills, conceits and opinions, and with as much uncharity as ignorance, doe erre I feare in points, not onely of our own, but on anothers salvation." The issue of church and sectarian "usurpation" is coolly distanced through the allusion to each "turning the key against" the other, an image that prepares the way for an even more discreet turn of phrase that leaves the whole matter of salvation still very much up in the air. Browne's use of the present tense in "we goe to heaven against each others wills" suggests a general sense of upward progress being made by everybody, as if there might be more than one Saint Peter after all; but the final clause narrows the passage, and we can only speculate on the mystery of who gets through the gate.

Despite being frequently fueled by the bizarre, one strand of Browne's wit always keeps moving us toward the center, toward a "reasonable" appreciation of both the "good life" and the good in life. As someone who has "seene and examined all," he enjoys the odd verbal coinage as well as the worldly flourish of a foreign phrase. He gives a courtier's *"Bezo las Manos"* to Fortune in describing the marvelous adventures of his life—"the escapes of dangers, and hits of chance" (1.17, p. 17). He has enough Greek on hand to mock the hot skirmishes among grammarians who "hack and slash for the Genitive case in *Jupiter"* (2.3, p. 59), and he can politely twit the reader with French examples of the "opprobrious Epithets wee miscall each other" (2,4). Indeed, the very fact that *Religio* is presented as not so much a studied work as a spontaneous creation in which, as the author confesses in the preface, he *"had not the assistance of any good booke, whereby to promote my invention or relieve my memory,"* makes the whole a virtuoso performance achieved without even a preliminary pen biting in order to bring forth a truant muse. Classical and European literature as well as the Bible are at his finger tips, Browne would have us believe. Thoroughly at ease with himself and the world, he urges that "A man may be in as just possession of Truth as of a City, and yet bee forced to surrender; tis therefore farre better to enjoy her with peace, then to hazzard her on a battell" (1.6, p. 6). Enjoying the city in peace is synonymous in *Religio* with keeping the positive values traditionally associated with urban life: manners, civility, and intelligence.

And yet if *Religio* underscores the comedy of the good life in which reason and moderation are given definite values, the work never presumes to insist that these virtues are self-sufficient. Browne is only a partial prototype of the eighteenth-century "amiable humorist." He certainly anticipates rational theologians like Isaac Barrow who remarked that "it is a scandalous misprision, vulgarly admitted, concerning Religion, that it is altogether sullen and sour requiring a dull, lumpish, morose kind of life, barring all delight, all mirth, all good humour." But he would have refused Barrow's utilitarian attempt to deny fancy a significant place in religious experience.[11] In Browne's individualistic and whimsical vision, the earthly city is continually being absorbed—sometimes at very odd angles—by the City of God. The comedy of manners keeps dissolving into a higher comedy of faith. To paraphrase Owen Felltham: if mirth is good for the body, meditation irradiates the soul.[12]

A perfect instance of this vertical climb occurs in part 1, section 11, which begins by wittily adapting a line from Horace to fit a decidedly Christian, even mystical, context: "In my solitary and retired imagination, (*Neque enim cum porticus aut me lectulus accepit, desum mihi*) I remember I am not alone, and therefore forget not to contemplate him and his attributes who is ever with mee, especially those two mighty ones, his wisedome and eternitie; with the one I recreate, with the other I confound my understanding." With its allusion to Horace's "when I withdraw to my couch or go off for a walk through the colonnade, I never neglect myself,"[13] Browne's opening line substitutes for the contemplation of the self the contemplation of God in an action that transposes the Horatian emphasis on the rational into a celebration of the irrational: "for who can speake of eternitie without a soloecisme, or thinke thereof without an extasie? Time we may comprehend, 'tis but five dayes elder then our selves, and hath the same Horoscope with the world; but to retire so farre backe as to apprehend a beginning, to give such an infinite start forward, as to conceive an end in an essence that wee affirme hath neither the one nor the other; it puts my reason to Saint *Pauls* Sanctuary." The satirist's couch becomes "Saint *Pauls* Sanctuary," a receding hall of paradoxes constructed out of Browne's perception of the vast discrepancy between man and God. But the comic note of well-being in Horace is not altogether eradicated in *Religio*. It is refined and elevated into a "recreation" that centers on the confounding of one's reason. "I love to lose my selfe in a mystery to pursue my reason to an *oh altitudo*" (1.9, p. 9), exults Browne in what has become the most famous in a long history of fideistic paraphrases on St. Paul's "O the depth of the riches both of the wisdom and knowledge of God!" (Romans 11:33).[14]

Browne's comedy of faith, like Kierkegaard's but without the torturous anxiety, springs from his recognition of the very impossibility of knowing God except through the conscious devaluation of the intellect. In passage after passage, section after section, the author of *Religio* keeps asking his haggard and unreclaimed reason "to stoope unto the lure of faith" (1.10, p. 10). He meditates on the "wingy mysteries in Divinity" (1.9, p. 9)—the Trinity, the Incarnation, and the Resurrection. He sends his reason to school to learn "the wisedome of Bees, Aunts, and Spiders" (1.15, p. 15). He turns rational criticism of Scripture on its head by widening the context for uncertainty: "Whether *Eve* was framed out of the left side of *Adam*, I dispute not; because I stand not yet assured which is the right side of a man, or whether there be any such distinction in Nature" (1.21, p. 22). "The whole Creation is a mystery, and particularly that of man," he solemnly observes and then ends a lengthy, technical account of the soul with a conclusion in which, except for discovering our general ignorance of ourselves, nothing is concluded: "Thus we are men, and we know not how, there is something in us, that can be without us, and will be after us, though it is strange that it hath no history, what it was before us, nor cannot tell how it entred in us" (1.36, p. 36).

Nothing, in fact, confirms Browne more in his faith than a wry smile or a good laugh generated by his recognition of the folly of human reason.[15] "Certainly it is not a warrantable curiosity, to examine the verity of Scripture by the concordance of humane history, or seek to confirme the Chronicle of *Hester* or *Daniel,* by the authority of *Megasthenes* or *Herodotus,*" he observes, and then adds: "I confesse I have had an unhappy curiosity this way, till I laughed my selfe out of it with a piece of *Justine,* where hee delivers that the children of *Israel* for being scabbed were banished out of Egypt" (1.29, p. 29). Browne's sense of the absurd keeps coming to his rescue: "I can answer all the objections of Satan, and my rebellious reason, with that odde resolution I learned of *Tertullian, Certum est quia impossibile est*" (it is certain because it is impossible—1.9, p. 9). And with a witty sleight-of-hand, he can make a virtue out of a necessity and convert a posture of weakness into a position of triumph:

Some beleeve the better for seeing Christ his Sepulchre, and when they have seene the Red Sea, doubt not of the miracle. Now contrarily I blesse my selfe, and am thankefull that I lived not in the dayes of miracles, that I never saw Christ nor his Disciples; I would not have beene one of those Israelites that passed the Red Sea, nor one of Christs Patients, on whom he wrought his wonders; then had my faith beene thrust upon me, nor should I enjoy that greater blessing pronounced to all that believe & saw not.

Seeing is not believing to Browne, or at least not believing in the same happy and slightly reckless way. However much he might "doubt" his external vision—his reason—he is not a "doubting Thomas" when it comes to matters of faith, as the witty allusion to the biblical story of his namesake reveals (John 20:29). Browne's discipleship is very much a matter of choice, and he signals his freedom through his exuberant sense of play.

The interweaving of comic play and personal election that runs

throughout *Religio* is, in fact, all but cinched at the end of part 1.
Meditating on the possibility of his salvation, of which Browne is
"confident and fully perswaded" but dares not take an oath, he runs
a circle around St. Paul's severe injunction to *"Worke out your salvation
with feare and trembling"* (1.59, p. 54). A humble soul conscious of
"her owne unworthinesse," Browne notes, needs no such trumpet
blast. But in the process of sidestepping a favorite Puritan text
which, as Calvin said, "honor[s] the Lord's power, while greatly
abashing ours,"[16] Browne promotes the antithesis of work, fear, and
trembling when he underscores the playfulness of imitating a paradox of Christ that also allows him to celebrate the comic implications of his election:

That which is the cause of my election, I hold to be the cause of my
salvation, which was the mercy, and beneplacit of God, before I was, or
the foundation of the world. *Before Abraham was, I am,* is the saying of
Christ, yet is it true in some sense if I say it of my selfe, for I was not
onely before my selfe, but *Adam,* that is, in the Idea of God, and the
decree of that Synod held from all Eternity. And in this sense, I say, the
world was before the Creation, and at an end before it had a beginning;
and thus was I dead before I was alive, though my grave be *England,* my
dying place was Paradise, and *Eve* miscarried of mee before she conceiv'd
of *Cain.*

Christ's paradoxical reply to the unbelieving Jews in John 3:58
("Before Abraham was, I am") stimulates in Browne an outpouring
of paradox, a rhetorical figure that Puttenham surnamed the "won-
derer."[17] In the sense that Dr. Johnson refused to honor,[18] Browne's
life in Christ is "a miracle of thirty yeares" because, like Christ's,
it reaches out through God to touch the beginning and the end,
the alpha and the omega, of time. But what enthralls us here is not
so much any definition of election and predestination for which
Christ's words might supply a proof-text as the vertical rush—the
sense of wonder—achieved through the witty compression of im-
possibilities. More than any oath might do, Browne's rhetoric works
to persuade us of the giddy rapture that accompanies the probability,
if not certainty, of salvation.

   To be sure, Browne's sense of comic play did not eradicate all
melancholy from his religious experience. *Religio Medici* certainly
possesses a ground beat of sobriety that justifies C. A. Patrides's
designation of Browne as "grave-merry," but even when the author

seems most dispirited, he always manages, in Joan Webber's memorable phrase, to pull "the sting from pain."[19] In the midst of meditating on his own corruption, for instance, he announces that "the man without a Navell yet lives in me" (2.10, p. 69), a witty circumlocution that prevents us from taking his (and our) fallen Adamic condition too seriously. As for the general horrors of death, Browne can press them into nonexistence by delivering a parodically literalistic reading of a biblical text:

All flesh is grasse, is not onely metaphorically, but literally true, for all those creatures we behold, are but the hearbs of the field, digested into flesh in them, or more remotely carnified in our selves. Nay further, we are what we all abhorre, *Anthropophagi* and Cannibals, devourers not onely of men, but of our selves; and that not in an allegory, but a positive truth; for all this masse of flesh which wee behold, came in at our mouths: this frame wee looke upon, hath beene upon our trenchers; In briefe, we have devoured our selves. (1.37, p. 36)

The elegiac touches surrounding Isaiah's "all flesh is grasse" (40:6–7) are quickly converted by Browne into morbid grist for his comic mill, a conversion signaled first by the odd coinage "carnified," meaning made into flesh, intensified through the mock horror over the *"Anthropophagi,"* and clinched in the burlesque reduction of the metaphoric to the literal in the phrase "this frame wee looke upon, hath beene upon our trenchers." Indeed, Browne's wish to deprive us of a genuine glimpse into the abyss of despair underlies his excision from the authorized 1643 text of the one line in *Religio* containing suicidal overtones: "that I detest mine owne nature, and in my retired imagination cannot withhold my hands from violence on my selfe."[20] Browne might suggest elsewhere that "every man is his owne *Atropos*" (2.4, p. 61), but he resisted offering himself as an example. His bouts with melancholy are not to be confused with a life-and-death struggle for the soul.

Criticism and the Anticomic Tradition

Browne's reluctance—or rather refusal—to dig too deeply into the dark corners of his heart has brought criticism that he bobbed only too easily on the surface of theology and resisted the self-consuming call of God. "Browne," writes Stanley Fish, "does not say to us 'awake, remember, change,' but 'take it easy, don't let it

bother you, let it be,' " while from a slightly different perspective
Joan Webber observes that "with Browne, one often has the sense
that the tragic insight is at best willed and at worst a cliché."[21]
These are honest and, to an extent, appropriate responses to *Religio,*
but as criticisms they also assume that there is something deeply
suspicious about a work whose basic strategy is affirmative and comic
rather than afflictive and potentially tragic. For Fish, Browne's
amiability betrays a fundamental indifference to the cry of the soul;
for Webber (and also for Fish), Browne's preoccupation with the
artful depiction of the self amounts to an escapist aesthetic: "whatever kind of tragedy or comedy the world may be (stage of fools,
devil's mockshow, hospital, dream, globe, or fable), it is not
remediable."[22]

Browne would readily have agreed with the first part of Fish's
criticism since he strongly resisted Puritan insistence on the de-
pravity of man, a vision that urged a tortuous investigation of the
sinful self ("awake, remember") and valued the conversion experience
as the only authentic sign of election ("change"). "I can hardly
think there was ever any scared into Heaven" (1.52, p. 49), he
remarked with a deadpan innocence that quietly dismantles the
rationale behind the hellfire and brimstone sermon. (Thomas Fuller
tells us that the great Puritan divine, William Perkins, "would
pronounce the word *Damne* with such an emphasis as left a doleful
Echo in his auditours ears a good while after.")[23] "That name and
compellation of *little Flocke,* doth not comfort but deject my devotion" (1.58, p. 53), Browne observed in distancing himself from
the Puritan ideal of a spiritual elite, a brotherhood of Saints, either
within or without the great wheel of the Church.[24] And though he
carefully distinguishes between his human and his Christian birth
and admits not "esteeming my selfe any thing, before I was my
Saviours" (1.45, p. 42), he does not translate this theological recognition into a formal principle: the spiraling meditations of *Religio,*
separated into discrete sections, militate against the sequential struc-
turing of events basic to all conversion narratives. If Fish eyes Browne
with suspicion for not saying "awake, remember, change," Browne
was equally suspicious of the bullying designs that could lurk behind
ardent declarations of faith: "Insolent zeales that doe decry good
workes and rely only upon faith," he wrote, adding "onely" in
1643 to give more teeth to his criticism, "take not away merit: for
depending upon the efficacy of their faith, they enforce the condition

of God, and in a more sophisticall way doe seeme to challenge Heaven" (1.60, p. 54).

Remarks such as these would also suggest that *Religio* does not quite say "take it easy, don't let it bother you, let it be," or that if it does, these amiable gestures do not constitute so much an attitude of indifference or escape as a defense of the *via media*. Taking it easy—enjoying one's self—is inseparable in Browne from both the proper devotional attitude and the proper church which allows for the fulfillment of this possibility. When he says that his "conversation . . . is like the Sunne's with all men, and with a friendly aspect to good and bad" (2.10, p. 68), he defends his mode of comic discourse and deportment that, through the pun on "Sunne," purports to be both humanistic and godly, natural and yet transcendental. Indeed, Browne's identification with a benevolent Christ is further reinforced by the underlying biblical echo, "But I say unto you which hear, 'Love your enemies, do good to them which hate you' " (Luke 6:27). To reject this pattern of imitation in *Religio* is synonymous with rejecting "the common spirit that playes within us"; and though Browne is never so blunt or presumptuous as to say that this action alone merits damnation, he does suggest that playfulness—"a friendly aspect to good and bad"—is very much an expression of charity "without which Faith is a meer notion, and of no existence" (2.1, p. 55).

As for the failure of *Religio* to be remedial, this criticism depends, of course, very much on the diagnosis of the illness. If the times have become overwrought, then it makes perfectly good sense, as Anna Nardo has argued, to prescribe some playful recreation in which tensions can be released through the exuberant but innocuous *"altitudos"* of wit.[25] One can be a little zany without becoming a zealot. In fact, by allowing for a little zaniness, one might even take some of the insolence out of zeal. "There is not any of such a fugitive faith, such an unstable belief, as a Christian," Browne reckoned (1.25, p. 25); and like Shakespeare ministering to infatuation, he sought to create an imaginative space—a "green world" of wit—in which instability could be celebrated, exhausted, and exorcised and "singular" minds readily reconciled to the great wheel of the church. Indeed, the rationale behind the addition of section 8 to the 1643 text emphasizes this point. Placed between the author's discussion of his heretical "greener studies" (1.6, p. 7) and his vertiginous exploration of the "wingy mysteries in Divinity" (1.9), this section simultaneously defends the via media as an acceptable place for the "singular" individual and underscores the exemplary nature of the author's subsequently eccentric but ultimately harmless exercise of faith: "for there is yet after all the decrees of counsells and the niceties of the Schooles, many things untouch'd, unimagin'd, wherein the libertie of an honest reason may play and expatiate with security and farre without the circle of an heresie" (p. 9).

To celebrate play, especially in 1643, was also the perfect strategy of a moderate, a way to use a buckler rather than a sword at a time when swords were being unsheathed. Playing seems antithetical to fighting, or to adopt Johan Huizinga's phrasing, it seems to lie "outside the reasonableness of practical life; has nothing to do with necessity or utility, duty or truth";[26] and yet it is also difficult to escape the notion that Browne's additional emphasis upon "recreation" in 1643 was an act of resistance against an increasingly powerful Parliament that under pressure from strict "anti-theater Puritan leaders"[27] sought officially to outlaw all forms of playing. In response to Charles's having raised his standard at Nottingham on 22 August 1642, it issued its famous order on 2 September to shut down the theaters: "whereas public Sports do not well agree with public Calamities; nor public Plays with the Seasons of Humiliation; this being an Exercise of sad and pious Solemnity, and the other being Spectacles of Pleasure, too commonly expressing lascivious Mirth and Leachery: It is, therefore, thought fit and ordained by the Lords and Commons, &c. That while those sad Courses and set Times of Humiliations do continue, public Stage-Plays shall cease and be forborne."[28] The injunction represented a triumphant moment for extremists like William Prynne, who had vehemently attacked the corrupting influence of the theaters in his voluminous *Histriomastix* (1633); and though the ordinance had no immediate liturgical bearing, it nonetheless gave, in its hostility to public sports, a signal about the fate of the bitterly disputed *Book of Sports*. Reissued by Laud in 1633 as a way to enforce conformity by insisting on the "lawful recreation" of games on Sundays, the book was burned by the hangman in 1643.

Playful and recreative, *Religio Medici* is hardly a closet version of *The Book of Sports* or a clandestine drama, but two lengthy passages attached to specifically recreative sections in *Religio* show that Browne was not going to subscribe to the new mood of imminent seriousness, or at least not in the way Parliament was legislating. The first of these additions occurs in part 1, section 13. Underscoring the general emphasis of part 1 on the first two cardinal virtues, faith and hope,[29] both early and revised versions begin with a declaration of worship: "That other attribute wherewith I recreate my devotion, is his wisedome, in which I am happy"; and in the portions added in 1643, Browne highlights, first through references to Solomon and then in an extended twenty-two-line poem with some closing commentary, the peaceful and solitary nature of his devotion. The additional portions do much to emphasize the nonviolent aspects of Browne's worship, as he recreates with obvious humility among the wonders of nature: "Teach me to soare aloft, yet ever so, / When neare the Sunne, to stoope againe below." But they also show him wielding the buckler with a deftly defensive touch. Just when the speaker of the poem is about to evaporate from this world in his innocent "buzzing" of praises to God, Browne returns in the prose addition to remark: "And this is almost all wherein an humble creature may endeavour to requite, and someway to retribute unto his Creator." "Almost all" is the key here. Browne sees the need for a few more words. Exchanging one book of God for another, nature for Scripture, he quotes Matthew 7:21 to the effect that not everyone who cries "Lord, Lord, Shall enter into the Kingdom of heaven; but he that doeth the will of my Father which is in heaven." The biblical allusion is deliberately modest, but it places the entire discussion of recreation within a scriptural frame that recollects, in a diminished key, the militant charge, "Beware of False Prophets, which come to you in sheep's clothing, but inwardly they are ravening wolves" (Matthew 7:15). This is an accusation that Milton, for one, had already hurled at the corrupt clergy in "Lycidas" in 1637; with a reticence befitting his moderate stance, Browne turns it back on the zealous prophets (like Milton and Prynne) of the early 1640s. In his act of recreation, his pastoral pursuits, he quietly urges that the will of heaven is best served not by those who, prophesying in Christ's name, attempt to cast out the devils and do "many wonderful works" (7:22), but by those who, stooping before the sun (Son), leave the wonderful works to God.

The other major interpolation in the 1643 text involving recreation occurs in part 2, section 11. In many ways a summation or epitome of the comic spirit of *Religio,* the addition is thematically congruent with the emphasis in part 2 on the third cardinal virtue, charity, a virtue which, though appearing in Browne after faith and hope, nonetheless claims priority in order of theological importance since without it "Faith is a meer notion, and of no existence" (2.1, p. 55). Browne is reversing Calvin's preference here, and in doing so he gives a particularly Anglican reading of the decalogue;[30] but his presentation of a charitable disposition is also significantly different from Laudian attempts to use charity as a means to browbeat Puritans. Claiming to give a "moderate" answer to Henry Burton, Peter Heylyn, for instance, invokes "charity," which "vaunteth not itself, is not puffed up, doth not behave itselfe unseemely," as a justification for his notion of rigid conformity declared on the title page in the quotation from 1 Peter 13–14: "Submit yourselves to every ordinance of man for the Lord's sake: whether it be to the king, as supreme; or unto governers, as unto them that are sent by him for the punishment of evildoers, and for the praise of them that do well."[31] Like Heylyn, Browne readily viewed the "flames of zeale" as a threat to charity, but his response to this perceived political conflict was not to insist that the zealous become charitable by submitting themselves to every ordinance of man but to urge that each person practice being charitable to himself: "how shall we expect charity towards others," he queried, "when we are uncharitable to our selves?" (2.4, p. 61).

Browne, who remarks in 2.13 that he has "two armes too few to embrace [him] selfe," heightened comic gestures like these into something like a comic principle in 1643 by extending and amplifying a statement about the self as a globe which he turns "round sometimes for my recreation" into a moment of rapturous self-worship:

The earth is a point not onely in respect of the heavens above us, but of that heavenly and celestial part within us: that masse of flesh that circumscribes me, limits not my mind: that surface that tells the heavens it hath an end, cannot perswade me I have any; I take my circle to be above three hundred and sixty, though the number of the Arke do measure my body, it comprehendeth not my minde: whilst I study to finde how I am a Microcosme or little world, I finde my selfe something more than the great. There is surely a peece of Divinity in us, something that was before the Elements, and owes no homage unto the Sun. Nature tels me I am the Image of God as well as Scripture; he that understands not thus much, hath not his introduction or first lesson, and is yet to begin the Alphabet of man. (2.11, p. 70)

The elaborate repetition of statement here, in which Browne keeps recreating from slightly different angles a transcendent, unlimited, divine version of himself, asks the reader to share in this pleasurable action, to experience momentarily the personal contentment that "wee call Happiness" (2,11), an experience in which through the stillness of syntax and idea we understand intensively the divinity behind the proverbial remark, "Charity begins at home" (2.4, p. 61). But if there is a rhapsodic element in this interpolation—one of the lines is included among those praised by the Norwich Quaker, Samuel Duncon[32]—the passage also serves to objectify the self in something like a "scientific" manner. We study Browne studying himself where every angle of vision, each perspective, discovers the same essential truth: the happy recognition that "There is *surely* a peece of Divinity in us" (my italics). Browne's taxonomic approach thus circumvents Heylyn's "uncharitable" attempt to institutionalize charity through an act of political authority bearing the imprimatur of Laud, but his giddy playfulness also elegantly opposes the radical discontent of Puritanism. In Browne's "Alphabet of man," there is finally no room for Prynne's extraordinary denunciation of mirth in *Histriomastix* in which he asserts that "Our Saviour, whose doctrine no Christian dares controll, hath denounced an woe to all those that laugh."[33] Browne's age in *Religio Medici,* a "miracle of thirty yeares," recollects through Christ the prelapsarian Adam who, at age thirty, was thought to be "created in the perfect age and stature of man" (1.39, p. 38). Both the coincidence and the cause that made this recollection possible are surely reasons to smile.

Writing about generic contamination in *Much Ado About Nothing,* John Traugott has argued that "comedy is a fantasy of triumph, giving an access of superiority, as though somehow—by wit, accident, fortune, the god's intervention—we had mastered the perverse will of contingent life to sink down into the inert or fly into incoherent bits and pieces. This instant of mastery has no future, being what is right and therefore timeless."[34] Like so many politicized autobiographies of the late 1630s and early 1640s, *Religio Medici* is preeminently a fantasy of triumph, an exposition in which the self seems to have mastered the perverse will of contingent life once and for all; but the triumph and the comedy are also necessarily interior and personal, reckoned by the oblique angles of wit, word-play, and paradox. Browne's God is the spirit that plays within, a figuration for the unexpected. He is not a deus ex machina, a god of history who will determine the shape of events to fit a predictable linear pattern and thus be the self-evident promoter of an elect nation. If Browne happily recorded the favor of Providence shining on England in "the victory of 88" (1.17, p. 17) when a Protestant country conquered the mighty Spanish Armada, he gives no sign, either within the text or in the preface, that England in the early 1640s retains its special status as a chosen nation "kindling her undazl'd eyes at the full midday beam."[35]

Browne's silence on this issue underlies, moreover, the embattled tone in the 1643 preface and helps to make acute the moment of mastery suggested by *Religio* itself. *"Certainly that man were greedy of life, who should desire to live when all the world were at an end"* is the troubling apocalyptic note sounded in the first line, cribbed from one of the more horrific moments in Seneca's *Thyestes*. Having learned of Atreus's mutilation of his nephews and of their being cannibalized by their father, the chorus in the play launches into a one-hundred-line description of cosmic chaos that concludes with the line, "Greedy indeed for life is he who would not die when the world is perishing." Browne's recollection of *Thyestes* sets his work squarely in the disruptive, immediate historical context of England, as do the subsequent lines on the abusive powers of the press defaming the name of *"his Majesty"* and parliament. All are part of an author's elaborate protest for even bothering to emend a text at a time when there are more momentous things happening than the pirating of a physician's religion, a protest that Dr. Johnson, for one, found hard to take at face value. But whatever other reasons might underlie the stated one of desiring to repair something within one's power, it is impossible to erase altogether the survivalist impulse contained in the opening reference from Seneca: *"Certainly that man were greedy of life, who should desire to live when all the world were at an end."* Written in a different key, the preface merges with the autobiography in identifying an author who resolutely refuses to lose his being.

Chapter Six
Pseudodoxia Epidemica, or Global Inquiries

If *Religio Medici* can be read in a single, albeit lengthy, sitting, as Sir Kenelm Digby discovered,[1] *Pseudodoxia Epidemica* contains enough material for nearly a lifetime of perusing. In almost every sense it is a remarkable book. It is uncommonly knowledgeable, it is uncommonly written, it is uncommonly speculative, and it is uncommonly long. It is the text that cinched Browne's reputation among his contemporaries for being "learned," and it is the text that, from a modern perspective, helps to place Browne among the producers of magisterial prose works in the seventeenth century, an elite group that includes the likes of Ralegh, Bacon, Burton, and Milton. It is also the book of Browne's likely to prove most troublesome to modern students of literature. Although the work delivers a "world view" of a particular individual, the reader approaching it as autobiography will be quickly baffled by what he or she finds. *Pseudodoxia* is not a history of personal opinions like *Religio Medici;* it is a critical history of the opinions of others. And though it is written with conviction and sometimes with humor, the feelings are not as immediately nor as generally accessible as those that animate *Urne-Buriall, The Garden of Cyrus,* or even *A Letter to a Friend,* all of which are profoundly shaped by the alternating rhythms of life and death.

Browne's topic is the epidemic of false truths that he found infecting nearly every branch of knowledge. The subject had received official approval from Bacon in *The Advancement of Learning* (1605), and it was clearly on the minds of many English and European thinkers, distinguished and undistinguished alike, in the earlier part of the seventeenth century. Browne cites in the 1646 preface the separate works of his fellow countryman and colleague, James Primerose, and his French counterpart, Laurent Joubert, as having preceded him in a limited way in this venture. In the 1650 edition he adds the name of the Italian physician Scipio Mercurio to this

list. And shortly after the first edition was published, he received
a letter of enthusiastic praise from a returning Englishman, Henry
Bate, who, having studied, traveled, and discoursed "with forraig-
ners," had "beene long in quest after most of those particulars
[queried in *Pseudodoxia*], and lamented the confident mistakes and
wormeaten errours of the age."[2] Descartes, too, on his way to discovering the argument on which the proof of his existence is based
in *The Discourse on Method* (1637), reported trafficking with the
problem of separating the customary and the traditional from the
certain and the absolute.

The topic of searching out vulgar errors was obviously a valued
activity among the polite and the learned for a variety of reasons.
It could have serious epistemological consequences, as it did for
Descartes. It might prove helpful for future research in a specific
field, as Bacon suggested. And it could provide opportunity for
sport and amusement, as Bate's letter indicates—something to do
while on the grand tour or enduring exile from a politically inhospitable homeland. All three of these motives intermingle in *Pseudodoxia,* a work that makes serious epistemological statements by
sporting with many popular—and some not so popular—errors in
an effort to advance learning at a moment when the gentry were
particularly likely to be idle and in need of some nourishment besides
feeding on political and religious controversy.

In the very broadest sense, *Pseudodoxia* is an encyclopedia written
from the underside of that tradition. The great works of Pliny,
Gesner, and Aldrovandi sought to collect all that had been said on
a particular subject, "all that ha[d] been *seen* and *heard,* all that
ha[d] been *recounted,* either by nature or by men, by the language
of the world, by tradition, or by the poets."[3] Browne's work proceeds
from the opposite perspective. It seeks to reduce the flow of indis-
criminate reportage. If we are "to purchase a clear and warrantable
body of Truth," he warns his readers at the outset, "we must forget
and part with much wee know" (p. 1), a warning that follows quickly
after an epigram from Julius Scaliger on the title page: *"Ex Libris
colligere quae prodiderunt Authores longe est periculosissimum; Rerum ips-
arum cognitio vera è rebus ipsis est"* (To cull from books what authors
have reported is exceedingly dangerous; true knowledge of things
themselves is out of the things themselves). Browne's stated purpose
in *Pseudodoxia* is to perform a "timely survey [of] our knowledge;
impartially singling out those encroachments, which junior com-

pliance and popular credulity hath admitted" (p. 1). And his criteria of truth, his means of judgment, are to be "experience" and "reason," not simply the past appearance of an idea or statement in print.

Book 1: "The Common Infirmity of Humane Nature"

Browne's "timely survey" begins in book 1 with a description of the origin and the general causes of error. Neither the origin (the Fall of man), nor the general causes cited (ignorance, credulity, laziness, a slavish adherence to authority, or susceptibility to the promptings of Satan) are categories unique to Browne, though they certainly bear the individual stamp of his being. Bacon had singled out a number of these features in *The Advancement* and again in *The New Organon* (see above, chapter 2), while criticism of the ignorant multitude was a common "humanist" practice. And, of course, it is nearly impossible to imagine anyone in the seventeenth century capable of thinking of error without also thinking of man's first act of disobedience in the Garden. If the opening book lays special claim to our attention—and I believe it does—it is not for its diagnostic subtlety or its conceptual breakthroughs; it is because, as a general introduction to the problem of error, it highlights, without rancor or contention, the urgency, the "timeliness," of the whole project.

In this book Browne writes from the podium/pulpit, not from the privacy of his study. There is here none of the coy indirection of *Religio*. False truths have reached epidemic proportions: "being now at greatest distance from the beginning of errour," he laments, we "are almost lost in its dissemination, whose wayes are boundlesse, and confesse no circumscription" (1.2, p. 14). This solemn note of muted apocalyptic concern keeps being sounded in various forms throughout the opening book; and though Browne, always the cool physician, never becomes panic-striken over the situation, the very gravity of his voice identifies someone deeply conscious of the moral, intellectual, and social implications of the Fall, and of the acute need to return at least a portion of the world to order.

In response to this situation, Browne marches through his topics with measured "high" seriousness. His discussion of the Fall, for instance, jettisons a whole series of interpretive "nicities" (p. 8) that might complicate the central message of his text: how Adam and Eve "were grossely deceived in their perfection," an observation repeated with solemn professorial regularity in the topic sentence of each paragraph: "They were deceived by one another, and in the greatest disadvantage of delusion,""They were deceived from themselves, and their owne apprehensions," "They were deceived through the conduct of their senses," "Againe, they might for ought we know, be still deceived in the unbeliefe of their mortality," and, in a final summary example, "Man was not only deceiveable in his integrity, but the Angells of light in all their clarity" (1.1, pp. 5– 9). Individual chapters are also broken down into numerically arranged units for ready assimilation. There are six instances of erroneous speech before the flood (1.2, pp. 10–14), five main points in which Satan commonly deceives mankind (1.10, pp. 58–66), and a seemingly comprehensive listing of authors, reminiscent of an epic catalog, whose works should be read with caution (1.8–9, pp. 46–57). Paragraphs, too, are often simply a tissue of examples, linked together to make a tour de force: "Thus the Priests of Elder time, have put upon them [the multitude] many incredible conceits . . . and thus also in some Christian Churches . . . there have not wanted, many strange deceptions. . . . Thus Theudas an Imposter was able to lead away foure thousand into the wildernesse. . . . Thus all heresies how grosse soever, have found a welcome with the people" (1.3, p. 19).

Details pile up, observations are amassed, single points amplified with multiple examples: all presented in order to make the reader apprehend on a visceral level the ubiquitous nature of error and the need for correction. Mistakes, for Browne, are never simply intellectual, a failure in the mechanics of reasoning, as they often are, for instance, with Hobbes (see *Leviathan,* 1.5). From "the fallacie of Æquivocation and Amphibologie . . . arose that calamitous error of the Jewes, misapprehending the Prophesies of their Messias, and expounding them alwayes unto literall and temporall expectations" (1.4, pp. 22–23). From the confusion of sign with the thing signified, "Idolatry first crept in," a "deplorable mistake" that reaches out to touch on those flammable contemporary disputes involving interpretation of the Eucharist and the Sabbath (p. 26). Indeed, given the Civil War context of *Pseudodoxia,* it is almost impossible to escape the sense of immediacy prompting Browne's decision to examine the separate arguments made by Cain and Lamech for rationalizing murder, the one despairing altogether of God's mercy, the other presuming it (1.2, pp. 12–13); just as his account of the dangerous stupidity of the multitude (1.3, pp. 15–21), without making any explicit references, seems to stare out at a world turned upside down in which brutality and political chicanery predominate.

Browne's imagination is relentlessly expansionist in this opening book; the single seed of the fall has yielded an epidemic of error. In any given passage, the curve of his prose can open up to our attention the ultimate implications of an action as casually expressed as rolling the stone in vain:

> And this is one reason why though Universities bee full of men, they are oftentimes empty of learning. Why as there are some which do much without learning, so others but little with it, and few that attaine to any measure of it. For many heads that undertake it, were never squared nor timbred for it. There are not onely particular men, but whole nations indisposed for learning, whereunto is required not onely education, but a pregnant Minerva and teeming constitution. For the wisdome of God hath divided the Genius of men according to the different affaires of the world, and varied their inclinations according to the variety of Actions to be performed therein, which they who consider not, rudely rushing upon professions and wayes of life unequall to their natures; dishonour not onely themselves and their functions, but pervert the harmony of the whole world. For if the world went on as God hath ordained it, and were every one implyed in points concordant to their Natures; Professions, Arts and Common-wealths would rise up of themselves; nor needed we a Lanthorne to finde a man in Athens. (1.5, p. 31)

There is nothing here so portentous as Ulysses' "untune that string, / And hark what discord follows" (*Troilus and Cressida,* 1.3, 109–10), though the message is essentially the same. Browne's passage simply presses ineluctably outward. Moving from his initial reference to individual men, to "whole nations," to the perverted "harmony of the whole world," to the "utopia" God promised if people only understood their nature, he generates a cosmic vision of people in the wrong calling, of a world, if not quite hopelessly out of joint, certainly in need of being reset.

If Browne's imagination is pointedly expansionist in this opening book, the arcs ultimately created serve to frame the single underlying dialectic of ignorance versus intelligence, submission to superstition versus admiration for wisdom, as best exemplified in the "rationall and well grounded precepts of Christ, whose life as it was conformable unto his doctrine, so was that unto the highest rules of reason"

(1.3, p. 17). This opposition is suggested in miniature in the chiastic
structure of phrases like "full of men" / "empty of learning" or "as
there are some which do much without learning, so others but little
with it." It achieves its greatest rhetorical moment in Browne's
depiction of the two ends of the intelligence spectrum: the ignorant
multitude and the wise man. In the first instance, Browne's withering portrait of the multitude, the traditional enemy of reason in
the Renaissance, is rivaled among seventeenth-century prose writers
only by Burton's for sheer sweep of incident and cumulative power
of denunciation. In fact, it is the one moment in his writings when
Browne explicitly aligns himself with Democritus. Some of the
details, too, are perhaps owing to *The Anatomy:* both authors deplore
mob violence; both quote from Acts 19:34 in which the multitude,
in rejecting Paul, cried out for two hours, "Great is Diana." Both
also represent the heresies welcomed by the people, and criticize
the ignorant for being continually abused by priests and politicians
alike.[4] But the force of Burton's satire—the battering strength of
his prose—invests the objects of his attack with an extraordinary
energy and power even if he is highly critical of their purpose: the
madness recounted in *The Anatomy* is full of sound and fury some
of which belongs to the author himself. Browne's criticism of the
vulgar, on the other hand, comes down from on high; it concentrates
on signifying the nothingness that accompanies the loss of intellect,
and it insists on a vast separation between the author and his subject.
Having choked "those tender sparkes, which Adam hath left them
of reason" (1.3, 17), the ignorant are represented as wandering in
a twilight of nonbeing:

> Their understanding is so feeble in the discernement of falsities, and
> averting the errors of reason, that it submitteth unto the fallacies of sence,
> and is unable to rectifie the error of its sensations. Thus the greater part
> of mankinde having but one eye of sence and reason, conceive the earth
> farre bigger then the Sun, the fixed Stars lesser than the Moone, their
> figures plaine, and their spaces from earth equidistant. For thus their sence
> enformeth them, and herein their reason cannot rectifie them, and therefore
> hopelesly continuing in mistakes, they live and dye in their absurdities;
> passing their dayes in perverted apprehensions, and conceptions of the
> world, derogatory unto God, and the wisdome of his creation. (1.3, p.
> 15).

In contrast to this depiction of the Cyclopean multitude, a vision
that concludes by dissolving social and economic boundaries to

consider any who resign their reason as "within the line of vulgaritie, and Democraticall enemies of truth" (p. 21), stands the wise man, the person capable of making "experiment by sence or enquiry by reason" (1.5, p. 30), the kind of man whom Browne seeks to challenge into action by a combination of flattery, warning, and deliberate exhortation. "The solid reason of one man, is as sufficient as the clamor of a whole Nation" (1.7, p. 42) is one way of describing the heroic potential involved in the pursuit of truth. Another is by characterizing him, in favorite Renaissance fashion, as an industrious Adam and type of Christ: through the sweat of his brow, he "may in some measure repaire our primarie ruins, and build our selves men againe" (1.5, p. 30). And a third is by offering a veiled threat that failure by the gifted to take up the challenge of a scientific inquiry "may perhaps fill up the charge of the last day" (p. 30). Despite Browne's willingness, stated in *Religio,* "to be but the last man, and bring up the Rere in Heaven" (1.58, p. 53), it is this third idea in particular that catches hold of his imagination as he turns a warning into an occasion for extolling what is sometimes referred to as the myth of Protestant individualism underlying the scientific quest.[5] The upward sweep begins:

For not obeying the dictates of reason, and neglecting the cryes of truth, we faile not onely in the trust of our undertakings, but in the intention of man it selfe, which although more veniall in ordinary constitutions, and such as are not framed beyond the capacity of beaten notions, yet will it inexcusably condemne some men, who having received excellent endowments, have yet sat downe by the way, and frustrated the intention of their habilities. For certainely as some men have sinned, in the principles of humanity, and must answer, for not being men, so others offend if they be not more; *Magis extra vitia quam cum virtutibus* [rather without vice than with virtue], would commend those, These are not excusable without an Excellency. For great constitutions, and such as are constellated unto knowledge, do nothing till they outdoe all; they come short of themselves if they go not beyond others, and must not sit downe under the degree of worthies. God expects no lustre from the minor stars, but if the Sun should not illuminate all, it were a sin in Nature. (1.5, pp. 30–31)

The marginal jotting in one copy of *Pseudodoxia* at this point by a supine reader of "excellent endowments" would seem to be exactly the response Browne was after: "O me!!"[6]

Books 2–4: From Minerals to Man

The opening book seems rooted in "prophecy," not in any millenarian sense of figuring forth a new Jerusalem but in the general way that Frank L. Huntley applies the term elsewhere to Browne: as "discovering" a profound truth.[7] Browne wants his audience to "see" into the epidemic nature of error—its origin and general causes—and to hear a voice tinged with the oracular, giving significance to everything that comes within its range and endowing the quest for knowledge with new vigor. Without quite declaring a holy war on error, Browne's prose in the opening book verges constantly on the apocalyptic. Swallowing "falsities for truths, dubiosities for certainties, fesibilities for possibilities, and things impossible as possibilities themselves" is presented, in deliberately swelling tones, as being never far from committing the grossest of mistakes: believing "that any thing is God" or that "there is no God at all" (1.5, pp. 28–29).

In the six books that follow, Browne works more from the library and laboratory than the lectern. Having alerted his audience to the "timeliness" of his venture, he embarks on a "survey" of the particular manifestations of error in the world about him—"timely" in this case applying to the controlled, "impartial," methodical nature of the quest. In these books, Browne is the embodiment of the patient researcher. He is the careful and punctilious inquirer "into Very many received Tenents and commonly presumed Truths"—to quote the subtitle of his work—not the announcer of "pseudodoxia epidemica." "Experience" and "reason" (buttressed by authority) are his principal weapons, and with them he sets out to return the world, piece by piece, if not to a state of innocence, at least to a place in which rationality rather than superstition has the larger share.

Browne's wanderings "in the America and untravelled parts of truth" (p. 3) partially follow the path of the great chain of being. The order of these six books, a recent critic succinctly observes,

generally reflects Browne's attempt to enlarge progressively the circle of his enquiry, for in considering various popular beliefs he moves from minerals to plants, animals, and eventually man, ascending the scale of creation (Books II–IV). Browne then further widens his focus to include man's pictorial representations of the created world (Book V) and problems related to geography, history, cosmology, and the nature of time (Book VI), finally concluding with a discussion of miscellaneous beliefs derived from secular and biblical history (Book VII). Not only does this encyclopedia encompass the circle of creation; it also spans the entire cycle of providential history from Creation and the Fall (Book I) to the Apocalypse and the Last Judgment (Book VI). The *Pseudodoxia Epidemica* thus embraces both the physical and "temporal circumscriptions" [6.1, p. 440] of the world.[8]

And, it should be added, the work also places man, "that amphibious piece betweene a corporall and spirituall essence" (*RM*, 1.34, p. 33)—the middle link in the universe—at the observing as well as the structural center of the whole.

Book 2, focusing on common tenets concerning "Minerall and vegetable bodies" (in that order), begins the journey. Browne starts by querying the general opinion that "Crystall is nothing else, but Ice or Snow," "of which assertion," he adds, "if prescription of time, and numerositie of Assertors, were a sufficient demonstration, we might sit downe herein" (p. 74). But Browne, does not, and his refusal is typical of his determination, especially in the early books, to get at the truth. "Upon a strict enquiry," he discovers that the balance of evidence, which includes the views of other writers, some of his personal observations, and his own deductions, is against this position. Browne then marches off on his longest journey in book 2 to consider questions concerning the lodestone, a topic of perennial interest to the seventeenth century. The two chapters draw heavily on Gilbert's *De Magnete* (1600), not yet translated into English,[9] whose views Browne seeks to champion; and underneath the lengthy, quasi-technical discussions, the citations of various authorities, and some crude and unintentionally amusing experiments, it is still possible to feel Browne's excitement over the issue of terrestrial magnetism. "This is probably that foundation the wisdom of the Creator hath laid unto the earth; in this sense we may more nearly apprehend, and sensibly make out the expressions of holy Scripture, as *Firmavit orbem terrae qui non commovebitur* [Psalm 93:1], he hath made the round world so sure that it cannot be moved" (p. 87). "Wonderful" is the word that directs many discussions, as Browne's enthusiasm seems generated not just by the neat dovetailing of natural philosophy and theology but also by how the two function as mutually reinforcing (and doubly comforting) explanations for an ordered universe.

The second of the two chapters also reveals Browne debunking some "wondrous strange" reports surrounding the lodestone. "Eusebius Nierembergius a learned Jesuit of Spain delivers, that the body of man is magneticall, and being placed in a boate, the vessell will never rest untill the head respecteth the North" (p. 104). Browne begins his laconic refutation with the remark: "if this be true, the bodies of Christians doe lye unnaturally in their graves." In a similar manner, Pliny's account that the shores of India are so abundant with "Loadstone mines and rocks . . . that it proves an adventure of hazard to passe those coasts in a ship with Iron nailes," amplified by "Serapion the Moore, an Author of good esteeme and reasonable antiquity," who argues that "there is no Iron in them [ships passing by] which flyes not like a bird unto these mountains," is summarily dismissed on the basis of recent reports of navigators, many of whom are "of our owne Nation" (pp. 106–7). As for relations involving the "magical" uses of the lodestone—its purpose in determining "the incontinencie of a wife" (p. 112), for instance, or its powers to create a "Sympathie" between two needles touched by it (p. 114)—these "conceits" show Browne, the advancer of knowledge, at his most indignant and humorous. "The Aeolus that blew" about the latter idea, Browne quips, "was Famianus Strada, that elegant Jesuit in his Rhetoricall prolusions" (p. 114).

The remaining chapters in the second book are conceived on a narrower scale. Browne's discussion of electricity is blandly bookish (4). His account of stones and jewels is a series of brief essays on the properties commonly ascribed to particular minerals (5). So, too, are the succeeding two chapters on vegetable and plants (6–7), the second of which, moving further up the chain of being, also inquires into popular errors concerning insects. These later chapters are more indebted to and animated by folklore traditions. They show Browne combating a variety of common beliefs attached to stones and plants: "Whether a Carbuncle . . . doth flame in the dark, or shine like a coale in the night" (p. 137), or whether the stones in "*Aarons* brestplate made a Jewel surpassing any" (p. 139). He takes on the "many Mola's and false conceptions" that swirl around the Mandrake—for example, its fertility associations, an idea that Donne plays with in his song "Go and catch a falling star," and the more grisly question of whether "it naturally groweth under gallowses and places of execution, arising from fat or urine that drops from the body of the dead" (p. 143). And he attempts to weed out legends, rooted frequently in pagan and monastic "superstition," that still cling to plants like the mistletoe, Rose of Jericho, and Glastonbury Thorn (pp. 147–50). The book then concludes with a list of vegetable fables expanded in the 1650 and 1658 editions: "That Flos Affricanus is poyson, and destroyeth dogs, in two experiments we have not found" (p. 158).

In many ways, the third book, "Of divers popular and received Tenents concerning Animals," forms the heart of *Pseudodoxia*. It is not at the structural center of the seven-book work; that honor goes to the fourth book, with its inquiries into popular errors involving man. But the third is by far the largest of the books, nearly twice as long as the shortest (7) and half again as long as the next largest (5–6). It is also, perhaps after the opening survey of the general causes of error, the book to which readers have most readily taken. The subject matter, on the whole, is generally familiar to even the casual naturalist: elephants, horses, doves, beavers, badgers, bears, wolves, deer, kingfishers, frogs, toads, salamanders, vipers, rabbits, snails, and so on. But it is not so familiar as to be routine. Browne has chapters on the basilisk, griffin, phoenix, amphisbaena, and unicorn; and, of course, the popular tenets Browne examines have generally passed so far out of currency that the modern, suburban reader might well feel that he has been suddenly transported into a land of make-believe. "That an Elephant hath no joynts" (3.1), "That a Bever to escape the hunter bites off his Testicles or stones" (3.4), "That a Salamander lives in the fire" (3.14), or "That the Chamaeleon lives onely by Aire" (3.21) sounds like material out of Lewis Carroll or ideas for a limerick by Edward Lear.

Browne, as usual, is essentially on our side here, or almost. These are not views he accepts. His account of the elephant, for instance, begins on a wonderful note of Aesopian mockery: "The first shall be of the Elephant, where of there generally passeth an opinion it hath no joynts; and this absurdity is seconded with another, that being unable to lye downe, it sleepeth against a tree, which the Hunters observing doe saw almost asunder; whereon the beast relying, by the fall of the tree falls also down it selfe, and is able to rise no more" (3.1, p. 160). His refutation of the view "That a Brock or Badger hath the legs of one side shorter than of the other" is less comical but no less certain: "an opinion perhaps not very ancient, [it] is yet very generall, received not only by theorists and unexperienced beleevers, but assented unto by most who have the opportunity to behold and hunt them dayly; which notwithstanding upon enquiry I finde repugnant unto the three determinators of truth, Authority, Sense and Reason" (3.5, p. 176). And in repudiating the old and apparently still current belief that a bear brings forth her young unformed and licks them into shape, Browne can become positively incensed: "Beside (what few take notice of) men hereby doe in an high measure vilifie the workes of God, imputing that unto the tongue of a beast, which is the strangest artifice in all the acts of nature, that is the formation of the Infant in the womb, not only in mankind, but all viviparous animals" (3.6, p. 179). Browne then presides over the "proper" interpretation of the phenomenon of birth like a high priest both respecting and protecting a mystery: "to behold it were a spectacle almost worth ones being, a sight beyond all, except that man had been created first, and might have seen the shew of five dayes after."

It is also in the third book that we are perhaps made most conscious of the difficulty of separating the essayist from the encyclopedist, the advancer of knowledge from the collector of opinions, the critic who wishes to reduce the traffic of false truths from the author who still desires to say all that might be said on a particular subject. Browne's respect for the written word, though guarded, remains enormous. Even when Browne is apparently attempting to resist the tyranny of its presence, authority still looms large in *Pseudodoxia*. He might in the preface (p. 3) identify himself as a David against Goliath; he might indict "a peremptory adhesion unto Authority," as having done "the greatest execution upon truth" (1.6, p. 32); he might even draw up a sizeable list of canonical authors who have played leading parts in the grand march of error: but Browne ultimately accepts the canon as it is and the prestige attached to writing as a potent weapon in mediating the truth. It is not enough for Browne simply to go out and examine the legs of a badger to see if they are shorter on one side. He wants to reexamine the question within the framework of the existing epistemological tradition, one that accords the written word an important, if no longer quite a divine, place.

Browne's desire to examine tenets involving "fabulous" creatures like the phoenix and the griffin, creatures beyond his "ocular" powers, is consequently an instance of his questioning on one level what he accepts on another. So, too, is the encyclopedic nature of many of the essays. Browne wants to have the last word here, not just in the sense of delivering a final blow to an already much pummelled view, like the old saw that swans "sing most sweetly before their death (3.27, p. 275); but also in the sense of exhausting his topic, of saying all there is to say. The latter feature is particularly visible in an essay like the one on the phoenix, in which the bulk of his considerable discourse occurs after the word "lastly." It is also present in the discursive nature of the essays themselves. As a number of critics have observed, Browne often uses the "inquiry" into a popular tenet simply as a point of departure, the excuse or occasion to consider a wide variety of topics, sometimes arranged only in the loosest fashion under the double or triple determinators of truth. And, of course, the drive for inclusiveness is present in the author's discourse—Browne's happy use of myth and metaphor even while he is constantly citing these features as frequent promoters of error.

To look for a moment at only one instance of Browne's rewriting the encyclopedic tradition from a more "critical" perspective: Browne's notorious account of the elephant (1.3) begins with a presentation of the "old and gray-headed errour," moves quickly through a citation of offending authors beginning with Aristotle, and then sets out to refute the opinion. His first line of attack— that it is difficult to conceive of a creature without joints walking— returns Aristotle to a position of authority ("as Aristotle teacheth") with no sense of contradiction. The paragraph concludes with a wildly mythologized *reductio ad absurdum:* we might just as well "expect a race from Hercules his pillars, or hope to behold the effects of Orpheus his harpe, when Trees found joints, and danced after his musicke." Browne then explores another contradiction (how can the vastest of animals not enjoy the position of rest "ordained unto all pedestrious animalls") with "proofs" partially borrowed from the pagan underworld with its tormented figures of Ixion, Sisyphus, and Tantalus. Further "evidence" is quickly marshaled from "obvious relations of history" (reports of elephants being able to walk on tightropes and dance to music), from grammarians, and "lastly" from contemporary reports, "whereof not many yeares past we have had the advantage in England" of seeing one. Having refuted an error "still alive and epidemicall," Browne then moves on to consider the origins of the mistake, which he locates in the "Cylindricall composure of the legs," and various other "concernments . . . which might admit of discourse": their teeth, genitals, even the possibility that elephants can write or talk.

Browne, of course, is right. Elephants do have joints in their legs, though Browne's near contemporary, George Herbert, would seem to think otherwise;[10] but few modern scientists are likely to be impressed by his approach. Like Pliny or Topsell, Browne is still very much fascinated and influenced by the "legend" of the creature, by the written tradition attached to the beast, even if in refuting some of the particulars he does not simply pass along the texts of previous authors in quite the wholesale fashion as Topsell does in his *Historie of Four Footed Beasts* (1607). "Experience" here plays a small role, as indeed it must, since Browne apparently has not seen the elephant itself. But this situation still does not prevent him from inquiring into the subject, and it certainly does not prevent him from passing along a few wild speculations, which, in fact, are part of the written tradition. The subject of talking elephants goes back to Pliny, as do Browne's other remarks respecting the legendary intelligence of the elephant. Browne's impulses here and throughout *Pseudodoxia* are, like those of the encyclopedists, textually based if not absolutely textually centered.

In the fourth book, Browne takes a further step up the chain of being. His topic is the "many popular and received Tenents concerning Man," and, not surprisingly, we are more aware here than anywhere else of Browne the physician: the student of anatomy who, with a copy of Galen in his hand, addresses first that favorite Renaissance topic of man's erect stature (1), moves on to question popular views concerning the heart (2), pleurisies (3), the ring finger (4), hands (5), the physics of swimming (6), weight (7), the passage of meat and drink (8), and sneezing (9), then branches out to consider, from a physiological perspective, certain racial issues— whether "Jews stink naturally" (10) or whether pygmies exist (11)— before concluding with several lengthy inquiries into medically related superstitions, one involving numerology ("Of the great Climactericall yeare, that is, sixty three"), the other astrology ("Of the Canicular or Dogdayes").

On the issue of erectness, Browne's "man" remains singular on technical grounds only. If we take "erectness" to mean, as Galen did, when the "spine and thigh bone are carried in right lines" (p. 291), fine; but not if we take it in the popular sense of meaning "largely opposed to pronenesse" (p. 292). By the latter definition, we are no different from penguins. Nor does our physical stature have anything to do with our wish "to looke up toward heaven" since "man hath a notable disadvantage in the eyelid; whereof [contrary to birds] the upper is farre greater then the lower" (p. 293). Whatever special dignity man might possess—and the suggestion of his dignity comes in largely by inference—it is only marginally connected to his physical stature. Although still at the center of the universe, he is hardly what George Herbert would call "all symmetrie" ("Man").

If in this opening chapter, man appears less than godlike, he is nonetheless not altogether forsaken. The continual, if not always steady, pressure of the fourth book is to urge man's special status in the universe as a *rational* amphibium. The note is struck at the outset when, defending Plato against misinterpretation, Browne defines *Sursum aspicere* as meaning not "to gape or looke upward with the eye but [for man] to have his thoughts sublime, and not onely to behold, but speculate their nature with the eye of the understanding" (p. 293). It is sounded again in the next chapter when Browne veers away from his discussion of the heart to uphold the assumption that "man proportionally hath the largest brain" (p. 296). Its echoes are heard, if only by implication, in the many discussions that identify popular tenets about man or men as grounded in custom, superstition, prejudice, or ignorance but not in reason. And it reaches its fullest extension in the last two chapters when, as a physician, Browne attempts to liberate his readers from a deterministic or fatalistic view of health care.

In the first of these, he returns to the theme of looking with the eyes of the understanding, a response now viewed as a problematic activity, and marshalls a series of learned, numerologically based arguments to dismantle the common conceit, "entertained with feare" (p. 334), that sixty-three is necessarily the "Climactericall and dangerous yeare" (p. 350) of a person's life. The second takes on the question of "the Canicular or Dogdayes," "commonly termed the Physitians vacation" since during this time all medication is supposed to be useless. It, too, is learnedly skeptical, relying on a vast amount of astrological lore to demolish an astrologically founded opinion. Browne's closing peroration, mingling an attachment to "a sober and regulated Astrology" with an earthly desire for survival, underscores the central, distinctive, and ultimately for Browne, preservationist role of reason in daily affairs:

We deny not the influence of the Stars, but often suspect the due appli-
cation thereof; for though we should affirme that all things were in all
things, that heaven were but earth celestified, and earth but heaven ter-
restrified, or that each part above had an influence upon its divided affinity
below; yet how to single out these relations, and duely to apply their
actions is a worke oft times to be effected by some revelation, and Cabala
from above, rather then any Philosophy, or speculation here below; what
power soever they have upon our bodies, it is not requisite they should
destroy our reasons, that is, to make us rely on the strength of Nature,
when she is least able to relieve us, and when we conceive the heaven
against us, to refuse the assistance of the earth created for us; this were
to suffer from the mouth of the Dog above, what others doe from the
teeth of Dogs below; that is, to be afraid of their proper remedy, and
refuse to approach any water, though that hath often proved a cure unto
their disease. (p. 365)

Books 5–7: The Greater World

The remaining three books move outward rather than upward.
Book 5 examines "many things questionable as they are commonly
described in Pictures" and includes a wide variety of topics—pel-
icans, grasshoppers, dolphins, biblical scenes and persons, saints,
mermaids and unicorns, to name only a few—that appeared in high
and low forms of art of the period and that usually receive from
Browne a few short paragraphs of analysis. The most curious is
probably his questioning "the Picture of Adam and Eve with Na-
vells" (5.5, pp. 377–79). The most abstruse involves his reckoning
the proper representation of the feast of "our Saviour at the Passe-
over," an inquiry that takes Browne through some of the great feasts
in Old Testament, Greek, and Roman history, the seating arrange-
ments and bathing and sleeping customs associated with each, all
of which, bolstered by a diagram describing "the feast of Perpenna"
and some exact grammatical attention given to the Bible, points to
the likelihood that Christ and his disciples ought to be rendered
not sitting but reclining, or to use Browne's phrase, in a position
of "decumbency" (6.6, pp. 380–87).

In these essays and throughout the book, Browne is the icon-
ographer, the historian of a trope or gesture, not the appreciator of
a specific work of art. When he detects deviations from the literal,
he is not afraid to rap the knuckles of some of the most famous
Renaissance artists. Both Michelangelo and Raphael are singled out

among the offenders who give Adam and Eve navels. (Their only "umbilicality," Browne solemnly informs us, is their spiritual link with God.) And Raphael again comes under fire for depicting Mary Magdalene on her knees, rather than standing, while washing Christ's feet (p. 386). Browne leaves little room for what we would call artistic license. These "authorities" are subject to the same kind of scrutiny as Aristotle; and though there are times when, Bible in hand, he can seem excessively Protestant in his quest for exactitude, his criticisms of the pictorial arts are notably free of iconoclasm. Browne exhibits none of the radical Puritan's fear that the form itself is idolatrous, only a concern that the representation is erroneous. When he speaks on one occasion of "The picture of the Creator, or God the Father in the shape of an old Man [as being] a dangerous piece" (22, p. 429), danger here refers to the power pictures have for inspiring social chaos: "in this fecundity of sects [it] may revive the Anthropomorphites." The word does not refer to the temptations pictures offer as an ersatz deity to be worshipped. When he talks elsewhere of the mystery of Moses' irradiation being "vilified," he is referring not to the dangerous impropriety of trying to represent a divine mystery in art. Rather, he is responding to a problem of textual corruption that has produced a situation in which a "horned" Moses might be only too readily and blasphemously confused with a pagan deity like Bacchus (9, pp. 390–91).

Book 6 reveals Browne at his most global, as a cultural relativist who refuses a simplifying, reductive view of the world—its history and some of its inhabitants. The fourteen chapters examine "sundry common opinions Cosmographicall and Historicall." Browne's topics include a series of related inquiries into temporal questions concerning the world (1–4), a celebration of "the wisedome of God in the site and motion of the Sun," in which, like Milton, he accepts a Ptolemaic view of the universe while praising the "grateful vicissitude" associated with providential order (5), a detailed refutation of the "vulgar opinion that the earth was slenderly peopled before the Flood" (6), separate inquiries into the supposed superiority of East over West (7), the reputed seven mouths of the Nile (8), the apparent redness of the Red Sea (9), and two lengthy investigations into "The Blackness of Negroes" (10–11), followed by a "digression concerning Blacknesse" that has earned him a small place in the history of color theory.[11] The book then concludes with two chapters added in 1650: one a brief essay on the origins of the gypsies (13); the other a potpourri of questions on cosmology designated simply "Of some others" (14).

The subject of greatest contemporary immediacy is probably his opening chapter, "Concerning the World and its temporall circumscriptions." Browne had already partially addressed the topic in *Religio Medici* when, subscribing to the general seventeenth-century notion of a decaying world, he declared that any attempt to determine exactly the "day and yeare" of the End "is not onely convincible and statute madnesse, but also manifest impiety" (1.46, pp. 43–44). He also revealed his general aversion to political prophecies in responding to a request to decode one "concerning the Future State of Several Nations" (*K*, 3, pp. 103–8). In *Pseudodoxia*, published during the Civil War, when prognostications were especially rife,[12] Browne amplifies his annoyance with predictions into a full-fledged skeptical attack on attempts to determine either the beginning or the end of the world. "That as it is presumption to enquire after the one, so is there no rest or satisfactory decision in the other" (p. 440). Browne's is the learned and conservative alternative to the chiliast's enthusiastic reckonings. First denying any authentic record from antiquity on the origins of the world, then playing biblical numerologists off against one another, Browne casts the possibility of a single, stable reading of temporal history into a dark web of complexity. Given this situation of uncertainty, the only "reasonable" conclusion is to recognize that "the ends of things are wrapt up in the hands of God" (p. 452); and given this conclusion the only "reasonable" thing to do is to accept a posture of quietism.

The topic of greatest social currency for a modern reader is likely to be the two chapters on "The Blacknesse of Negroes." In reading these broadly inquisitive and unbigoted essays, there is a danger of turning Browne into "our contemporary." (The problem is less likely to occur with his discussion of Jews in book 4, which redetermines a number of the old prejudices in new ways.) Browne is not writing of blacks in a modern liberal vein in which the issue of "human equality" is stressed, an idiom completely foreign to seventeenth-century England. He is studying a particular scientific problem: the question of why things, or in this case people, are the color they are. But as invariably happens in *Pseudodoxia*, Browne rarely accepts the commonplace or vulgar opinion, and in advancing his own views on pigmentation in Negroes, he dispels some old racial myths and stereotypes. The first chapter is given over to rebutting the simple view that dark complexions can be explained on the basis of people living in the torrid zone. The second redresses the old belief, still popular in the author's day, that blackness is a sign of God's punishment (see, for instance, *Othello,* 1.2.62–81). Browne's tentatively phrased, Neoplatonically informed explanation of the origins of blackness will not be accepted in many corners today, but it does have its own logic as well as place in the history of embryology,[13] and the passage certainly helps to illuminate why the imagination is so vital a function in his writings. You are what you read:

It may be perpended whether it [blackness] might not fall out the same way that Jacobs cattell became speckled, spotted and ringstraked, that is, by the power and efficacy of Imagination; which produceth effects in the conception correspondent unto the phancy of the Agents in generation, and sometimes assimilates the Idea of the generator into a realty in the thing ingendred. For, hereof there passe for currant many indisputed examples; so in Hippocrates wee reade of one, that from an intent view of a picture conceaved a Negroe; And in the history of Heliodore of a Moorish Queene, who upon aspection of the picture of Andromeda, conceaved and brought forth a faire one. And thus perhaps might some say was the beginning of this complexion, induced first by Imagination, which having once impregnated the seed, found afterward concurrent co-operations, which were continued by Climes, whose constitution advantaged the first impression. (p. 513)

The final book of *Pseudodoxia* is the most heterogeneous. It combines examination into some tenets "deduced from the History of holy Scripture" with a further inquiry into opinions about historical topics that range in subject matter from the cessation of oracles (12), to the death of Aristotle (13), to "divers other relations," including the story of Averroes, "now common in every mouth, of the woman that conceived in a bath, by attracting the sperme or seminall effluxion of a man admitted to bathe in some vicinity unto her" (16)—a fable still current in the legend of folktales about sex, despite Browne's attempt to scotch it. The book then concludes with a single chapter entitled "Of some relations whose truth we feare." As Robbins notes, it seems almost a "whimsical inversion of the drift of the entire work."[14]

Browne's inquiry into false opinions derived from Scripture certainly verifies his opening wish, stated in the preface, to evade "the frowne of *Theologie*" (p. 3). None of the topics addressed here is even remotely "controversial," in the political or doctrinal sense of that word. Nor do the essays brush against some of the more explosive issues of the day, as happens in *Religio Medici*. Indeed, the opening inquiry into the particular species of the forbidden fruit toys with the frivolous nature of its own speculations: "Since therefore after this fruit curiosity fruitlessly enquireth, and confidence blindly determineth, we shall surcease our Inquisition, rather troubled that it was tasted, then troubling our selves in its decision" (7.1, p. 539). Although Browne does extract a serious moral from his useless meanderings here, he certainly seems, in addressing disputed topics like Methuselah's age, the birth order of Noah's three sons, and the mandrakes of Leah, the perfect embodiment of his own rule in *Religio* that "there is yet after all the decrees of counsells and the niceties of the Schooles, many things untouch'd, unimagin'd, wherein the libertie of an honest reason may play and expatiate with security and farre without the circle of an heresie" (1.8, p. 9). Whether John the Baptist lived on locusts and honey while in the wilderness is not likely to cause a wide ripple of commotion at any moment in the history of scriptural hermeneutics.

Nonetheless, as happens throughout *Pseudodoxia*, Browne's humane intelligence overtakes us in ways that are rarely possible to predict. His inquiry into the "conceit" that "John the Evangelist should not dye" (7.10, pp. 562–67) is, among the biblical topics, perhaps the most notable instance of how he can suddenly catch us up in the drama of interpretation. The essay is one of the longer ones in this book. It appears right after his uninspired account of John the Baptist, and before another with the unpromising title of "More compendiously of some others." It also involves a theme on which Browne is almost invariably interesting: death, or, in this case, repudiating a "miraculous" interpretation held by some Catholics that John did not die. And it affords us one of the best views of how an author known for his fine nuances and shades of meaning can practice a finely nuanced reading of his own on a text that he considered "one of the hardest Books I have met with" (*K*, 3, p. 3) but still thought capable of being fathomed by the intellect if not altogether plucked of its mystery.

Browne sets the problem before us succinctly and without overstatement. This is not a major issue, hardly "weightier than that of Joseph the wandring Jew [7.17, p. 597]; yet being deduced from Scripture, and abetted by Authors of all times, it shall not escape our enquiry." Browne is not simply tilting at a windmill; Scripture, especially, encourages the conscientious interpreter, as does the canon of misinterpreters itself, which includes various biblical commentators from the fourth to the sixteenth century as well as Dante, who alludes to John in the *Paradiso* 25.124. With a brief nod to the immediate biblical context, Browne then delivers the relevant quotation from John 21:21–22: "It is drawne from the speech of our Saviour unto Peter after the prediction of his martyrdome; Peter saith unto Jesus, Lord, and what shall this man do? Jesus saith unto him, If I will that he tarry untill I come, what is that to thee? follow thou me; then went this saying abroad among the brethren that this disciple should not dye."

"Drawing" seems to be also the perfect metaphor for describing how Browne carefully extracts the proper reading from the text. (In an oft-quoted passage from book 1, Browne, in fact, identifies the practice of "exantlation," or drawing out, as the method sanctioned by wise men in describing how truth, lying at the bottom of a well, is slowly recovered—1.5, p. 30.) After his citation of misinterpreters, Browne, in good Protestant fashion, first reexamines the biblical text, where he finds the opinion refuted by John himself: "Yet Jesus said not unto him, He shall not die; but, if I will that he tarry till I come, what is that to thee" (21:23). A further look at the Bible, this time Revelation, assures Browne that it is doubtful that "tarry" could be interpreted as meaning untombed until the Apocalypse, an anomalous condition reserved for Enoch and Elias only. His doubt is quickly reinforced by a review of the relevant patristical authorities who note the time and place of the evangelist's burial. Browne then turns to discover the origins of the error, which he locates primarily in a tonal misconstruction of John 21:23 (not surprisingly, Browne favors a softer, more conditional, reading of Christ's rebuke to Peter); secondarily in various legends stemming from the belief that John was the disciple for whom Jesus felt the greatest affection; and lastly in a combination of attitudes generated by the evangelist's "escape of Martyrdrom," a textual corruption, and by unfounded reports that no corpse was ever discovered in the tomb. His conclusion then moralizes the correct reading on a grand note that, in its concentrated focus on the folly of human attempts at earthly perpetuity, looks ahead to *Urne-Buriall:*

Some indeed have beene so affectedly vaine as to counterfeit Immortality, and have stolne their death in a hope to be esteemed immortall; and others

have conceived themselves dead: but surely few or none have falne upon
so bold an errour, as not to thinke that they could dye at all. The reason
of those mighty ones, whose ambition could suffer them to be called gods,
would never be flattered into Immortality, but the proudest thereof, have
by the daylie dictates of corruption convinced the impropriety of that
appellation. And surely, although delusion may runne high, and possible
it is that for a while a man may forget his nature, yet cannot this be
durable, for the inconcealeable imperfections of our selves, or their dayly
examples in others, will hourely prompt us our corruption, and lowdly
tell us we are the sons of earth. (7.10, p. 567)

The essay is impressive in its thoroughness. It is also impressively
even in tone. In discrediting a Catholic miracle, Browne is neither
the zealous nor the reluctant reformist, but a conscientious inquirer
after the truth. It remains memorable, however, for another reason:
the obvious sympathy the author has for his subject, and more
particularly for John himself. Browne's "correct" reading of Scripture
fully restores the Evangelist to human status. In the essay, John is
not the quasi-transcendental figure of either a miracle story or a
fresco painting. He lives *and* he dies; and though he outlives the
other disciples and escapes martyrdrom, which is perhaps one reason
why Browne is attracted to him, he does not escape suffering.
Browne is not remembered, with Donne and Herbert, for his intimate response to the Passion, but his depiction of John at the
crucifixion, witnessing Christ's sorrow, shows how deeply he could
imagine and value that response in another:

Now why among all the rest John only escaped the death of a Martyr,
the reason is given; because all others fled away or withdrew themselves
at his death, and he alone of the Twelve beheld his passion on the Crosse;
wherein notwithstanding, the affliction that he suffered could not amount
unto lesse then Martyrdome: for if the naked relation, at least the intentive
consideration of that passion, be able still and at this disadvantage of time,
to rend the hearts of pious contemplators; surely the neare and sensible
vision thereof must needs occasion agonies beyond the comprehension of
flesh, and the trajections of such an object more sharply pierce the martyr'd
soule of John, then afterward did the nayles the crucified body of Peter.
(p. 564).

John is ultimately a doctor's hero. Others turn away, but he must
stay and assimilate the "neare and sensible vision" of another's suf-

ferings—extraordinary as they are in this case—into his daily experience.

Conclusion

Pseudodoxia is too large to be circumscribed within a single chapter. At best, it is only possible to suggest its vast diversity of subject matter and some of the responses these topics elicited from Browne, responses ranging in tone from humor (of many kinds), to indignation, to irritation, to deep concern, and ranging in approach from a patient—some would call it a pedantic—examination of sources, to some sound and not so sound reasoning, to documented experiments. In Browne's day, it was chiefly valued as an important contribution to the advancement of knowledge, second only to Bacon's in some readers' minds. Walter Charleton, physician-in-ordinary to Charles I and later a member of the Royal Society, viewed it in a nearly heroic light: along with Bacon, Browne is seen as discovering a mode of discourse comparable to the dignity of Latin— the international language of learned communities—in which the most sublime thoughts could be rendered into their native tongue.[15] Browne's multitextured language did not, of course, become the language favored by the Royal Society, nor is it likely to be favored by scientists today. But its failure to replicate itself among a later generation of significant thinkers should not be confused with stylistic and intellectual obsolescence in its own day. *Pseudodoxia* had a wide contemporary audience: the six editions published during the author's lifetime tell us this much; and some of its more influential readers, like Robert Boyle and Joseph Glanville, were at the center of the scientific community and especially prized the careful, inquiring mind they found in *Pseudodoxia*. If one ingredient in a revolution—whether political, religious, or scientific—involves the popularization of a key idea, Browne's work played its part by helping to authorize a community of researchers who, above all, were urged to value the unbelligerent search for truth during an especially captious moment in history.

As for its place in a broader view of history, *Pseudodoxia* must inevitably, if only partially, be grouped with important seventeenth-century texts, like Hobbes's *Leviathan,* that helped to bring about "the decline of magic," to borrow a portion of the title of Keith Thomas's encyclopedic study of popular belief in Browne's day (see

note 12 above). "Inevitably," of course, because even while contributing some vulgar errors of its own, the avowed purpose of
Pseudodxia is to question the uncritical acceptance of customs, tenets,
and superstitions, passed on from one generation to the next; "partially" because the work retains, rather than relinquishes, a theo-
logically centered view of the universe. Only those most ardently
committed to a progressively "enlightened" vision of history, like
the nineteenth-century historian Henry Thomas Buckle, have found
it difficult to imagine how the "superstitious" author of *Religio
Medici* could also have written *Pseudodoxia Epidemica*. Basil Willey
is certainly much closer to the mark when he notes that, in the later
work, Browne's Satan is "akin to Milton's in the breadth of his
views and the scope of his strategy."[16] Rather than being exorcized
by "reason" and "experience," the figure of the devil frames the
entire investigation, appearing in both the opening and closing
chapters of the work.

It is in this skeptical, postlapsarian context, moreover, that the
last chapter assumes special immediacy. The chapter is usually excluded from editions of Browne's selected works, but it ought to
be better known since it encapsulates perfectly the author's lingering
suspicions, increasingly visible in the later books, over man's power
to do anything more than *"in some measure* [to] repaire our primarie
ruins"* (1.5, p. 30; my italics), a small qualifying phrase that thoroughly distinguishes Browne from Bacon and the latter's more zealous followers.[17] Whether the chapter constitutes a "whimsical
reversal" of all that has gone before is unclear. Perhaps recognizing
its completely undermining potential, Browne attached a quotation
from Lactantius to the end of the second edition of 1650, in which
the project of clearing away error is once again reaffirmed: *"Primus
sapientiae gradus est, falsa intelligere"* (the first step toward wisdom
is to understand what is false).

But whatever precise ironic value we assign to this chapter, it is
finally impossible to escape its chastening power in the way it
readmits a fully demonic view of man that lies ultimately outside
of the corrective intelligence but still shadows the inquiring mind.
The chapter is given over to "some relations whose truths we feare,"
stories of past atrocities that could easily serve as a script for a
Senecan or Jacobean tragedy: parricide, necrophilia, murder, revenge, damnation, and so on, stories that Browne records in disbelief
but does not attempt to challenge, except to question the very act

of recording them (though he does not follow his own advice), which in turn leads him to "commend the wisdome and goodnesse of Galen, who would not leave unto the world too subtile a Theory of poysons; unarming thereby the malice of venemous spirits, whose ignorance must be contented with Sublimate and Arsenick. For, surely there are subtiler venenations, such as will invisibly destroy, and [be] like the Basilisks of heaven" (p. 608). In a moment like this, with its fearful admission of the human potential for self-destruction on a grand scale, *Pseudodoxia* speaks more directly to our age than any of Browne's other writings.

Chapter Seven

Motives for Metaphor: *Urne-Buriall* and *The Garden of Cyrus*

Urne-Buriall and *The Garden of Cyrus* are certainly Browne's ripest studies; indeed, they are among the ripest of any studies written in English. Published together in 1658, near the close of the Interregnum, the two essays reflect an extraordinarily seasoned sensibility ranging with ease over a vast terrain of knowledge. Browne imagines human experience in its most distilled, even archetypal, essentials, a distillation signaled in part by the governing emblems in each work of graves and gardens, while the two essays radiate outward to connect with some of the larger rhythms of sixteenth and seventeenth-century aspirations: the splendid monumentalizing desires of man given renewed sanction during the Renaissance; and the nearly endless fascination in that period, extending into the eighteenth century, with the metaphor of the garden as an earthly paradise. The two essays are also the most patterned of Browne's writings. Each is divided into five chapters, suggesting the five-act structure of drama; and this mirroring design draws immediate attention to the multiple ways in which the vision of one serves to illuminate the particular achievement of the other. The essays too are unique in Browne for the special privilege they make of friendship; both are dedicated to close acquaintances and show the author comfortably situated among the Norfolk gentry. And, of course, both essays contain some of the most opulent language Browne or anyone has ever used.

Urne-Buriall: Going Underground

Urne-Buriall is no ordinary record of an archaeological dig. The immediate occasion generating the essay involved the "discovery" of some forty or fifty urns, buried "not a yard deep," in "a Field

120

of old *Walsingham"* (p. 94); but as Browne makes clear in the
dedicatory epistle to Thomas Le Gros, he was inspired to write of
the event not for the usual antiquarian reasons of preserving detail
for posterity, but in order to "run up [the reader's] thoughts upon
the ancient of dayes, the Antiquaries truest object" (p. 84). To
Browne's hieroglyphical imagination, the sudden appearance of the
urns assumed preternatural significance. Although he describes the
occasion in chapter 2 as being the product of a simple human
action—digging—he presents the event in the dedicatory epistle
as the work of some larger, more mysterious, agency. "We were
hinted by the occasion," he observes, "not catched [by] the opportunity to write of old things, or intrude upon the Antiquary. We
are coldly drawn unto discourses of Antiquities, who have scarce
time before us to comprehend new things, or make out learned
Novelties. But seeing they arose as they lay, almost in silence among
us, at least in short account suddenly passed over; we were very
unwilling they should die again, and be buried twice among us"
(p. 84). Browne never specifies exactly what the occasion "hinted,"
only that it required being written about; and though there is a
temptation for the careful reader to see in the figure of the urns
rising from their graves a type of the Resurrection, it is also the
nature of *Urne-Buriall* to leave connections vague and subliminal,
under rather than overstated, at least until the fifth chapter when
Browne emerges from the "Subterranean world" (p. 89) to deliver
his extended oracular pronouncement emphasizing how, except for
"The man of God" (p. 123), "Diuturnity is a dream and folly of
expectation" (p. 122).

Browne also makes clear in the epistle to Le Gros that his method
of running up the reader's "thoughts upon the ancient of dayes"
will involve, paradoxically, undermining, from various angles, our
sense of significance and self-sufficiency. The genteel, opening paragraph in which the author describes how "The Funerall pyre was
out" and "men took a lasting adieu of their interred Friends" turns
suddenly back on itself to ponder a series of paradoxes: "But who
knows the fate of his bones, or how often he is to be buried? who
hath the Oracle of his ashes, or whether they are to be scattered?"
The questions immediately challenge the limits of human knowledge, tease the intellect out of thought, and ask us to recall the
Browne of *Religio Medici* who both loved to pursue his reason to an
"oh altitudo!" and perceived that "the wisest heads prove at last,

almost all Scepticks, and stand like *Janus* in the field of knowledge" (2.8, p. 66). But there are important differences between the two works. In *Religio,* the witty play of paradox dominates. We are always conscious of the youthful author shadow-boxing with his reason, striking a variety of poses, of which the graveling of intellect is one stance among several. In *Urne-Buriall,* the play has been subdued to the somber theme; or rather the play is increasingly subsumed by the theme of human vanity, as the process of subjugating reason to faith in the interest of confirming the special virtues of anonymity becomes the end toward which everything in the essay moves. In the consciously apocalyptic vision of *Urne-Buriall,* human aspiration is not so much trivialized as shown to be splendidly wanting. Its energies are redetermined in the great last chapter toward celebrating a Christian triumph in which the reward of living "by an invisible Sun within us" (p. 123) takes on both an immediate and final significance.[1]

The five chapters cut progressively deeper arcs that separate the known from the unknowable. In doing so, they also render a speaker more and more aware of the gulf that divides the incidental from the essential, the local and contingent from the ultimate and the ineradicable. "In the deep discovery of the Subterranean world," to quote the first words of the essay, "a shallow part would satisfie some enquirers," but not Browne. His is an imagination that presses outward and deeper, that measures his topic from many perspectives, until our usual systems of measurement are called eloquently into question.

The opening chapter plays with surfaces. It is easily the least perplexed and most overtly witty of the five. If, echoing Horace, Browne promised Le Gros that he was not going to "pisse" upon the ashes of the dead, he is also not going to be so respectful of his subject, at least at the outset, as to refuse all opportunities for some funereal humor. His division of the problem of "corporall dissolution" into two categories—"simple inhumation" (burying) and "burning"—allows him to detail some of the "phantasticall" and "singular contrivances" that nations have invented in order to dispose of the dead. The twenty paragraphs document a wide variety of practices. Most are thumbnail sketches, brief, masterfully executed "character" studies, devoted to revealing the customs of a particular nation or group of nations; and almost all contain some odd verbal twist, a moment of false solemnity, a fastidiously mannered phrase, a pun, bizarre image, quotation, or allusion, that keeps the whole funeral operation at a slightly comic distance.

The snippet about the Egyptians is typical in possessing many of these mock delicacies: "The Ægyptians were afraid of fire, not as a Deity, but a devouring Element, mercilesly consuming their bodies, and leaving too little of them; and therefore by precious Embalments, depositure in dry earths, or handsome inclosure in glasses, contrived the notablest wayes of integrall conservation. And from such Ægyptian scruples imbibed by *Pythagoras,* it may be conjectured that *Numa* and the Pythagoricall Sect first waved the fiery solution" (p. 92). This is all done with a very straight face, but the image of a fastidious Pythagoras "imbibing" an Egyptian custom, which includes "precious Embalments"—an image further rarefied by the allusion to his followers as causally "wav[ing] the fiery solution"—certainly takes some of the fear out of the opening reference to the merciless devouring powers of fire. The epicurean habits of the Egyptian embalmers seem fully appreciated by this speaker, just as he is bemused by the inexplicable crudities involved in the practices of another, less cultured nation: "The old *Balearians* had a peculiar mode, for they used great Urnes and much wood, but no fire in their burials, while they bruised the flesh and bones of the dead, crowded them into Urnes, and laid heapes of wood upon them" (p. 92). No further comment is offered or perhaps is needed. Browne simply goes on to describe the more civilized ceremonies used by the Chinese, who "without cremation or urnall interrment of their bodies, make use of trees and much burning, while they plant a Pine-tree by their grave, and burn great numbers of printed draughts of slaves and horses over it."

In keeping with the "phantastic" note of the opening survey, yet hinting at the larger occasion underlying his discourse, Browne includes a description of the Resurrection near the end of the chapter that describes what is surely one of the most comical escapes from the grave on record:

Nor in their long co-habitation with Ægyptians, [the Jews] crept into a custome of their exact embalming, wherein deeply slashing the muscles, and taking out the brains and entrails, they had broken the subject of so entire a Resurrection, nor fully answered the types of *Enoch, Eliah,* or *Jonah,* which yet to prevent or restore, was of equall facility unto that rising power, able to break the fasciations and bands of death, to get clear

out of the Cere-cloth, and an hundred pounds of oyntment, and out of
the Sepulchre before the stone was rolled from it. (p. 94)

Only on one occasion does Browne register perplexity—a "wavering
conjecture" over the possible significance of David's "treble calling
out after *Absalom*" (p. 94). Otherwise, in the opening chapter, he
is an observer of peculiarities, occasionally offering a rational explication of a custom (p. 89), but usually allowing the "phantasticall" to speak for itself.

In chapter 2, however, problems abound. Although they are
limited by the historical nature of the inquiry at this point, they
challenge the cool levity of the Horatian opening. Browne narrows
his focus to the particular urns in question and, through observation
and reason, attempts to determine both the proprietors of the urns
and their date. The idiom here is tentative and conjectural, though
not radically uncertain. As an archaeologist of sorts, Browne is
operating in the grey area of probability, defined in *Pseudodoxia* as
involving "a staggering assent unto the affirmative, not without
some feare of the negative" (7.18, p. 604). "That these were the
Urnes of *Romanes* from the common custome and place where they
were found, is no obscure conjecture" (p. 95); "Nor is it improbable
that the *Romanes* early possessed this Countrey." These possible
answers are set against the greater difficulties of supplying an accurate date for the urns: "Then the time of these Urnes deposited,
or precise Antiquity of these Reliques, nothing [is] of more uncertainty" (p. 97). Eventually, though, Browne does stagger to a conclusion, incorrect as it turns out: "the most assured account will
fall upon the *Romanes,* or *Brittains Romanized*" (p. 101). On the basis
of the plate in the original edition, the urns were later identified
as Saxon; but even without this additional bit of knowledge, Browne's
mention of "falling" works to deprive "the most assured account"
of much assurance, and the chapter ends, appropriately, on a further
slide—with Browne raising a question about why "the Anglesea
Urnes are placed with their mouths downward" (p. 101).

In the third chapter, Browne is knee-deep in mortality, writing
from "the Land of Moles and Pismires" (p. 106). An eyewitness of
human corruption, he looks deliberately beyond or through the
"Playstered and whited Sepulchres" of antiquity mentioned in the
opening sentence (p. 101) to record the pathetic inevitability of

bodily dissolution, a vision explicitly humanized at the outset and extended to the reader when Browne compares the "commmon form" of the urns with their necks lying in the earth to "our Nativity" in the womb (p. 102). In this chapter, everything is in the process of dissolving. Discovering "Lachrymatories, or Tear-bottles," Browne imagines the "passionate expressions of their surviving friends" (p. 103). His momentary trumpeting of the survival of "our little Iron pins," which have outlasted iron reliques found in the monument of King Childerick, gives way to the pathetic recognition that "in the space of a few moneths, they begin to spot and betray their green entrals" (p. 104). *"Plato's* historian of the other world, lies twelve days incorrupted, while his soul was viewing the large stations of the dead"; Browne thinks it requires a "hazardable peece of art" simply "to keep the corps seven dayes from corruption" (p. 107). In this chapter, ashes meet with ashes, dust with dust: well-burned bones leave "almost allwayes a morsell for the Earth, whereof all things are but a colonie; and which, if time permits, the mother Element will have in their primitive masse again" (p. 109).

And yet for all of its pathos, the chapter also resists the larger implications of its dying fall. In the land of moles and pismires, Browne remains still oddly attached to the superfluities of his own worldly and scientific wit. A resonant phrase such as "The certainty of death is attended with uncertainties, in time, manner, places," though sometimes viewed as marking a tonal turning point in the work, is short-circuited by a continual valuation of the physical world: "Let Monuments and rich Fabricks, not Riches adorn mens ashes" (p. 107), Browne proclaims. Even the grotesque sequence, "To be gnaw'd out of our graves, to have our sculs made drinking-bowls, and our bones turned into Pipes, to delight and sport our Enemies, are Tragicall abominations, escaped in burning Burials" (pp. 109–10), reveals a speaker less interested in the afterlife than in the indecorous use of objects in this life. Browne is still very much a connoisseur of antiquities in this chapter. He tells us where to seek relics (p. 109). He imagines "the Aromaticall Liquors" found in the urns as far exceeding "the Palats of Antiquity" (p. 103). He values the discovery of bones because they allow him to "figure" the body (pp. 110–11); and though the chapter does conclude with an allusion to the Resurrection, as did the opening one, the event is imagined in thoroughly topographical terms, as if, despite the warning to the contrary given in the Book of Common Prayer involving the burial of the dead, it really might be to a person's future advantage to have all his bones in one place (p. 111).

It is the fourth chapter that draws together this nexus of themes involving burial customs, questions, and bodily dissolution and begins the process of revaluing them in the light of the larger metaphysical ironies of Christian salvation. The heightened mood is sounded at the outset: "Christians have handsomely glossed the deformity of death, by careful consideration of the body, and civil rites which take of[f] brutall terminations. And though they conceived all reparable by a resurrection, cast not off all care of enterrment" (pp. 111–12). In the course of the chapter, Browne attends to the various glosses supplied by both pagans and Christians—the position of the body in the grave, the ritual strewing of flowers, and so on—and he places increasing pressure on determining the motives and propriety of these gestures, especially those of pagan worship. "That they buried a peece of money with them as a Fee of the *Elysian Ferriman,* was a practise full of folly. But the ancient custome of placing coynes in considerable Urnes, and the present practice of burying medals in the Noble Foundations of *Europe,* are laudable wayes of historicall discoveries, in actions, persons, Chronologies; and posterity will applaud them" (pp. 114–15).

In contrast to his actions in the first chapter, Browne is no longer simply an observer of peculiarities but a critic of them, and his criticisms, moreover, strike a progressively more plangent note as he questions both the irrationality of numerous customs and the way fictions—or glosses—of death presume to rationalize the unknown: "Why the Female Ghosts appear unto *Ulysses,* before the *Heroes* and masculine spirits? Why the *Psyche* or soul of *Tiresias* is of the masculine gender; who being blinde on earth sees more than all the rest in hell . . ." (p. 115). These questions defeat the intellect, and when Browne reintroduces the image of the womb in this chapter, he does so now to raise ultimate questions about the limitations of human knowledge involving the afterlife: "The particulars of future beings must needs be dark unto ancient Theories, which Christian Philosophy yet determines but in a Cloud of opinions. A Dialogue between two Infants in the womb concerning the state of this world, might handsomely illustrate our ignorance of the next, whereof methinks we yet discourse in *Platoes* denne, and are but *Embryon* Philosophers" (p. 116).

The whole discourse then begins to turn in an explicitly theological direction by pivoting not on any complex doctrinal matter but on a fundamental rule of faith. "It will therefore, and must at last appeare, that all salvation is through Christ" (*RM*, 1.54, p. 51). Or as Browne says in the more subdued tone of *Urne-Buriall:* "Happy are they, which live not in that disadvantage of time, when men could say little for futurity, but from reason. Whereby the noblest mindes fell often upon doubtfull deaths, and melancholly Dissolutions" (p. 117). Although present only by inference, revelation is the missing ingredient here. Socrates, mentioned at the beginning of the chapter as being exemplary for disdaining the body and valuing the soul, is now reintroduced, along with Cato, as an exemplary spiritual failure almost too sad to contemplate: "With these hopes *Socrates* warmed his doubtfull spirits, against that cold potion, and *Cato* before he durst give the fatall stroak spent part of the night in reading the immortality of *Plato,* thereby confirming his wavering hand unto the animosity of that attempt" (p. 117). Whatever virtues reason might possess, these are seen as not just negligible but completely helpless when it comes to speculating on the afterlife, a matter not at all for the intellect but for faith. Without the latter, Browne reminds us, we can only despair at our situation: "It is the heaviest stone that melancholy can throw at a man, to tell him he is at the end of his nature; or that there is no further state to come, unto which this seemes progressionall, and otherwise made in vaine. . . . But the superiour ingredient and obscured part of our selves, whereto all present felicities afford no resting contentment, will be able at last to tell us we are more then our present selves; and evacuate such hopes in the fruition of their own accomplishments" (pp. 117–18).

Dr. Johnson thought that the turn at the end of chapter four could "never be too frequently recollected."[2] Most have since reserved this judgment for the fifth chapter. One of *the* splendid examples of the grand style in English prose, the chapter has always been given special status in Browne studies, its lines likened by De Quincey to "a melodious ascent as of a prelude to some impassioned requiem breathing from the pomps of earth, and from the sanctities of the grave," compared by Symonds to the lofty rhyme of Milton, dubbed by Saintsbury as the quintessence of baroque prose, and analyzed by more recent critics for its subtle metrical effects—almost always with attention to its stately rhythms.[3] If there is a danger as well as irony in viewing the chapter as a literary monument, it comes from identifying its merits largely in terms of local stylistic flourishes, the sublime falling of clauses, when much of its achievement lies in how it both incorporates and redetermines material in the first four chapters. Surely some of the splendor of the opening lines, "Now since these dead bones have already out-lasted the living ones of *Methuselah,*" is in the portentous drumbeat of simple Anglo-Saxon diction; but the sense of prescience here, of this chapter being like the fifth act of a drama, also derives from the fact that the urns, completely out of sight in the fourth chapter, suddenly and for the only time in *Urne-Buriall* assume front stage in the opening address. If Browne can mention to Le Gros how it "was an hit of fate and honour beyond prediction" that these urns "should arise so opportunely to serve your self," the remark seems to apply equally well to us in beginning the fifth chapter. The delimiting of reason at the end of chapter 4, even if in the service of faith, is finally not the whole plot of *Urne-Buriall.*

The fifth chapter turns a perception of faith as historical accident into a perception of faith as magnanimously felt experience. At the end of chapter four, it seems to be simply, albeit inexplicably, just bad luck to have been born before Christ: "Happy are they, which live not in that disadvantage of time" (p. 117). Equally diffident is the author's rationalization of faith as a convenient solution to the melancholy arising from the problem "that there is no further state to come, unto which this seemes progressionall, and otherwise made in vaine" (p. 117). Nowhere in his writings does Browne seem to be more the doctor prescribing the proper pill. In the fifth chapter, however, the Pauline "new man" surfaces. As Walter Davis has suggested, "this chapter acts out the discovery of Christian Faith,"[4] not though in the traditionally (and to Browne's mind suspiciously) zealous manner of a self-declared regeneration in which personal sins are scrutinized and eradicated in the light of Christian grace. The drumbeats signal a transformation that shows Browne recasting Christian faith into something like its fundamental role, embracing all godly persons, and from which both the mordant ironies and triumphant comforts of the last chapter arise.

From a doctrinal perspective, the key lines occur immediately after the often-quoted paradox that sums up the futility of attempting to find perpetuity in the material world:

There is nothing strictly immortall, but imortality; whatever hath no beginning may be confident of no end. All others have a dependent being, and within the reach of destruction, which is the peculiar of that necessary essence that cannot destroy it self; And the highest strain of omnipotency to be so powerfully constituted, as not to suffer even from the power of it self. But the sufficiency of Christian Immortality frustrates all earthly glory, and the quality of either state after death, makes a folly of post-humous memory. God who can only destroy our souls, and hath assured our resurrection, either of our bodies or names hath directly promised no duration. (p. 123)

George Williamson has pointed out that Browne here distills the teachings of St. Paul on the Resurrection (1 Corinthians 15), and he quotes from verses 43–44: "It is sown a natural body; it is raised a spiritual body. . . . For this corruptible must put on incorruption, and this mortal must put on immortality."[5] But also relevant are Paul's earlier remarks in which he introduces the subject of the Resurrection to his listeners. Verses 12–17 describe how, without belief in the Resurrection, the whole idea of Christian faith is a charade: "And if Christ be not risen, then *is* our preaching vain, and your faith *is* also vain" (v. 14). Browne made a similar point in *Religio Medici* when he remarked that "the life therefore and spirit of all our actions, is the resurrection" (1.47, p. 45).

It would be wrong to overdramatize the rhetorical force of this passage in *Urne-Buriall,* but in the context of the several, very witty, clinical and topographical references to the Resurrection made earlier, and within the rhythmic structure of the chapter itself, which drives incessantly at human vanity, the reference that "God hath *assured* our resurrection" (my italics) stands out in its elemental simplicity. As in the teachings of Paul, the recovery of this truth serves as the essential underpinning for all preaching. In Browne's case, it allows him to picture man in his glorious shortcomings as well as in his potential state of heroic anonymity, "Ready to be any thing, in the extasie of being ever, and as content with six foot as the Moles of *Adrianus*" (p. 125). And it lies behind his final act of jettisoning the whole issue of burial customs in the quotation from Lucan appended to the treatise: "*Tabesne cadavera solvat* / *An rogus haud refert"* (it matters not whether corpses burn on the pyre or decompose with time).

The magnificent cadences of the fifth chapter work steadily to undermine the monumentalizing instincts of man in order to secure a victory for humility and privacy. Browne's great subject here is time, the present moment in all its hapless, earthly mutations as set against the ultimate measure of worldly aspirations—eternity. The first word of the chapter is "now"; "ever" is one of its last. Between these temporal poles, Browne fuses a Solomonic awareness that "all is vanity" with the Johannine vision of apocalyptic history, the combination of which places present attempts at human perpetuity in a doubly ironic and futile light:

Pagan vain-glories which thought the world might last for ever, had encouragement for ambition, and finding no *Atropos* unto the immortality of their Names, were never dampt with the necessity of oblivion. Even old ambitions had the advantage of ours, in the attempts of their vain-glories, who acting early, and before the probable Meridian of time, have by this time found great accomplishment of their designes, whereby the ancient *Heroes* have already out-lasted their Monuments, and Mechanicall preservations. But in this latter Scene of time we cannot expect such Mummies unto our memories, when ambition may fear the Prophecy of *Elias,* and *Charles* the fifth can never hope to live within two *Methusela's* of *Hector.*

And therefore restlesse inquietude for the diuturnity of our memories unto present considerations, seems a vanity almost out of date, and superanuated peece of folly. We cannot hope to live so long in our names, as some have done in their persons, one face of *Janus* holds no proportion unto the other. 'Tis too late to be ambitious. The great mutations of the world are acted, or time may be too short for our designes. To extend our memories by Monuments, whose death we dayly pray for, and whose duration we cannot hope, without injury to our expectations, in the advent of the last day, were a contradiction to our beliefs. We whose generations are ordained in this setting part of time, are providentially taken off from such imaginations. And being necessitated to eye the remaining particle of futurity, are naturally constituted unto thoughts of the next world, and cannot excusably decline the consideration of that duration, which maketh Pyramids pillars of snow, and all that's past a moment. (pp. 119–20)

Monuments themselves are part of the "great mutations of the world," a point Browne "hits" at here and throughout the chapter, and no time remains to build new ones. The whole meditation—its elegant alliterations ("Pyramids pillars of snow"), grave word play ("Mummies unto our memories"), and solemn Latinate echoings ("Oblivion," "ambitions," "preservations," "considerations," "expectations," "mutations," "generations")—seems to run up flat and collapse in the face of the single, simply stated conclusion that "all that's past a moment." But Browne's leveling vision goes deeper. Any attempt at perpetuating an outer identity is interpreted as not only vainglorious and futile in light of eternity; it is also subject to the equally vast ironies of human history itself: "In vain we compute our felicities by the advantage of our good names, since bad have equall durations; and *Thersites* is like to live as long as *Agamemnon*. . . . Oblivion is not to be hired: The greater part must be content to be as though they had not been, to be found in the Register of God, not in the record of man" (p. 121). Who would not, Browne queries, "rather have been the good theef, then *Pilate?*"

Edmund Gosse wittily crowned Browne "the laureate of the forgotten dead"[6] because of his elevation in the fifth chapter of the unnamed over the named, the pious anonymously enrolled in God's record versus the impious infamously seeking to enroll their names in human history. There is certainly ample justification for this remark, but it is also only a partial perception of the author's motives in this chapter and in *Urne-Buriall* as a whole. As Browne mentions in the epistle to Le Gros, his aims are twofold: "to preserve the living, and make the dead to live, to keep men out of their Urnes, and discourse of humane fragments in them" (p. 84). Having spoken of human fragments in the first four chapters, and in the fifth raised these speculations to include "question[s] above Antiquarism" (p. 119) involving the mutability of all earthly things, Browne resists the strongly apocalyptic implications of his own argument in favor of a message of preservation and continuity, one that identifies the triumph of Christianity not with any motions of outward militancy but with privacy and humility, with the virtues of being below rather than above ground.

The great beginning of the fifth chapter, in fact, glosses the urns for their exemplary method of surviving "quietly . . . under the drums and tramplings of three conquests"; and though Browne goes on to interpret the urns also as "Emblemes of mortall vanities; Antidotes against pride, vain-glory, and madding vices" (p. 119), the value of quietism as a mode of continuing in this world as well as the proper preparation for the next is reasserted at the conclusion as a fundamental feature in his climactic celebration of Christianity:

Happy are they whom privacy makes innocent, who deal so with men in this world, that they are not afraid to meet them in the next, who when they dye, make no commotion among the dead, and are not toucht with that poeticall taunt of *Isaiah.*

Pyramids, Arches, Obelisks, were but the irregularities of vainglory, and wilde enormities of ancient magnanimity. But the most magnanimous resolution rests in the Christian Religion, which trampleth upon pride, and sets on the neck of ambition, humbly pursuing that infallible perpetuity, unto which all others must diminish their diameters, and be poorly seen in Angles of contingency. (p. 124)

Browne's defense of humility here is purposefully broad, designed to present "the Christian Religion" unified in its triumph over an easily identified common enemy—the "wilde enormities of ancient magnanimity." The only rule of faith involves charity, one to which most can readily subscribe; and even if it is a virtue more prized by Anglicans than Puritans, Browne's rejection of monuments in the final chapter would certainly seem consonant with a Puritan dislike of icons. Indeed, during the Civil War and Interregnum in Puritan-dominated Norwich, the building of monuments commemorating the dead nobility, which had been a thriving business, slackened noticeably.[7] But Browne's embrace is also not quite evenly distributed. The "poeticall taunt of *Isaiah,*" tantalizingly withheld from the reader, edges the text with its unspoken apocalyptic warning ("How hath the oppressor ceased! the golden city ceased! The Lord hath broken the staff of the wicked, *and* the sceptre of the rulers" [14:4–5]) and its subsequent celebration of the delivery of Israel from Babylon. Browne is not, prophetlike, calling for a deliverance but using a prophetic allusion that looks out upon an immediate political situation to give support to those who, like the urns, are living "under ground." In Browne's "Christian Religion," triumph is finally a feature of hiddenness and obscurity: "Happy are they whom privacy *makes* innocent" (my italics).

Thomas Le Gros would have understood this "survivalist" reading of the urns on a firsthand basis. We know almost nothing of Le Gros other than that he was the only son of Browne's close friend and patient Charles Le Gros, of an ancient family going back to the time of King Stephen (1135–54), and that upon the death of his father in 1656, he inherited Crostwick Hall.[8] The funereal tone of *Urne-Buriall,* its concern with antiquity, continuity, and transcendence would thus be all immediately appropriate, and Browne's remark in the epistle that "I look upon you as a Gemme of the old Rock" (p.85) seems obviously recollective of the father. But one piece of information about Thomas has drifted down that tells us something about his private activities during the Interregnum. In one of the most pathetic accounts involving the sufferings of the clergy sequestered under the Puritan takeover of the church, Le Gros figures in a fully charitable context, dealing "so with men in this world" that he might not be "afraid to meet them in the next." An eyewitness reports how one Thomas Campbell, "forced from his Rectory of Swafield" in Norfolk in 1643 and "with wife and four children, reduced to starvation diet," was by the "assistance of Dr. [Bernard] Hales, late Master of Peterhowse [1660–63], one Mr.Thomas Le Gross of Crostwight in Norfolk, and some other good friends [kept] from starving, till ye Restauration of King Charles ye Second."[9]

We have no way of knowing for sure whether Browne was familiar with Le Gros's underground activities, though it would seem almost certain given his close ties with the family; but he was, without question, aware of the sequestered status of the clergy, and perhaps at no time more acutely than when he was working on *Urne-Buriall,* between May 1656 and 1 May 1658.[10] On 9 September 1656, Browne's longtime friend, Joseph Hall, died, with Browne attending him in his last days. Commemorated in a funeral sermon preached at Peter Mancroft by their mutual friend, John Whitefoot, Hall, also known as the "Christian Seneca," was presented to the Anglican community as a signal reminder of the unjust treatment of the righteous minister at the hands of the Puritan authorities. Whitefoot's sermon refers at the outset to Hall's generally acknowledged sequestration, in which he was "muzzled *from the "Enjoyment"* of his ecclesiastical appointments, and then proceeds *"towards a Demonstration that* Prelacie and Piety *are not such inconsistent things, as some would make them; and that the Men which are of, or for that Order, should not be excluded (as by the* Monopolizers *of that Name they now are) from the number of* Saints."[11]

Browne was present at Whitefoot's "excellent funerall sermon," which he recollects more than twenty years later in *Repertorium,* where he also delivers a brief character sketch of Hall along the lines of Whitefoot's suffering servant: "My Honord freind Bishop Joseph Hall, Deane of Worcester, and Bishop of Excester, was buryed at Heigham, where hee hath his monument, who in the Rebellious times, when the Revenues of the church were alienated, retired unto that surburbian parish, and there ended his dayes: being above fourscore yeares of age. A person of singular humillity, patience and pietie."[12] But it is at the end of *Urne-Buriall*, with its buried reminiscences from the funeral sermon,[13] that the commemoration of the neo-Senecan values for which Hall stood, his alienated piety, speaks with greatest communal resonance: "Happy are they whom privacy makes innocent." Without writing hagiography and hence begging the question of sanctification, an issue Browne always viewed with suspicion, his generalized celebration of "pious spirits" in *Urne-Buriall* is, nonetheless, not quite a celebration of anonymity but a recollection of the special virtues of anonymity that speak to the disestablished. Twenty years later, when the church was fully visible and there was no longer any need for an Anglican to meditate on the "Subterranean world," Browne thought it no vanity to supply a number of names to "the Tombs and Monuments in the Cathedrall Church of Norwich." "In the time of the late civill warres," many had been "torne and taken away."[14]

The Garden of Cyrus and the Generation of Wit

" 'Tis too late to be ambitious" is the mordant close of *Urne-Buriall* mocked by the very notion of a sequel. *The Garden of Cyrus* is a typologically appropriate addition to *Urne-Buriall* since, as Browne suggests in the prefatory epistle to his "Worthy and Honored Friend, Nicholas Bacon," *"the delightfull World comes after death, and Paradise succeeds the Grave. Since the verdant state of things is the Symbole of the Resurrection, and to flourish in the state of Glory, we must first be sown in corruption"* (p. 87). Perhaps because Browne sensed the potentially indecorous nature of attaching *Urne-Buriall* to a work directed to one of the more "monumentalized" families in East Anglia, there is a hint of apology here for "conjoyn[ing] these parts of different Subjects"; but, as Frank Huntley has definitively shown, these two essays were designed to be read together.[15] One concerns death, the other life. One is a Solomonic lament on human limitation, the other a Baconian celebration of human potential; one a meditation on fragments, the other an encomium to order and continuity; one written to sustain the pious in their obscurity, the other composed to entertain a member of the Norfolk gentry at his leisure. Both essays gain clarity of meaning through juxtaposition; and it seems fully appropriate that the last works Browne himself saw published should not only attempt to strike a balance between two worlds, but that a vision of order and generation—a vision not just of sustaining but of producing—should prevail.

Like *Urne-Buriall, The Garden of Cyrus* is no ordinary scientific treatise. Browne disclaims at the outset writing the usual *"Herball"* or attempting to *"erect a new Phytology." "Of old things we write something new,"* he remarks, and then goes on to emphasize the singular nature of both his audience and his creation:

You have been so long out of trite learning, that 'tis hard to finde a subject proper for you; and if you have met with a Sheet upon this, we have missed our intention. In this multiplicity of writing, bye [incidental] and barren Themes are best fitted for invention; Subjects so often discoursed confine the Imagination, and fix our conceptions unto the notions of fore-writers. Besides, such Discourses allow excursions, and venially admit of collaterall truths, though at some distance from their principals. (p. 86)

The *"bye and barren Theme"* that Browne fits for invention is the quincunx. "The term derives from quinque-unciae, or five-twelfths of a unit of weight or measure, and was used by the Romans to denote an arrangement of five trees in the form of a rectangle, four occupying the corners, one the center, like the cinque-point on a die, so that a massing of quincunxes produces long rows of trees with the effect of lattice-work."[16] Doubtless, as Jeremiah Finch suggests in following out one of the author's footnotes, Browne owes a principal debt to two sixteenth-century gardening treatises, one by Baptiste Della Porta, the other by Benoit Court, for bringing this figure to his attention; but it is Browne's idea alone to *"illustrate the excellency of this order"* by considering, as he says in the subtitle, "The Quincunciall, Lozenge, or Net-work Plantations of the Ancients, Artificially Naturally [and] Mystically." There is, to be sure, something at least slightly fantastic about a quincuncial encomium. "A reader, not watchful against the power of his infusions," warns Dr. Johnson, "would imagine that decussation was the great business of the world, and that nature and art had no other purpose than to exemplify and imitate a Quincunx."[17] But Johnson's response also reveals how attractive he found the whole presentation to be.

Browne's five chapters are given over to ennobling both a particular order and the person who can imagine, search out, and create order. In doing so, the essay makes it nearly impossible to draw a sharp line between the scientific and the artistic imagination, or even between the artistic and the divine mind. Both scientist and artist are engaged in reading God's book, and both author and God are engaged in the process of writing the book—in Browne's case, one with a quincuncial pattern to it. And all are engaged, at various levels, with ordering reality. If the work can seem at times of admittedly little significance, as surely happens in places in the third chapter, it is the very nature of *The Garden of Cyrus*—raising a large creation from a *"bye and barren theme"*—to question our usual modes of granting significance. In what is still one of the best commentaries on the essay, Johnson thought *Cyrus* belonged with the mock epics of Homer, Virgil, and Spenser. I think there is an important difference, however. In Browne, it is never quite possible to know where epic ends and mockery begins. Browne does not simply attribute grand sentiments to trivial subjects. He blends the two together so that the grand and the incidental are part of a single vision.

The opening chapter is given over to identifying the heroic genealogy of the quincunx—to constructing its legendary status from various historical perspectives. Its strategy is simple, but for a modern reader unfamiliar with either the two Cyruses of antiquity or the stature of Cyrus the Elder in the Renaissance, it is also in danger of being lost amid the swirl of mythological and biblical references that begin to accrue with the opening sentence. Cyrus the Elder, the Cyrus of Xenophon's *Cyropaedia,* the founder of the Persian empire and liberator of the Jews from Babylonian captivity, was reckoned to be one of the great heroes of antiquity, the proper subject for an epic poem. He had been praised by both Sidney and Spenser in this capacity, and he makes an early appearance in Browne's treatise. But this is not the Cyrus of *The Garden.* "Our magnified *Cyrus*" comes from Xenophon's *Oeconomicus;* he is the younger son of Darius II, and it is through association with him that Browne elevates both husbandry and "quincuncial ordination":

Not only a Lord of Gardens, but a manuall planter thereof: disposing his trees like his armies in regular ordination. So that while old *Laertes* hath found a name in *Homer* for pruning hedges, and clearing away thorns and bryars; while King *Attalus* lives for his poysonous plantations of *Aconites,* Henbane, Hellebore, and plants hardly admitted within the walls of Paradise; While many of the Ancients do poorly live in the single names of Vegetables; All stories do look upon *Cyrus,* as the splendid and regular planter. (p. 131)

"Disposing his trees like his armies," Cyrus has inevitably invited comparison with Marvell's Fairfax, who, having retired from his post as comander in chief of the Parliamentary forces in 1650, is imagined in "Upon Appleton House" as laying out his garden along military lines—imitating the Cinque Ports, no less. But the difference between Browne's and Marvell's use of this trope is that Browne reflects none of Marvell's ambivalence over gardening as an alternative to the active life. Cyrus combines the two roles, and in this act of easy assimilation allows marginal figures like Browne and Bacon to think big about their task, a point reinforced by the spacious procession of quincuncial possibilities that follows, as Browne traces the ancestry of this figure back through the *"Heroes"* of the Old Testament to the Garden of Eden itself, where the chapter concludes.

Browne's opening description of early gardens, including Eden, is notably bereft of nostalgia. He is not writing of lost paradises, but of continuity, of the inevitability of order that lies not below ground or in the deep recesses of history, but all around. When Browne begins chapter 2, his first sentence, in direct contrast to the gnomic, isolating pronouncements introducing chapters in *Urne-Buriall,* insists quietly on the organic nature of design, his own included: "Nor was this only a form of practice in Plantations, but found imitation from high Antiquity, in sundry artificiall contrivances and manuall operations" (pp. 135–36). Although *Cyrus* is the most carefully structured of Browne's works, with the chapters arranged to approximate a Platonic hierarchy spelled out in the running chapter headings to the 1658 text, it uses the divisions to underscore, not to question, the unity of reality itself. With a sentence that looks casually backward and forward, the second chapter seems to exfoliate, to grow, out of the first.

It is in this chapter, too, where decussation becomes the great business of the world, not just the work of a few exemplary heroes. The chapter is an extraordinary assemblage of quincuncial artifacts taken mostly from high antiquity and arranged in no particular order. Browne finds his figure in "The Triumphal Oval, and Civicall Crowns of Laurel, Oake, and Myrtle"; in the crown of Charles V; in "the radiated, and starry Crown, upon the head of *Augustus*, and many succeeding Emperors" (p. 136); in "The beds of the antients" as well as their "triumphall seats"; "in the old game of *Pentalithismus*, or casting up five stones to catch them on the back of their hand" (p. 138); in the figure of Roman armies (pp. 139–40); even in the "Labyrinth of *Crete*," which, though not one "of the seven wonders" of the world is made from "a Copy exceeding all the rest" in nobility (p. 141). There are exceptions to the quincuncial rule, as Browne had said would be the case in the prefatory epistle to Bacon. "The neat *Retiarie* Spider" (p. 138) weaves according to a different law of nature, "which is beyond the common art of Textury," but the insect is valued no less as both an example and creator of order.

The third chapter, the middle of *The Garden of Cyrus*, is devoted to nature, with Browne discovering his quincunxes not in the artifacts of the past but in the immediate, burgeoning world around him: "Now although this elegant ordination of vegetables, hath found coincidence or imitation in sundry works of art, yet is it not also destitute of naturall examples, and though overlooked by all, was elegantly observable, in severall works of nature" (p. 142). "Elegant" is the key word sounded twice here and repeated throughout this, the longest, chapter. Browne almost always reserved the term for describing his response to the beauty he found in God's two books, and this chapter is certainly one of the most richly textured evocations of the creation in all of seventeenth-century literature:

The same [quincuncial pattern] is observably effected in the *Julus, Catkins,* or pendulous excrescencies of severall Trees, of Wallnuts, Alders, and Hazels, which hanging all the Winter, and maintaining their Networke close, by the expansion thereof are the early foretellers of the Spring, discoverable also in long Pepper, and elegantly in the *Jules* of *Calamus Aromaticus,* so plentifully growing with us in the first palmes of Willowes, and in the Flowers of Sycamore, Petasites, Asphodelus, and *Blattaria,* before explication. After such order stand the flowery Branches in our best spread *Verbascum,* and the seeds about the spicous head or torch of *Tapsas Barbatus,* in as fair a regularity as the circular and wreathed order will admit, which advanceth one side of the square, and makes the same Rhomboidall. (p. 143)

One does not have to be a horticulturist of Nicholas Bacon's stature to share fully Browne's delight in "the flowery Branches in our best spread *Verbascum,*" or to appreciate the quietly energizing wit of "torch of *Tapsas Barbatus,*" or to admire how something as hugely awkward as "pendulous excrescencies" can hang on something as simple as a walnut tree and also serve as a harbinger of spring, or to wonder just how the "long pepper" got to be next to the *"Calamus Aromaticus."* In these passages, Browne makes us aware that the quincunx functions as a marvelous device not so much for revealing an absolutely fixed scheme of order in nature as for realizing one of the most favored ideas of nature in the seventeenth century: a concord of discords.

It is also in this chapter that we are perhaps made most conscious of the revisionary nature of *The Garden*—that one of its purposes has been to recollect and redetermine in a positive direction the skeptical attitudes toward knowledge at the core of *Urne-Buriall.* This practice, of course, has been going on implicitly in various ways, imagistically and thematically, since the opening allusion to Apollo, the God of light and order, in the first sentence; but in the third chapter, the epistemological contrast between the two works becomes explicit. At its center, the "decussation" of the whole essay, Browne includes a lengthy, fairly technical, account of his search for the generative origins in plants. The "digression," casually introduced with "by the way," departs momentarily from the hunt for quincunxes and is, like his inclusion of "the neat *Retiarie* Spider," a principal exception to the particular pattern he has been tracing. As a report on his research into "the plastic principle" exemplified in seeds, the digression emphasizes the potentiality, not the futility, of human inquiry, and the section concludes, appropriately, with a series of questions involving the subject of germination that look forward to a future point of resolution. Like everything else in *The Garden,* Browne views the inquiries as "enlarging," not delimiting, the nature of his discourse. They grow naturally out of a concern with seeds, which grows naturally out of a concern with quincuncial patterns in nature. And when the chapter concludes with a slightly dreamy account of motion, it captures in miniature a sense of the quietly restless energy that animates both the investigatory process itself and the rhythms of the creation: "Even Animals near the Classis of plants, seem to have the most restlesse motions. The Summerworm of Ponds and plashes makes a long waving motion; the hair-worm seldome lies still. He that would behold a very anomalous motion, may observe it in the Tortile and tiring stroaks of Gnat-worms" (p. 158).

With the running heading, "The Quincunx Mistically Consid-ered," the last two chapters carry the wavy expansion of *The Garden* to its ultimate level: the universal significance attached to the num-ber 5. The first of these—chapter 4—concentrates principally on the "delights" and "commodoties" of quincuncial plantation by proposing to "enlarge with additionall ampliations" (pp. 158–59) the brief descriptions of Virgil and Varro cited in the opening chapter. By "commodities," Browne means the productive virtues of this order, the natural arguments favoring this form of planting: healthy root structure, ample foliage, protection from the wind, ease of watering and so forth, topics treated mainly in the first half of the chapter (pp. 159–64). By "delights," Browne means the aesthetic values of this order. The second half of the chapter con-centrates on the pleasures provided by geometrical figures associated with lozengelike shapes in both the individual plants and in their groupings, in which the "oppposite ranks of Trees standing like pillars in the *Cavedia* of the Courts of famous buildings, and the *Portico's* of the *Templa subdialia* of old; Somewhat imitating the *Peristylia* or Cloyster buildings, and the *Exedrae* of the Ancients, wherein men discoursed, walked and exercised" (p. 165). Browne also takes up issues of color, of perspective, and of echoes, familiar topics in seventeenth-century gardening books, now rarefied by quasi-technical accounts of decussation. The whole chapter is then "graced" by three mystical glosses on the "Letter X," first from an Egyptian, then a Platonic, and finally from a Christian, Neoplatonic point of view.

In moving from commodities, to delights, to hieroglyphic glosses, from an initial discussion of root structures to a concluding vision of Christ placed crosswise in the universe, the fourth chapter stretches in an increasingly vertical and recondite direction, expanding in the last two paragraphs by speculating on the most esoteric of coinci-dences. The fifth chapter caps this ascent by carrying Browne into the mystical mathematics of the universe. "To enlarge this contem-plation unto all the mysteries and secrets, accomodable unto this number, were inexcusable Pythagorisme," he begins, apologetically, but then embarks on a numerological romp that yokes together justice, the number of leaves on flowers, five fingers, the "Conjugall or wedding number of Antiquity" as well as the "five wise and foolish Virgins" waiting for the bridegroom, "Cabalistical accounts" of the "character of Generation, declared by the Letter *He,* the fifth in [the Hebrew] Alphabet," the stability and sphericity of the number, the five mice of 1 Samuel 6:4, St. Paul's preference for five words in a known tongue, and starfish—to name only some of the abstrusities assembled here (pp. 170–72).

Numbers, of course, were thought to reflect the ultimate order underlying the creation of the universe. John Dee articulates this view in his preface to Henry Billingsley's translation of Euclid's *Elements* (1570), a work Browne cites in *Pseudodoxia* (p. 414): "All thinges (which from the very first originall being of thinges, have bene framed and made) do appeare to be Formed by the reason of Numbers. For this was the principall example or patterne in the minde of the Creator."[18] To view art and nature quincuncially is to recognize a significant pattern running throughout the corporeal world. To meditate on the numerological meaning of the quincunx is to approach more nearly the "ordainer of order"—to borrow Browne's euphemism for God at the end of the essay—since the special virtue of numbers was their mediatorial function. They linked the natural with the supernatural, the changeable with the unchangeable. *"Thynges Mathematicall,"* writes Dee, "being (in a maner) middle, betwene thinges supernaturall and naturall: are not so absolute and excellent, as thinges supernatural: Nor yet so base and grosse, as thinges naturall: But are thinges immateriall: and neverthelesse, by materiall things hable somewhat to be signified."

Browne's final litany of queries involving the number 5 consequently assumes some of the features of a mystical chant. "If any shall further quaery why magneticall Philosophy excludeth decussations, and needles transversly placed do naturally distract their verticities," Browne begins, and then continues,

Why Geomancers do imitate the Quintuple Figure, in their Mother Characters of Acquisition and Amission. . . . Why five must be only left in that Symbolicall mutiny among the men of *Cadmus?* Why *Proteus* in *Homer* the Symbole of the first matter, before he setled himself in the midst of his Sea-monsters, doth place them out by fives? Why the fifth years Oxe was acceptable Sacrifice unto *Jupiter?* Or why the Noble *Antoninus* in some sence doth call the soul it self a Rhombus? He shall not fall on trite or triviall disquisitions. (p. 173)

As Frank Huntley writes in what is certainly one of the best analyses of *The Garden,* "the answers are not amenable to reason; man can only wonder. But there it is, laid out in a panoply intended to overburden the mind."[19]

And yet *The Garden of Cyrus* does not end in a rapturous swirl of questions. It closes, rather, with a quintessentially Brownean gesture: with the author pointing to his own ingenuity as a maker of conceits, as an inventor of propositions for "acuter enquirers," of which the quincunx serves as a model. This bit of self-flattery is then expanded into a "call" for others to search out *"quaternios"* (the perfect number: $1 + 2 + 3 + 4 = 10$) and "figured draughts" (p. 174) in nature, before the whole passage closes with Browne gradually succumbing to the pleasures of sleep. Like the last chapter of *Urne-Buriall,* these concluding paragraphs have always been counted among the author's most exquisite. "It is a marvel," observes Laurence Stapleton,[20] "that the writer who could thus link so many discrepant facts retains at the last a hope worthy of the scientist." The "marvel," I think, is not lessened if we remember that Browne "invented" *The Garden of Cyrus* for a kinsman of Francis Bacon: it simply adds a social dimension to a gesture that is both comic and heroic. However dizzying the search for quincunxes has become, Browne has not forgotten his immediate audience.

Indeed, as Browne begins in the most outrageous fashion to draw the curtain on his work, our sense of *The Garden* as an evening's entertainment is further reinforced:

But the Quincunx of Heaven runs low, and 'tis time to close the five ports of knowledge; We are unwilling to spin out our awaking thoughts in the phantasmes of sleep, which to[o] often continueth praecogitations; making Cables of Cobwebbes and Wildernesses of handsome Groves. Beside *Hipprocrates* hath spoke so little and the Oneirocriticall Masters, have left such frigid Interpretations from plants, that there is little encouragement to dream of Paradise it self. Nor will the sweetest delight of Gardens afford much comfort in sleep; wherein the dulnesse of that sense shakes hands with delectable odours; and though in the Bed of *Cleopatra,* can hardly with any delight raise up the ghost of a Rose. (p. 174)

Surely, as Coleridge remarked of this and the succeeding paragraphs, there could hardly be a more elaborately conceived rationale for going to bed.[21] Browne seems to be reincarnating, in fact, the role Sir Kenelm Digby imagined for him in reading *Religio Medici* late into the evening: "this good natur'd creature I could easily perswade to bee my Bedfellow, and to wake with mee as long as I had any edge to entertaine my selfe with the delights I sucked from so noble a conversation."[22] Without climbing into the reader's bed, Browne delivers one of the coziest exits in English prose, leaving us with a blissful dormative that quietly insists on the superiority of the author's "invention"—his "waking thoughts"—to anything that dreams might produce.

In turning the text back on itself and its creator, Browne also makes of his *Garden* what conservative poets, especially, were claiming for gardens in general: a place of leisure and retirement, a refuge from the political hurly-burly of the Protectorate, a retreat where quincuncial games can be played and a nutcracker might be described in such a way as to keep even *"a serious Student in the highest* arcana's *of Nature"* like Nicholas Bacon busy for more than a single evening. This, indeed, is one view of gardens expressed by John Evelyn in a letter to Browne written shortly after the publication of *The Garden of Cyrus.* Evelyn was venturing his hopes of establishing "a society of the *Paradisi Cultores,* persons of antient simplicity, paradisean and hortulan saints," in which the pursuit of "innocent, pure, and usefull diversions might enjoy the least encouragement, whilst brutish and ambitious persons seeke themselves in the ruines of our miserable yet dearest country."[23] Early on in the essay, Browne, too, had underscored the idea of the garden as both a retreat from strife and a place of pleasure in recording that "garden" and "Buckler" are derived etymologically from the same Hebrew root (p. 130). And his own preference for Cyrus the planter over Cyrus the liberator, the "Lord of Gardens" described by Xenophon in his *Oeconomicus* rather than the Lord's "annointed" recorded in the Old Testament (cf. especially 2 Chronicles 36:22–23; Ezra 1:1–2; and Isaiah 44:28, 45:1), suggests that he might have been attempting to turn a politically controversial figure in an explicitly pastoral direction.[24]

When Browne closes his eyes at last, he does so with a knowing wink of sublime political indifference: "Though *Somnus* in *Homer* be sent to rowse up *Agamemnon,* I finde no such effects in the drowsy approaches of sleep. To keep our eyes open longer were but to act our *Antipodes.* The Huntsmen are up in *America,* and they are already past their first sleep in *Persia.* But who can be drowsie at that howr which freed us from everlasting sleep? or have slumbring thoughts at that time, when sleep it self must end, and as some conjecture all shall awake again?" (pp. 174–75). This is an author who is going to sleep out the Trojan War, who can conceive of a westward vision of destruction, moving from Persia to America, only as it passes him by. His waking thoughts are reserved solely for the Last Judgment. This forward glance is meant to be not threatening but consoling, as if Browne's last act here is to play the comforter with a small *c* and to leave his readers with a message of peace.[25]

Browne's closing salutation in which wrath and dissension are momentarily imagined and then dissolved in the great wakening at the End also suggests the suturing potential inherent in the discourse. Approximately one month before *Urne-Buriall* and *The Garden of Cyrus* were registered with the Stationer on 9 March 1657/ 58, Edward Reynolds, in a typically "conciliatory" sermon on Philemon 3: 15–16 ("Let us walk by the same rule, let us mind the same thing"), urgently requested "how much it is *incumbent* upon those whom the Prophet calleth *Healers* [Isaiah 3:7] to put their helping hand to prevent further Ruines, and *to close* up the Breaches of *Sion* again."[26] *The Garden of Cyrus* never overtly presents itself as politically motivated, nor does Browne present himself in any obvious way as a healer. We see in the figure of Cyrus only the ideal landlord removed from any immediate historical context. Perhaps we are meant to think of the absent Charles, but such connections are made only by the reader and they could, at any rate, apply to the still healthy Cromwell. But Browne's text does "preach" latitude, not as a religious requirement or a social necessity, but as a fact of nature, a feature built into the structure of the universe, perceived and proven by the observing-creating author and scientist, who understands that exceptions exist even within the ingenious order of quincuncial rule. In *The Garden of Cyrus,* many things walk by the same rule but not quite everything. There will always be "the neat" but nonconforming *"Retiary* Spider," the decussation at the center that forms a digression, perhaps even the quincuncial-minded orb weaver who is himself happily "beyond the Common art of Textury." If *Urne-Buriall* looks within to offer special solace to the displaced, *The Garden* looks outward and suggests the universal rightness of tolerance.

Nonetheless, despite the clarity of its design, its genteel political shadings, and its marvelous final pages, *The Garden of Cyrus* will never be in danger of becoming the object of cult worhip, as happened with *Urne-Buriall* in the nineteenth century. The work was written to please a specific person, the only work Browne saw through publication with this intention. In an age of rarefied learning, it is self-consciously recondite. But its difficulty can be and sometimes has been exaggerated by critics who balk at the central experience of the essay: "delight," a word that resounds from beginning to end, regardless of whether Browne is talking about art or nature or the universe, or is simply conveying his response to the rich play of coincidence that he sees everywhere about him—a word, moreover, that assumes almost talismanic significance because it would seem to have been so thoroughly erased from the lexicon by the somber rhythms of *Urne-Buriall*. This is not to suggest that the subject matter of *The Garden* is without meaning or to deny its obscurity in places. It is to suggest that the principal appeal of the work—and of the mind creating it—is its ability to keep opening outward, absorbing and assimilating the surrounding world, while admitting exceptions, and, in doing so, turning a remote improbability—the quincunx—into a possible explanation for what Browne tentatively identifies in *Religio Medici* as "a universall and common Spirit to the whole world" (1.32, p. 33).

The peculiar idiom, and I would say with Johnson the great attraction of the work, is the *"insinuating"* nature of its argument, *"insinuating"* being the adjective Browne uses to describe the pleasure he found in *"Garden Delights"* (p.87). In contrast to *Religio Medici*, the author does not try here to impress us at every opportunity with the novelty of his being; nor, as with *Pseudodoxia*, does he wage a global campaign against vulgar errors. In these works, as with *Urne-Buriall*, there is a constant testing of limits: personal, intellectual, and spiritual. But however abstruse *The Garden* might be, Browne seems thoroughly at ease with his project. Structurally and rhetorically, his design steals upon us, expanding through negative statements that include far more than they exclude; through conditional phrases that keep radiating outward without reaching a point of closure; and through an occasional, magi-like, embrace of the cosmos, alongside of which the more modest desire for a vision of quincuncial order resonates. The beguiling aspect of *The Garden* is how it admits simultaneously both Johnson's definition of it as "a sport of fancy" and Frank Huntley's description of it as "a revelation of a profound truth that requires an act of faith." These two impulses are never very far apart in Browne. In *The Garden of Cyrus*, they seem inseparable.

Chapter Eight
Christian Morals and After

When Abraham Cowley, poet, Royalist, and future member and celebrator of the Royal Society, complained in 1656 of the withering of wit that accompanied troubled times,[1] he struck a note of self-pity indirectly challenged and criticized by Browne, whose works—at least the ones he saw through the press—all appeared during the Civil War and the Interregnum. Although hardly heroic in the conventional sense, *Religio Medici, Pseudodoxia Epidemica, Urne-Buriall* and *The Garden of Cyrus* quietly present in large Browne's own advice in *Christian Morals:* "Comply with some humors, bear with others, but serve none" (1.23, p. 211). These works are all remarkably individualistic. Without being a polemicist, Browne serves no one humor or one person, even when he is attempting to advance learning; and he remains studiously aloof from controversy, at least in the narrow sense of that word. The image he projects is of someone unruffled by the political moment, or rather, as someone who chooses to look through it and concentrate on more enduring matters, matters that involve him in inscribing and reinscribing the values of continuity and order, regardless of whether the topic involves a celebration of self, the repudiation of vulgar errors, or the recognition of some deep essential truth running through the universe.

Browne's final work, or the work generally assumed to be his last—*Christian Morals*—will always be seen as less inventive, less witty, less verbally resourceful, less intellectually demanding, less moving, than his other major achievements. Although reported by Edward to be the "choicest" of his father's writings and "a continuation of *Religio Medici* drawne up in his elder years,"[2] *Christian Morals* bears only a superficial thematic resemblance to Browne's first work. It is admonitory, not speculative, deliberately didactic not autobiographical. Its generic affiliations are rather with the vast literature of conduct in the Renaissance, shaped by a taste for proverbs and maxims, by the Sermon on the Mount, the Pauline epistles, and the ethics of Aristotle, than with the essay tradition, in which the rhythms of personal exploitation and discovery are paramount. Polonius, not Montaigen, is Browne's not too distant kin; and as with Polonius, Browne can seem at times in need of more matter and less art: "Strive not to run like *Hercules* a furlong in a breath: Festination may prove Precipitation: Deliberating delay may be wise cunctation, and slowness no sloathfulness" (1.33, p. 216).

It might well seem that only a dutiful and respectful child would consider preserving precepts like these, let alone think of calling them the "choicest" of a father's writings; but it would be wrong to view this work as simply evidence of an imagination in retrograde beginning to parody earlier accomplishments. To be sure, most of the topics have appeared elsewhere in the canon and frequently more than once: the abiding concern with charity in its many forms, the reluctance to endorse a single pattern of imitation or plain pathway to heaven, a respect for classical wisdom that does not presume to displace the ultimate truths found in the Bible, the fascination with Pythagoras and a cyclical view of history, a measured appreciation for intellectual and scientific progress—to name only some of the more familiar themes. And at least some of the actual material was published in other contexts. Browne might not be responsible for the fact that sections 1–5, 7–11, 13–16, 18—19, and 30 in Part 1 were printed in 1690 as part of the ending of *A Letter to a Friend,* but he also did not blush over including a passage taken from the end of *Urne-Buriall* in order to conclude the later work. *Christian Morals* will always produce moments of déjà vu, moments when, because of thematic similarities or the appearance of a high number of reduplicative phrases, we might be tempted into agreeing with Solomon, one of Browne's favorite authors, that there is nothing new under the sun, only the reworking of old ideas and attitudes (Ecclesiastes 1:9).

But *Christian Morals* does have its rewards. Laurence Stapleton is surely right to remark that in this work "there is a deeper knowledge of what is human than in any previous writing of Browne," a sentiment anticipated in greater detail by Frank Huntley when, comparing this work with *Religio Medici,* he finds in it "a more seasoned wisdom, a greater humility, a more vivid eschatology, and a more patterned style."[3] To some, this might seem to be making a virtue out of a necessity, but in wisdom literature, it is the seasoning that counts—the sense that these precepts seem well-weighed, judicious, sane, distinguished not so much by the single and singular perspective as by the general truth of the observation. The witty turn is finally less prized than the notion of an idea being plumbed; and it is this slow turning of an idea, a deliberateness achieved in part by a conscious patterning of expression, that sets *Christian Morals* apart from Browne's other writings and illuminates the work at its best. The slow turn gives gravity to the voice, stability to the expression, dignity to human life.

We can witness the seasoning process, in fact, in one of the more celebrated passages from *Christian Morals* on the subject of forgiveness. A briefer version appears at the end of *A Letter to a Friend:* "Let not the Sun in *Capricorn* go down upon thy Wrath, but write thy Wrongs in Water; draw the Curtain of Night upon Injuries; shut them up in the Tower of Oblivion, and let them be as tho they had not been. Forgive thine Enemies totally, and without any Reservé of hope, that however, God will revenge thee" (*LF*, p. 194). The more expanded and altered account reads:

Let not the Sun in Capricorn go down upon thy wrath, but write thy wrongs in *Ashes*. Draw the Curtain of night upon injuries, shut them up in the Tower of Oblivion and let them be as though they had not been. *To forgive our Enemies, yet hope that God will punish them, is not to forgive enough. To forgive them our selves, and not to pray God to forgive them, is a partial piece of Charity.* Forgive thine enemies totally, and without any reserve, that however God will revenge thee. (*CM*, 1.15, pp. 207–8; my italics)

Both versions develop out of Paul's warning in the Epistle to the Ephesians: "Be ye angry, and sin not: let not the sun go down upon your wrath" (4:26). Both are also embellished with learned allusions glossed in the margins (the sun in Capricorn signifying the time of year when the days are shortest; the Tower of Oblivion, a Persian prison in which whoever was put "was as it were buried alive, and it was death for any but to name him"). But the second is certainly the more memorable of the two. The slight change from "water" to "ashes" at the outset signals a deeper response to the problem of forgiveness and of the hidden difficulty inherent in Paul's command, "Be ye angry, and sin not," a problem amplified in the addition of the patterned cadences beginning "To forgive our Enemies, yet hope that God will punish them." These lend both a ritualizing solemnity to the passage, as if Browne is exorcizing anger itself, and also the suggestion of his own involvement: "thine Enemies" is now accom-

panied by "our Enemies." We might not be impressed by the
originality of the idea in either version; indeed, we ought not to be
since Browne is simply giving voice to a central New Testament
belief. But in the second version, at least, we might be impressed
by the centrality of the voice itself: penitential, as if the speaker
knows the problem from the inside out, and yet still very much in
control of his idiom as he presses the notion of total forgiveness to
its logical and rhetorical limit.

If the passage on forgiveness helps to illustrate in miniature the
seasoning process itself—the manner in which a single perception
is layered with thought—it seems almost inevitable that one of the
most resonant sections in all of *Christian Morals* should concentrate
on the wisdom acquired through age. Part 3, section 22 (p. 241)
might well be called "the character of an elderly person." It is
"essayistic" rather than instructional, loosely meditative rather than
compact and didactic; and its presence reminds us, once again, that
while Browne certainly valued the pithy utterance—the sturdy
stance—the natural reach of his mind favored more extended forms
of discourse in which he could gradually tease meaning out of an
idea. The passage is striking, indeed moving, for many reasons, but
one stands out from the others. In *Religio Medici,* Browne had played
at being old. In *Christian Morals,* he no longer plays but registers
a thoroughly mellowed statement on the losses and gains of life, a
statement that, as we might expect, describes the world and man's
place in it as neither simply a vale of tears—a perspective offered,
for instance, by the Puritan divine, Lewis Bayly, in his "Meditation
on the Miseries of Old Age"—nor a place of innocence in which
"one entertains the harmless day / With a well-chosen book or care,"
to quote from Henry Wotton's "Character of a Happy Life."[4] Browne's
version asks us to share not just in the sweet and sour of aging but
in a vision of life remarkable for its fullness; and though not quite
a valediction, it comes as close to being a "final" statement as
anything he ever wrote.

The six paragraphs offer six perspectives on old age: the septu-
agenarian as "a curt Epitome of the whole," as "the best judge of
Time," as outliving his own progeny and friends, as a good judge
of the character of others, as a reflector on "the great intention of
his Being," and as someone who, feeling the "Emptiness of all
things," begins to long for the next life. The paragraphs do not
develop a single line of argument. They explore, rather, different

attitudes, different emotional reaches—the pleasures of knowing, the sorrows of being forgotten, the delight of expectation. But the particular phrase that sticks in the mind and underlies the others involves reflecting on how far one has "performed the great intention of his Being, in the Honour of his Maker; whether he hath made good the Principles of his Nature and what he was made to be; what Characteristick and special Mark he hath left, to be observable in his Generation; whether he hath Lived to purpose or in vain, and what he hath added, acted, or performed, that might considerably speak him a Man." Browne can imagine loss, even despair; he can also imagine a world of transcendent bliss. But he cannot finally imagine a life without purpose, and the purpose does not strictly involve preparing the self for the possibility of a better life to come. Leaving one's mark in the here and now is important. The wish to be observed *must* be observed, as the delight Browne finds in this life—the "deep Gust of the World"—seems irrepressible even (or rather, especially) when he is writing about leaving it. The final paragraph hangs graciously on this paradox:

In such an Age Delights will be undelightful and Pleasures grow stale unto him; Antiquated Theorems will revive, and *Solomon's* Maxims be Demonstrations unto him; Hopes or presumptions be over, and despair grow up of any satisfaction below. And having been long tossed in the Ocean of this World, he will by that time feel the In-draught of another, unto which this seems but preparatory, and without it of no high value. He will experimentally find the Emptiness of all things, and the nothing of what is past; and wisely grounding upon true Christian Expectations, finding so much past, will wholly fix upon what is to come. He will long for Perpetuity, and live as though he made haste to be happy. The last may prove the prime part of his Life, and those his best days which he lived nearest Heaven.

Browne is describing here not a rejection of the world but a gradual turning away from it, a turn, moreover, that ultimately concludes by incorporating a vision of the "prime part" of life in this world. Such finely tuned acts of inclusion are the very substance of Browne's wisdom in *Christian Morals*.

The "Special Mark He Hath Left"

Whatever current value we place on *Christian Morals* today, its significance cannot be underestimated in at least one respect: it served as the occasion for the first substantial, scholarly assessment of Browne. Dr. Johnson's biographical and critical introduction to the author, attached to his sparsely annotated edition of the work, was published in 1756; it was later called by Boswell one of his "best biographical performances."[5] Although other "lives" by Dr. Johnson have since become more famous, there can be no denying its importance, both as an independent critical document and as a landmark in the history of Browne criticism. Before its publication, Browne was a noted scientist, physician, and antiquarian. He had been the subject of some brief biographical sketches, often defending or denying his religious orthodoxy, and portions of his works were occasionally quoted and commended by purveyors of good taste like Addison. After Johnson's "life," it was possible to think of Browne as an *author*—as someone with a substantial corpus of works, varying in significance, purpose, and originality, who could be valued for his thought as well as his linguistic attributes, and whose prose style, after being much mimicked and then largely abandoned, could be seen as beginning to exert a lasting pressure on the English language.

Johnson was, in many ways, Browne's ideal reader. Versed in the physical sciences, especially anatomy, chemistry, and physiology, a devout member of the Church of England, an essayist, moralist, and lexicographer, he responded energetically, though not always favorably, to Browne's matter and manner. By the time he wrote his "life," he had already composed a number of biographical sketches of physicians and scientists. He had also "Englished," very freely, Juvenal's tenth satire, which he entitled "The Vanity of Human Wishes" (1749), completed the gargantuan series of *Rambler* essays (1750–52), and published his *Dictionary* in two volumes (1755). Browne figures frequently in the *Dictionary,* as we might expect. How formative an influence he was, in turn, on the latter's prose is another matter and has been the subject of speculation ever since 1788 when the Reverend Vicesimus Knox, a minor essayist in the manner of Addison and Steele, accused Johnson of selecting Browne as his stylistic model for *The Rambler.* The charge, now "generally thought" to be true according to Knox—a collective sentiment that Saintsbury was to repeat some 100 years later[6]—is hardly substantiated and hovers around Johnson's latinisms and the grand and sometimes pompous sweep of his prose. The most telling echoes have been located by Jeremiah Finch,[7] but the stylistic relationship between the two authors remains to be worked out in detail.

Despite Johnson's just measuring of Browne's career and canon, however, there is a real sense of Browne's being "discovered" by the romantics—at least that is how Charles Lamb felt when, after perhaps coming across a copy of *Religio Medici* in a bookstall in London, he began to read deeply in Browne's works and made certain that his friends, including Coleridge and Wordsworth, did the same.[8] Lamb's Browne was also not Johnson's. The Solomonic scientist and moralist valued by Johnson became preeminently a personality, a visionary eccentric, whose imagination colored and shaped all he observed, especially the natural world. *Religio Medici,* which had been only a part of the edifice, was now the centerpiece, flanked by the last chapters of *Urne-Buriall* and of *The Garden of Cyrus.* The author whom Johnson regarded at a distance was in the process of being enthusiastically assimilated into the consciousness of a generation of readers and of one prose stylist in particular.

Lamb's writings are saturated with Brownean moments, allusions, and recollections. From tellingly off-hand *"altitudos"* like "I love to lose myself in other men's minds," to direct quotation (or misquotation), " 'At my nativity,' says Sir Thomas Browne, 'my ascendent was the earthly sign of Scorpius,' " to similar responses to the sound of bells, "I never hear it without a gathering-up of my mind to a concentration of all the images that have been diffused over the past twelve months" (Browne had written "I could never hear the *Ave-Mary* bell without an elevation"), Lamb sufficiently possessed and reincarnated the earlier essayist until he finally had to write an essay entitled "Imperfect Sympathies" to mark off—and then only superficially—a distance between the two men.[9]

Lamb obviously found in Browne a kindred spirit, a model for his own expressive whimsy that so differentiates him from the eighteenth-century Addisonian essayist, as well as a fellow companion in pursuit of the arcane and the archaic. If Browne had his *Urne-Buriall,* Lamb had his "Old China." If Browne worshipped quincunxes, Lamb delighted in roast pig. If Browne could apprehend in *Christian Morals* an elderly man being forgotten in his own lifetime (3.22), Lamb could respond by attempting to recover his elders from oblivion ("My Relations"). If Browne loved to dream in prose, so did Lamb. There are important differences between the two. Lamb's

vision is finally domestic and nostalgic, Browne's progressively
cosmic; but with the crucial help of both Coleridge, whose letter
to his sister celebrating Browne's multiple achievements appeared
in *Blackwood's Magazine* (November 1819), and De Quincey, who
responded rhapsodically to the sound of Browne's prose in "The
Elements of Rhetoric," which was also published in *Blackwood's*
(December 1828), Lamb was instrumental in creating an audience
for his author, who could now be read as the proto-romantic par
excellence of the seventeenth century.

As such, Browne became an object of cult worship as well as a
source of genuine inspiration to later writers. James Crossley was
among the former. A second generation romantic, antiquarian, bib-
liophile, and editor of Browne, Crossley found *Urne-Buriall* and *A
Letter to a Friend* particularly suited to his macabre imaginings: "Like
the female magician, in The Arabian Nights Entertainment, [Browne]
loved to leave the habitations of the living, and take his repast amid
the charnel houses of the dead."[10] This kind of impressionistic
mimicry became a commonplace of the period, though none did it
better than Crossley. He was almost certainly responsible for producing the "Fragment on Mummies," a ghoulish forgery with a
long history of duping editors and readers. Despite containing a
number of anachronisms, the most conspicuous of which is perhaps
the late eighteenth-century "Vampirism," the fragment is still preserved by Keynes, who courteously leaves it to the reader "to judge
whether Browne would have owned to its verbal extravagances, or
would ever have gusted so irreverent a pleasantry."[11]

A more comprehensive and productive assimilation of Browne lay
in a different direction. As F.O. Matthiessen pointed out some years
ago,[12] American romantics, including Emerson, Melville, Thoreau,
and, to a lesser degree, Dickinson, responded deeply to Browne and
to other "metaphysicals" in a number of ways and for a number of
reasons. Emerson found in him a version of his self-reliant man.
Melville, dubbing Browne "a kind of 'crack'd Archangel,'" urged
in *Mardi:* "Be Sir Thomas Browne our ensample, who, while ex-
ploding 'Vulgar Errors', heartily hugged all the mysteries in the
Pentateuch" (chapter 13). And Thoreau attached particular significance to Browne's view of the self as microcosm. As for the special
marks he left on these authors, Browne's signature is most visible
in Melville: in his diction—the doublets as well as puns; in his
cadences—the gradual roll of a paragraph; in his skeptical inquiries

into nature; and in the generally metaphysical quality of his mind in which time and eternity are constantly coalescing.[13] Indeed, what is astonishing about Melville is how much of Browne he was capable of echoing: portions of *Religio Medici, Pseudodoxia Epidemica, Urne-Buriall, The Garden of Cyrus,* even some of the *Miscellany Tracts.* With Emerson, there are fewer instances of ventriloquism, despite his being called by Longfellow "the Chrysostom and Sir Thomas Browne of the day"; but the connections are there, although they await fuller exploration, and would certainly seem to originate in the authority Emerson found in Browne and other early writers for the essay as a place for a full and powerful display of the mind—of man thinking.[14] With Thoreau, the Brownean traces are perhaps the subtlest of all, but given the temperamental and scholarly affinities between the two men, they are certainly suggestive. No one who has read both authors can finish *Walden* without thinking of Browne's cosmic musings at the end of *The Garden of Cyrus.*[15]

If Browne was part of the vital center of American romanticism—indeed, in some ways more vital to it than to English romantics—he also became favorite fare for late Victorian essayists. Walter Pater's decision to devote a general "appreciation" to Browne seems, in retrospect, almost inevitable: the highly cultivated response of one stylist leisurely picking his way through the writings of another and casting everything he saw in the crepuscular glow of his own prose.[16] So too do the responses of J. A. Symonds, Leslie Stephen, and, if we wish to think of him as a late Victorian, Lytton Strachey.[17] These were essayists attempting to return, to some degree, to their prose roots, men of letters seeking to "discover" the essence of an earlier writer and, as it were, to allow others the opportunity to breathe in the aroma. Although all were in one way or another indebted to Coleridge for their guiding perceptions, each found a slightly different aspect of the author to emphasize. Pater was struck by Browne's "charm of absolute sincerity," Stephen by the author's "humor"; Symonds and Strachey admired the "deliciousness" of his prose. No cultural sage or prophet, Browne made little impression on Carlyle, Arnold, and Ruskin, but his apparent indifference to the present touched a wistful chord among a generation of writers intoxicated, in varying degrees, by their own cultural belatedness.

The present century has, on the whole, read Browne more soberly, more with an ear to Strachey's warning that "If one fails in the style of Pascal, one is merely flat; if one fails in the style of Browne, one is ridiculous. He who plays with the void, who dallies with eternity, who leaps from star to star, is in danger at every moment of being swept into utter limbo, and tossed forever in the Paradise of Fools."[18] Except for an occasional attempt at mimicry, as happens rather badly in E. M. Forster's short story, "The Celestial Omnibus," Browne has been more often the subject of serious scholarship than a source of immediate inspiration. This is not to deny him a potentially significant place in the vision of a writer like Jorge Luis Borges, fascinated as he is with labyrinths and a cyclical view of history,[19] or to sever him altogether from a modern purple prose essayist like William Gass—one thinks especially of his *On Being Blue: A Philosophical Inquiry*—or even to downplay his appeal to readers outside of English literature classes (Browne has been well served in this century by medical humanists); it is simply to note that the principal interpretive energies in this century have been devoted to analyzing and understanding the author in a variety of scholarly, historical, and critical contexts. Browne did not, in contrast to Donne, need to be "discovered" by Eliot. Indeed, Eliot was highly suspicious of Browne, as he was of Milton and Tennyson, for his "seductive" aural sensibility.[20] But Browne surely came of age with the renewed interest in the seventeenth century that accompanied Eliot's attempt to champion "metaphysical" poetry.

The Browne whom we meet today is likely to seem less quaint than he did to the late nineteenth century—more clearly representative of the "Janus-faced" nature of the age in which he lived, to borrow Basil Willey's shorthand description of the period, which is borrowed in part from Browne. In a century described as being "half scientific and half magical, half skeptical and half credulous, looking back in one direction to Mandiville, and forward to Newton,"[21] Browne occupies a central place. In reading him, we seek and acquire much "seventeenth-century background." Indeed, one of the great virtues of modern scholarship in general has been to connect Browne to some of the larger intellectual, social, and literary concerns of the period, and to render him thereby less of an oddity.

But it is also surely a mistake to claim too central a place for Browne in the canon of English literature. Even at his most popular, his appeal has largely been because he inhabits the byways of literary discourse, not the mainroads. If prose is "the younger art,"[22] later than poetry and drama, the pleasures of the essay are still primarily those associated with the individual talent and not with the tradition. And Browne's talents are remarkably individual. He survives as a countervoice to the expected; he draws strength from his obvious sense of difference, a difference that permeates the surface and lodges itself in the dark mysteries of life and human potentiality. As William Gass has remarked, Browne's is an art that puts the "soul inside the sentence."[23] He might not do so with every sentence, and we might not always read him for this reason, but when he does, it is tempting to paraphrase Frost and say "to do this to prose is why he came."[24]

To subsist in lasting Monuments, to live in their productions, to exist in their names, and prædicament of *Chymera's,* was large satisfaction unto old expectations, and made one part of their *Elyziums.* But all this is nothing in the Metaphysicks of true belief. To live indeed is to be again our selves, which being not only an hope but an evidence in noble beleevers; 'Tis all one to lye in St *Innocents* Church-yard, as in the Sands of *Aegypt:* Ready to be any thing, in the extasie of being ever, and as content with six foot as the Moles of *Adrianus.* (*UB,* p. 125)

Where but in Browne, amid the grand obliquities of Pauline regeneration, could the drive toward contentment include so many outlandish turns?

Notes and References

Please note that works that appear both immediately below *and* in the *Selected Bibliography* receive full citation in the latter entry.

Preface

1. For specific versions of each, see respectively: Margaret L. Wiley, *The Subtle Knot: Creative Scepticism in Seventeenth-Century England* (London, 1952), 137–60; Arno Löffler, *Sir Thomas Browne als Virtuoso* (Nuremberg, 1972); Jeremiah S. Finch, *Sir Thomas Browne: A Doctor's Life of Science and Faith* (New York, 1950); Stanley E. Fish, *Self-Consuming Artifacts: The Experience of Seventeenth-Century Literature* (Berkeley, 1972), 353–73; Lytton Strachey, "Sir Thomas Browne," in *Books and Characters, French and English* (New York, 1922), 31–44; Egon Stephen Merton, *Science and Imagination in Sir Thomas Browne* (New York, 1949); Leonard Nathanson, *The Strategy of Truth: A Study of Sir Thomas Browne* (Chicago, 1967); and Frank Livingstone Huntley, *Sir Thomas Browne: A Biographical and Critical Study* (Ann Arbor, 1962). My conciliatory and inclusive view of the critical tradition is anticipated in a remark by Joan Webber, *The Eloquent "I": Style and Self in Seventeenth-Century Prose* (Madison, 1968): "One never knows where to begin or end in analyzing his work. To greatly varying degrees, all his critics are right. But it is impossible to wait long and patiently enough to discover whether the pattern that changes like a *trompe l'oeil* before one's eyes has changed for the last time, or whether there is still another dimension qualifying all the others" (151). Her critical skepticism, of course, does not prevent her from attempting to get the picture right.

Chapter One

1. *The Diary of John Evelyn,* ed. E. S. de Beer, 6 vols. (Oxford: Clarendon Press, 1955), 3:594 (spelling slightly modernized).
2. The basic biographical sources for Browne are *Religio Medici;* the Reverend John Whitefoot, "Some Minutes for the Life of Sir Thomas Browne," in *Posthumous Works* (1712); Samuel Johnson's "Life of Browne," in his edition of *Christian Morals* (1756); "Sir Thomas Browne," *European Magazine* 40 (1801):89–90 (remarks by Dr. White Kennett); Simon Wilkin, "Supplementary Memoir," in *Sir Thomas Browne's Works,* 4 vols. (London, 1835–36), vol. 1; Jeremiah S. Finch, *Sir Thomas Browne: A Doctor's Life of Science and Faith* (New York, 1950); Joan Bennett, *Sir Thomas Browne*

(Cambridge, 1962), chaps. 1–2; and Frank Livingstone Huntley, *Sir Thomas Browne: A Biographical and Critical Study* (Ann Arbor, 1962). Edmund Gosse's *Sir Thomas Browne* (London, 1905) is outdated and too speculative to be reliable. Wilkin's account of the family tree should be supplemented by Charles Williams, "The Pedigree of Sir Thomas Browne," *Norfolk Archaeology* 15 (1904):109–13. It should also be remembered that *Religio Medici* is, above all, an imaginative piece of literature in which *"there are many things delivered Rhetorically, many expressions therein meerely Tropicall"*; it needs to be read cautiously as autobiography. On this last point see N. J. Endicott, "Some Aspects of Self-Revelation and Self-Portraiture in *Religio Medici*," in *Essays in English Literature from the Renaissance to the Victorian Age*, ed. Millar MacLure and F. W. Watt (Toronto: University of Toronto Press, 1964), 85–102.

3. G. C. R. Morris, "Sir Thomas Browne's Nativity," *Notes & Queries* 228 (1983):420–21.

4. Finch, *Sir Thomas Browne*, 26.

5. Wilkin, *Sir Thomas Browne's Works*, 1:cx.

6. Johnson's "Life of Browne" is made conveniently available in *Sir Thomas Browne: The Major Works*, ed. C. A. Patrides (Harmondsworth, 1977), 483–511. All further references to Johnson's "life" will be to this edition. The above quotation appears on p. 484.

7. Wilkin, *Sir Thomas Browne's Works*, 1:cx.

8. N. J. Endicott, "Sir Thomas Browne as 'Orphan,' with Some Account of his Stepfather, Sir Thomas Dutton," *University of Toronto Quarterly* 30 (1961):180–210.

9. Whitefoot, *Posthumous Works*, xxviii.

10. Huntley, *Sir Thomas Browne*, 48.

11. Ibid., 90–98. See also Sir Geoffrey Keynes, *A Bibliography of Sir Thomas Browne*, rev. ed. (Oxford, 1968), 3.

12. *Complete Prose Works of John Milton*, ed. Don M. Wolfe et al., 8 vols. to date (New Haven: Yale University Press, 1953–), 2:366–67 (*Of Education*).

13. John Mulder, *The Temple of the Mind: Education and Literary Taste in Seventeenth-Century England* (New York: Pegasus, 1969), 21.

14. *Pseudodoxia Epidemica*, ed. Robin Robbins, 2 vols. (Oxford, 1981), 1:xxix.

15. Quoted by Finch, *Sir Thomas Browne*, 31.

16. See Mulder, *Temple of the Mind*, 22–23, and Huntley, *Sir Thomas Browne*, 7–12.

17. Whitefoot, *Posthumous Works*, xxix.

18. Finch, *Sir Thomas Browne*, 37.

19. Arthur F. Leach, *A History of Winchester College* (London: Duckworth & Co., 1899), 322.

20. Mark H. Curtis, *Oxford and Cambridge in Transition* (Oxford: Clarendon Press, 1959), chaps. 4, 9.

21. H. M. Sinclair and A. H. T. Robb-Smith, *A Short History of Anatomical Teaching in Oxford* (Oxford: Oxford University Press, 1950), 11.

22. Phyllis Allen, "Medical Education in 17th-Century England," *Journal of the History of Medicine* 1 (1946):115–43.

23. Huntley, *Sir Thomas Browne*, 36.

24. Ibid., 39–40.

25. *Dictionary of National Biography*, 12:295.

26. Thomas Lushington, *The Resurrection Rescued* (London, 1659), 48. See also Frank L. Huntley, "Dr. Thomas Lushington (1590–1661), Sir Thomas Browne's Oxford Tutor," *Modern Philology* 81 (1983):14–23.

27. Quoted from George B. Parks, "Travel as Education," in *The Seventeenth Century*, ed. Richard Foster Jones (Stanford: Stanford University Press, 1951), 266.

28. See *RM*, 1.21, 2.8.

29. Keith Thomas, *Religion and the Decline of Magic* (New York: Charles Scribner's Sons, 1971), 8–9.

30. Ibid., 6.

31. A. Batty Shaw, "Sir Thomas Browne's Meadow," *Notes & Queries* 216 (1971):295–99.

32. See Thomas, *Religion and the Decline of Magic*, 5.

33. Whitefoot, *Posthumous Works*, xxxii.

34. For information on Joan Carlile, see Margaret Toynbee and Gyles Isham, "Joan Carlile (1606?–1679)—An Identification," *Burlington Magazine* 96 (1954):275–77, and Toynbee, "Some Friends of Sir Thomas Browne," *Norfolk Archaeology* 31 (1955–57):377–94.

35. Bennett, *Sir Thomas Browne*, 10.

36. Ibid.

37. Wilkin, *Sir Thomas Browne's Works*, 1:lxxiv.

38. Quoted from Dorothy Tyler, "A Review of the Interpretation of Sir Thomas Browne's Part in a Witch Trial in 1664," *Anglia* 54 (1930):187.

39. Malcolm Letts, "Sir Thomas Browne and Witchcraft," *Notes & Queries* 11, 5th ser. (1912):221–23.

40. Keynes, *Bibliography*, 193.

41. Whitefoot, *Posthumous Works*, xxxiv–xxxv.

42. Information on the contemporary reception of *Religio* is contained in Keynes, *Bibliography*, 3–51, 171–91, and in Frank L. Huntley, "The Publication and Immediate Reception of *Religio Medici*," *Library Quarterly* 25 (1955):203–18.

43. Henry Peacham, *The Complete Gentleman*, ed. Virgil B. Heltzel (Ithaca, N.Y.: Cornell University Press, 1962), 120.

44. Keynes, *Bibliography*, 176.

45. Wilkin, *Sir Thomas Browne's Works*, 1:352.

46. Keynes, *Bibliography*, 188, 191.

47. For a more thorough listing, see Robbins, ed., *Pseudodoxia Epidemica*, l:xxi

48. Curtis, *Oxford and Cambridge*, 131.

49. Quoted from Robbins, ed., *Pseudodoxia Epidemica*, l:xlv, which gives the most recent, authoritative account of the book's immediate reception and influence.

Chapter Two

1. *Coleridge on the Seventeenth Century*, ed. Roberta Florence Brinkley (Durham, 1955), 448.

2. Pater's essay is reprinted in *Appreciations* (London: Macmillan, 1922), 124–60. Modern studies taking Browne's scholarship more seriously include: Gordon Keith Chalmers, "Sir Thomas Browne, True Scientist," *Osiris* 2 (1936):28–79; Egon Stephen Merton, *Science and Imagination in Sir Thomas Browne* (New York, 1949); Jeremiah S. Finch, *Sir Thomas Browne* (New York, 1950); Joan Bennett, *Sir Thomas Browne* (Cambridge, 1962); Frank Livingston Huntley, *Sir Thomas Browne* (Ann Arbor, 1962); Robert Ralston Cawley and George Yost, *Studies in Sir Thomas Browne* (Eugene, Oreg., 1965); and Leonard Nathanson, *The Strategy of Truth: A Study of Sir Thomas Browne* (Chicago, 1967).

3. Michael Hunter, *Science and Society in Restoration England* (Cambridge: Cambridge University Press, 1981), 9. It should be noted that "science" in seventeenth-century usage retained its Latin meaning denoting "knowledge" in general; it was not until the nineteenth century that the word acquired the more specialized connotation honored today designating a specific branch of learning. I will be using it in its modern, more restricted, sense.

4. *The Works of George Herbert*, ed. F. E. Hutchinson, 2d ed. (Oxford: Clarendon Press, 1945), 160 ("The Pulley").

5. Rosalie L. Colie, "Dean Wren's Marginalia and Early Science at Oxford," *Bodleian Library Record* 6 (1960):549.

6. Christopher Hill, *Intellectual Origins of the English Revolution* (Oxford: Clarendon Press, 1965), 25. See also Max Weber, *The Protestant Ethic and the Spirit of Capitalism* (1905; reprint, New York: Charles Scribner's Sons, 1958); Robert K. Merton, *Science, Technology and Society in Seventeenth-Century England* (1938; reprint, New York: Howard Fertig, 1970); and Richard S. Westfall, *Science and Religion in Seventeenth-Century England* (New Haven: Yale University Press, 1964). For a recent survey skeptical of attempts to align the development of science with a specific branch of Protestantism, see Hunter, *Science and Society*, 113–35.

7. *Aubrey's Brief Lives,* ed. Oliver Lawson Dick (1949; reprint, Ann Arbor: University of Michigan Press, 1962), 130.

8. Francis Bacon, *Of The Advancement of Learning* (book 1), in *The Works of Francis Bacon,* ed. James Spedding et al., 15 vols. (Boston: Taggard and Thompson, 1860–64), 6:97.

9. Richard H. Popkin, *The History of Scepticism from Erasmus to Spinoza,* rev. ed. (Berkeley: University of California Press, 1979), 126–27, 129–50.

10. Bacon, *Works,* 8:76–90.

11. Charles Webster, *The Great Instauration: Science, Medicine, and Reform, 1626–1660* (London: Duckworth & Co., 1975), 25.

12. Hunter, *Science and Society,* 13–17, Barbara J. Shapiro, *Probability and Certainty in Seventeenth-Century England* (Princeton: Princeton University Press, 1983), 45–61, and I. Bernard Cohen, *Revolution in Science* (Cambridge, Mass.: Harvard University Press, 1985), 146–51.

13. Thomas Sprat, *History of the Royal Society* (London, 1734), 35.

14. Paolo Rossi, *Francis Bacon: From Magic to Science,* trans. Sacha Rabinovitch (London: Routledge & Kegan Paul, 1968), 27.

15. Bacon, *Works,* 6:127.

16. Quoted by Rossi, *Francis Bacon,* 10, from Bacon's *De Sapientia Veterum* (Of the wisdom of the ancients).

17. Michael Hattaway, "The Theology of Marlowe's *Doctor Faustus,*" *Renaissance Drama,* n.s., 3 (1970):53.

18. For Bacon's rejection of Plato and Neoplatonism, see Rossi, *Francis Bacon,* 51–59. The fullest discussion of Browne's considerable debts to Neoplatonism is Leonard Nathanson's *The Strategy of Truth.*

19. Shapiro, *Probability and Certainty,* 4.

20. Bacon, *Works,* 8:501 *(Advancement of Learning, 3.4).*

21. *Pseudodoxia Epidemica* ed. Robin Robbins, 2 vols. (Oxford, 1981), 1:xxviii–xxxiv.

22. R. F. Jones, *Ancients and Moderns: A Study of the Rise of the Scientific Movement in Seventeenth-Century England,* 2d ed. (Berkeley: University of California Press, 1965), 29.

23. Johnson, "Life of Browne," in *Sir Thomas Browne,* ed. C.A. Patrides (Harmondsworth, 1977), 492.

24. Huntley, *Sir Thomas Browne,* 204–23. An earlier version of this argument appeared in "Sir Thomas Browne: The Relationship of *Urn Burial* and *The Garden of Cyrus,*" *Studies in Philology* 53 (1956):204–19.

25. Bacon, *Works,* 6:132.

26. Huntley, *Sir Thomas Browne,* 215–18.

27. Although Browne barely figures into the argument of Anthony Low's *The Georgic Revolution* (Princeton: Princeton University Press, 1985), his study sheds much interesting light on the general cultural resistance

to representing labor in earlier seventeenth-century literature, a resistance still present in Browne, despite his Baconian connections, and which is felt perhaps nowhere more keenly in his published writings than at the end of *The Garden of Cyrus* when his courtly wit pastoralizes Vulcan's smithy into a vegetable shop.

28. Marie Boas Hall, "Thomas Browne Naturalist," in *Approaches to Sir Thomas Browne,* ed. C. A. Patrides (Columbia, Mo, 1982), 178–87.

29. Merton, *Science and Imagination,* 51.

30. Hall, "Thomas Browne Naturalist," 185.

31. Chalmers, "Sir Thomas Browne, True Scientist," 28–79, esp. 77–79.

32. Shapiro, *Probability and Certainty,* 70–73.

33. Nehemiah Grew, *The Anatomy of Plants* (London, 1682), 80.

Chapter Three

1. Richard Hooker, *Of The Laws of Ecclesiastical Polity,* 2 vols. (London: J. M. Dent & Sons; 1907), 1:95.

2. John Booty, "Hooker and Anglicanism," in *Studies in Richard Hooker,* ed. W. Speed Hill (Cleveland: Case Western Reserve, 1972), 211.

3. *The Works of Francis Bacon,* ed. James Spedding et al., 15 vols. (Boston: Taggard and Thompson, 1860–64), 12:88.

4. A. G. Dickens, *The English Reformation* (New York: Schocken Books, 1964), 249–54.

5. Ibid., 269.

6. Patrick Collinson, *The Religion of Protestants: The Church in English Society, 1559–1625* (Oxford: Clarendon Press, 1982), 81. See also Nicholas Tyacke, "Puritanism, Arminianism and Counter-Revolution," in *The Origins of the English Civil War,* ed. Conrad Russell (London: Macmillan, 1973), 119–43, esp. 130–31.

7. Bacon, *Works,* 12:88.

8. D.P. Walker, *The Decline of Hell: Seventeenth-Century Discussions of Eternal Torment* (London: Routledge & Kegan Paul, 1964), 4.

9. Ibid., 9–10.

10. Ibid., 6.

11. Nathanson, *The Strategy of Truth* (Chicago, 1967), 111–41.

12. Thomas Fuller, *The Worthies of England* (London, 1684), 484.

13. R. W. Ketton-Cremer, *Norfolk in the Civil War: A Portrait of a Society in Conflict* (London: Faber & Faber, 1969), 79; Ketton-Cremer reduces this number slightly.

14. *True News From Norwich* (London, 1642), 7.

15. Joseph Hall, "Bishop Hall's *Hard Measure*" (1647), in *The Works of Joseph Hall* (London, 1714), xvii.

16. "The Norwich Subscription for the Regaining of Newcastle, 1643," *Norfolk Archaeology* 18 (1914):149–60. The original manuscript is in the Norfolk and Norwich Record Office.

17. Huntley, *Sir Thomas Browne* (Ann Arbor, 1962), 27–29.

18. Jeremiah S. Finch, *Sir Thomas Browne* (New York, 1950), 167.

19. Ibid., 128–29.

20. Ketton-Cremer, *Norfolk in the Civil War,* 158–59, 194.

21. Quoted from John T. Evans, *Seventeenth-Century Norwich: Politics, Religion, and Government, 1620–1690* (Oxford: Clarendon Press, 1979), 223. The document, in the Norfolk and Norwich Record Office, is reproduced in *An Address from the Gentry of Norfolk and Norwich to General Monck in 1660,* ed. Hamon Le Strange and Walter Rye (Norfolk, 1913).

22. Edward Reynolds, *Works* (London, 1679), 931, 933, 937.

23. See I. M. Green, *The Re-establishment of the Church of England, 1660–1663* (New York: Oxford University Press, 1978), chap. 1.

24. Reynolds, *Works,* 1031–41.

25. Ibid., 1035.

26. Ibid., 1037.

27. W. K. Jordan, *The Development of Religious Toleration in England,* 4 vols. (London: George Allen & Unwin, 1932–40), 2:448.

28. This suggestion is made by Michael Wilding, "*Religio Medici* in the English Revolution," in *Approaches to Sir Thomas Browne,* ed. C. A. Patrides (Columbia, Mo., 1982), 100–101.

Chapter Four

1. Austin Warren, "The Style of Sir Thomas Browne," *Kenyon Review* 13 (1951):675.

2. *Coleridge on the Seventeenth Century,* ed. Roberta Florence Brinkley (Durham, 1955), 439.

3. Alexander Ross, *Medicus Medicatus* (London, 1645), dedicatory epistle.

4. Stanley Fish, *Self-Consuming Artifacts: The Experience of Seventeenth-Century Literature* (Berkeley, 1972), 367. Defending Browne against Fish's description of him as "The Bad Physician" has become something of a minor industry in Browne criticism. See, for instance, the measured rebuttal by Frank J. Warnke, "A Hook for Amphibium: Some Reflections on Fish," in *Approaches to Sir Thomas Browne,* ed. C. A. Patrides (Columbia, Mo., 1982), 49–59.

5. Strachey, "Sir Thomas Browne," in *Books and Characters, French & English* (New York, 1922), 38. Like Strachey, Browne was notably skeptical of attempts to fix an absolute standard in taste: "For beauty is determined by opinion, and seems to have no essence that holds one notion with all" (*PE,* 6.11, p. 522).

6. *Selections from Ralph Waldo Emerson,* ed. Stephen E. Whicher (Boston: Houghton Mifflin Co., 1957), 265 ("Experience").

7. Samuel Johnson, "Life of Browne," in *Sir Thomas Browne,* ed. C. A. Patrides (Harmondsworth, 1977), 508.

8. James Joyce, *Ulysses* (1914; reprint, New York: Random House, 1961), 394.

9. *Coleridge on the Seventeenth Century,* ed. Brinkley, 414.

10. Edward G. E. Bulwer-Lytton, "Sir Thomas Browne's Works," *Edinburgh Review* 64 (October 1836):31.

11. Johnson, "The Life of Sir Thomas Browne," 508.

12. George Williamson, "The Purple of *Urn Burial,*" *Modern Philology* 62 (1964):115.

13. Douglas Bush, *English Literature in the Earlier Seventeenth Century,* 2d ed. (Oxford: Clarendon Press, 1962), 357.

14. *The Works of Francis Bacon,* ed. James Spedding et al., 15 vols. (Boston: Taggard and Thompson, 1860–64), 6:119.

15. See, Ted-Larry Pebworth, "Not Being, but Passing: Defining the Early English Essay," *Studies in the Literary Imagination* 10, no. 2 (Fall 1977):17–27. Like all students of Renaissance and seventeenth-century prose, I am indebted in the following discussion to the pioneering essays of Morris Croll, collected in *Style, Rhetoric, and Rhythm,* ed. J. Max Patrick et al. (Princeton, 1966) and R. F. Jones, reprinted in *The Seventeenth Century: Studies in the History of English Thought and Literature from Bacon to Pope* (Stanford: Stanford University Press, 1951). Among recent general works devoted to historical study of seventeenth-century style, I have found especially useful Robert Adolph, *The Rise of Modern Prose Style* (Cambridge, Mass.: MIT Press, 1968), and Joseph Anthony Mazzeo, "Seventeenth-Century English Prose Style: The Quest for a Natural Style," *Mosaic* 6 (1973):107–44. Alvin Vos, " 'Good Matter and Good Utterance': The Character of English Ciceronianism," *Studies in English Literature* 19 (1979): 5–18, attends alertly to the caricature Bacon produced of Asham and the occasional simplifications it has inspired among later critics determined to see English Ciceronians as either empty of or unconcerned with content.

16. Robert Burton, *The Anatomy of Melancholy,* ed. Holbrook Jackson (1932; reprint, New York: Random House, 1977), 32 ("Democritus Junior to the Reader").

17. Croll, *Style, Rhetoric, and Rhythm,* 210.

18. Adolph, *Rise of Modern Prose Style,* 152–56.

19. Robert Boyle, *Certain Physiological Essays* (London, 1661), 1–36.

20. Whitefoot, *Posthumous Works,* xxxii.

21. See, respectively, the present author's "Browne's Revisions of *Religio Medici,*" *Studies in English Literature* 25 (1985):145–63, and Finch's "Early Drafts of *The Garden of Cyrus,*" *PMLA* 55 (1940):742–47. Joan

Bennett, *Sir Thomas Browne* (Cambridge, 1962), 230–40, also has good things to say about the stylistic changes Browne made to *Christian Morals*.
22. See Frank Huntley, *Sir Thomas Browne* (Ann Arbor, 1962), chap. 12. Objecting to Huntley's hypothesis, N.J. Endicott (*TLS*, 15 September 1966, 868) has argued—to my mind unpersuasively—against Loveday as the subject and Pettus as the recipient. If important questions remain involving the occasion of the letter and the identity of the "friends," Huntley's theory is still too well anchored in historical circumstance to be dismantled largely on the grounds of a problematic textual dispute. See also the letter by Karl Josef Holtgen (*TLS*, 20 October 1966, 966) and Huntley's response to both scholars (*TLS*, 9 February 1967, 116) as well as note 26 below.
23. Huntley, untitled review of *The Prose of Sir Thomas Browne*, ed. Norman Endicott, in *University of Toronto Quarterly* 37 (1968):408–15. See also, Frank Livingston Huntley, *Essays in Persuasion on Seventeenth-Century English Literature* (Chicago: University of Chicago Press, 1981), 114–25.
24. Walter Pater, "Sir Thomas Browne," in *Appreciations* (London, 1922), 152–53. Symond's remarks on *A Letter* appear in the introduction to his edition of *Religio Medici, Urn Burial, Christian Morals, and Other Essays* (London: Walter Scott, 1886), xxiv.
25. N. J. Endicott, "Sir Thomas Browne's *Letter to a Friend*," *University of Toronto Quarterly* 36 (1967):68–86; quotation is taken from p. 75.
26. Endicott's argument with Huntley involving the identity of the deceased (see note 22 above) depends largely on who the reader takes to be the subject (Scaliger or the patient) of the sentence beginning: "And this serious Person, tho no *minor* Wit, left the Poetry of his Epitaph unto others." Endicott favors Scaliger on the basis of a sophisticated but dubious reading of the manuscript. (See Huntley's rejoinder noted above.) The matter cannot be settled on textual grounds alone, and if context as well as a belief in the integrity of *The Letter* means anything, it certainly points to the patient as being "this serious Person." Browne is clearly talking at this point in the work about the patient's indifference to posterity, of which his refusal to pen his own epitaph serves as another instance. Moreover, despite his habits of amplification, Browne never altogether forgets the patient, who forms either the point of departure or return of all the author's thoughts. If the deceased is not the "serious Person" being referred to here, this paragraph becomes notable as the single exception to this practice and is the one obvious instance of an excrescence. Loose as it is, Browne's sense is clear; it might be roughly paraphrased: "as prolific as Scaliger was, he chose only five words for his epitaph; the victim, not of Scaliger's stature, though no minor wit, wrote none at all."

27. *Lamb's Criticism,* ed. E. M. W. Tillyard (Cambridge: Cambridge University Press, 1923), 68. The reference to Browne appears in "Mackery End in Hertfordshire."

28. *Coleridge on the Seventeenth Century,* ed. Brinkley, 448.

Chapter Five

1. See Margaret Bottrall, *Every Man a Phoenix: Studies in Seventeenth-Century Autobiography* (London: John Murray, 1958), chaps. 2–3, and Paul Delany, *British Autobiography in the Seventeenth-Century* (London: Routledge & Kegan Paul, 1969). Recent criticism on autobiography as a genre has become a major industry, but very little of it bears on writers of the seventeenth century. See, for instance, *Autobiography: Essays Theoretical and Critical,* ed. James Olney (Princeton: Princeton University Press, 1980), and the bibliography included in it.

2. Anne Drury Hall, "Epistle, Meditation, and Sir Thomas Browne's *Religio Medici,*" *PMLA* 94 (1979):234–46. Browne's debts to Montaigne have been a matter of curiosity ever since Thomas Keck's annotations to *Religio* in 1656, but no one has yet been able to speak with assurance about the *Essaies* as a "source" for *Religio.* See John Mulder, "Literary Scepticism: Montaigne and Sir Thomas Browne," *Dissertation Abstracts* 24 (1964):5389 (University of Michigan). The failure to locate a single "source" for *Religio* has, of course, not precluded scholarly attempts to record parallels and possible borrowings from other works, the most interesting of which is perhaps Allan Pritchard, "Wither's Motto and Browne's *Religio Medici,*" *Philological Quarterly* 40 (1961):302–07.

3. Henry Fielding, *Tom Jones,* ed. Fredson Bowers, 2 vols. (Oxford: Clarendon Press, 1974), 1:127.

4. *Coleridge on the Seventeenth Century,* ed. Roberta Florence Brinkley (Durham, 1955), 438.

5. Joan Webber, *The Eloquent "I": Style and Self in Seventeenth-Century Prose* (Madison, 1968), chap. 6, esp. 154–56.

6. See A. M. Luyendijk-Elshout, "Thomas Browne and the Study of Anatomy at Leiden," in *Sir Thomas Browne M.D. and the Anatomy of Man,* ed. J. A. van Dorsten (Leiden: E. J. Brill, 1982), 11–15. Browne's reference to "Fabrick" is presumably a reminiscence of Vesalius's anatomical work, *De Humani Corporis Fabrica* (On the fabric of the human body).

7. Leslie Stephen, "Sir Thomas Browne," in *Hours in a Library* (London: John Murray, 1917), 268. A. C. Howell, "Sir Thomas Browne as Wit and Humorist," *Studies in Philology* 42 (1945):564–77, surveys early responses to Browne's wit in their historical context and samples specific passages from the different works. See also C. A. Patrides, " 'The Best Part of Nothing': Sir Thomas Browne and the Strategy of Indirection,"

in *Approaches to Sir Thomas Browne,* ed. Patrides (Columbia, Mo., 1982), 31–48.

8. George Meredith, "An Essay on Comedy," in *Comedy,* ed. Wylie Sypher (New York: Doubleday, 1956), 49.

9. Quoted by Sypher, "The Meanings of Comedy," in ibid., 196.

10. Hall, "Epistle," 241.

11. *The Works of the Learned Isaac Barrow,* 3 vols, (London, 1686), 3:125, and *Several Sermons Against Evil-Speaking* (London, 1678), 80–81. Stuart M. Tave's *The Amiable Humorist: A Study in the Comic Theory and Criticism of the Eighteenth and Early Nineteenth Centuries* (Chicago: University of Chicago Press, 1960), 3–15, identifies Barrow's pivotal role in the gradual secularization of "good nature" and "cheerfulness" as criteria for the proper mode of wit. It should also be mentioned that the subject of religious joy often became a vehicle for the repression of dissidents. In a sermon on 1 Thessalonians 5:16, the same passage that spurred Barrow to deny the lumpishness of faith, Donne, rather extraordinarily, interrupts his preaching to remind some in the congregation "to testifie their devotion by more outward reverence" unless they wished to be reprimanded by "our Officers" (*The Sermons of John Donne,* ed. George R. Potter and Evelyn M. Simpson, 10 vols. [Berkeley: University of California Press, 1953–62], 10:222).

12. Owen Felltham, *Resolves, A Duple Century* (London, 1628), 43.

13. Horace, *Satires,* 1.4.133–34. I am quoting from the translation by Smith Palmer Bovie, *Satires and Epistles of Horace* (Chicago: University of Chicago Press, 1959).

14. R. J. Schoeck, *"O Altitudo!* Sir Thomas Browne, Scriptures, and Renaissance Tradition," *English Language Notes* 19 (1982):402–08.

15. Browne's place in the Renaissance revival of skepticism has been suggestively outlined by Louis I. Bredvold, *The Intellectual Milieu of John Dryden* (1934; reprint, Ann Arbor: University of Michigan Press, 1956), 40–46.

16. John Calvin, *Selections from His Writings,* ed. John Dillenberger (New York: Doubleday, 1971), 399. (*Institutes of the Christian Religion,* 3.2.23).

17. George Puttenham, *The Arte of English Poesie,* ed. Gladys Doidge Willcock and Alice Walker (Cambridge: Cambridge University Press, 1936), 225–26.

18. Johnson, "Life of Browne," in *Sir Thomas Browne,* ed. C. A. Patrides (Harmondsworth, 1977), 487–88.

19. Patrides, " 'The Best Part of Nothing,' " 33; Webber, *Eloquent "I,"* 181. On the issue of Browne's "merry-sadness," it is worth quoting Walter Savage Landor, who is, in turn, quoted approvingly by Meredith:

"Genuine humor and true wit require a sound and capacious mind, which is always a grave one" (*Comedy*, ed. Sypher, 19).

20. The line is preserved in Jean-Jacques Denonain's edition of *Religio Medici* (Cambridge, 1953), 103 (*RM*, 2.7).

21. Fish, *Self-Consuming Artifacts: The Experience of Seventeeth-Century Literature* (Berkeley, 1972), 372; Webber, *Eloquent "I,"* 182.

22. Webber, *Eloquent "I,"* 183.

23. *The Poems of Richard Corbett*, ed. J. A. W. Bennett and H. R. Trevor-Roper (Oxford: Clarendon Press, 1955), xxxi–ii. It should be noted that in the authorized version Browne corrected the final line from "Thy will be done though in my owne damnation" (MSS, 1642) to "Thy will be done, though in my owne undoing." The latter is not only less portentous but positively ambiguous if we think that in *Religio* the author has been "undoing" or revealing himself to the reader, a sense that is perfectly consonant with the essay format as described by Montaigne when he speaks in the preface to his *Essaies* of portraying "my selfe fully and naked." "Damnation" is thus not only erased from the text, but the possibility of it has been considerably softened by the suggestion, necessarily oblique given Browne's distrust of zealous proclamations, that his writing has been directed by the hand of God.

24. Raymond B. Waddington, "The Two Tables in *Religio Medici*," in *Approaches to Sir Thomas Browne*, ed. Patrides, 93–94. See also J. Sears McGee, *The Godly Man in Stuart England: Anglicans, Puritans, and the Two Tables, 1620–1670* (New Haven: Yale University Press, 1976), 171–234.

25. Anna K. Nardo, "Sir Thomas Browne: *Sub Specie Ludi*," *Centennial Review* 21 (1977):311–20.

26. Johan Huizinga, *Homo Ludens: A Study of the Play Element in Culture* (1944; reprint, Boston: Beacon Press, 1955), 158.

27. Margot Heinemann, *Puritanism and Theater: Thomas Middleton and Opposition Drama under the Early Stuarts* (Cambridge: Cambridge University Press, 1980), 235. This quotation notwithstanding, Heinemann's study is valuable for dispelling the prejudice of earlier generations that Puritans across the board were opposed to theater.

28. Quoted from the *Complete Prose Works of John Milton*, ed. Don M. Wolfe et al., 8 vols. to date (New Haven: Yale University Press, 1953–), 2:4–5.

29. Huntley, *Sir Thomas Browne*, (Ann Arbor, 1962), 107–17.

30. Calvin, *Selections from His Writings*, 419–21. (*Institutes*, 3.2.41–42.) See also Waddington, "The Two Tables in *Religio Medici*," 81–99.

31. Peter Heylyn, *A Brief and Moderate Answer to the Seditious and Scandalous Challenges of Henry Burton* (London, 1637), preface.

32. *Works*, ed. Wilkin, 1:352.

33. John Prynne, *Histriomastix* (London, 1633), 294. Browne defends a "laughing" Jesus as a sign of Christ's humanity in *PE,* 7.26, p. 588.

34. John Traugott, "Creating a Rational Rinaldo: A Study in the Mixture of the Genres of Comedy and Romance in *Much Ado About Nothing,*" *Genre* 15 (1982):176.

35. *Complete Prose Works of John Milton,* ed. Wolfe, 2.558 *(Areopagitica).*

Chapter Six

1, Kenelm Digby, *Observations Upon Religio Medici* (London, 1643), 2.

2. *Pseudodoxia Epidemica,* ed. Robbins, 2 vols (Oxford, 1981), 1:xxxix–xl.

3. Michel Foucault, *The Order of Things: An Archaeology of the Human Sciences* (New York: Random House, 1973), 40.

4. Burton, *The Anatomy of Melancholy,* ed. Holbrook Jackson, (1932; reprint, New York: Random House, 1977), 325–46, esp. 334 (pt. 3, sec. 4, mem. 1, subs 2).

5. Christopher Hill, *The Century of Revolution, 1603–1714* (1961; reprint, New York: W. W. Norton & Co., 1982), 77–80.

6. *Coleridge on the Seventeenth Century,* ed. Roberta Florence Brinkley (Durham, 1955), 451.

7. Frank L. Huntley, *"The Garden of Cyrus* as Prophecy," in *Approaches to Sir Thomas Browne,* ed. C. A. Patrides (Columbia, Mo., 1982), 132–33.

8. Achsah Guibbory, "Sir Thomas Browne's *Pseudodoxia Epidemica* and the Circle of Knowledge," *Texas Studies in Literature and Language* 18 (1976):489.

9. Robbins, ed., *Pseudodoxia Epidemica,* 2:725.

10. *The Works of George Herbert,* ed. F. E. Hutchinson, 2d ed. (Oxford: Clarendon Press, 1945), 121 ("Providence," l. 140).

11. Allen G. Debus, "Sir Thomas Browne and the Study of Colour Indicators," *Ambix* 10 (1962):29–36.

12. Keith Thomas, *Religion and the Decline of Magic* (New York: Charles Scribner's Sons, 1971), 342–43.

13. See Charles W. Bodemer, "Materialistic and Neoplatonic Influences in Embryology," in *Medicine in Seventeenth Century England,* ed. Allen G. Debus (Berkeley: University of California Press, 1974), 183–213, esp. 197–200.

14. Robbins, ed., *Pseudodoxia Epidemica,* 2:1141.

15. Ibid., 2:645.

16. See, respectively, Henry Thomas Buckle, *History of Civilization*

in England, 3 vols. (London: Longmans, Green, & Co., 1871), 1:365–66, and Basil Willey, *The Seventeenth Century Background* (1934; reprint, New York: Doubleday & Co., 1953), 60.

17. Guibbory, "Sir Thomas Browne's *Pseudodoxia Epidemica*," 493–99.

Chapter Seven

1. In viewing *Urne-Buriall* as in some sense "mimetic," I have been influenced by Leonard Nathanson, *The Strategy of Truth* (Chicago, 1967), chap. 7, and by Walter R. Davis, *"Urne Buriall:* A Descent into the Underworld," *Studies in the Literary Imagination* 10 (Fall 1977):73–87, but I differ from each in what I see as both the progress and, to some degree, the end of Browne's discourse. All modern discussions of the skeptical and paradoxical aspects of *Urne-Buriall,* including mine, owe a principal debt to James M. Cline, *"Hydriotaphia,"* in *Five Studies in Literature,* ed. B. H. Bronson et al., *University of California Publications in English* 8, no. 1 (1940):73–100.

2. Johnson, "Life of Browne," in *Sir Thomas Browne,* ed. C. A. Patrides (Harmondsworth, 1977), 492.

3. Thomas De Quincey, "Elements of Rhetoric," *Blackwood's Magazine* 24 (December 1828):894; Symonds, ed., *Religio Medici, Urn Burial, Christian Morals, and other Writings* (London: Walter Scott, 1886), 20; and Saintsbury, *A History of English Prose Rhythm* (London: Macmillan, 1912), 180–91.

4. Davis, *"Urne Buriall,"* 81.

5. Williamson, "The Purple of *Urn Burial,"* *Modern Philology* 62 (1964):114.

6. Gosse, *Sir Thomas Browne,* 205.

7. C. L. S. Linnell, *Norfolk Church Monuments* (Ipswich: Norman Adlard & Co., 1952), 13–14.

8. For information on Le Gros, see *Norfolk Archaeology* 3 (1852):91.

9. R. W. Ketton-Cremer, *A Norfolk Gallery* (London: Faber & Faber, 1948), 109–10.

10. *The Works of Sir Thomas Browne,* ed. Geoffrey Keynes, 4 vols. (London, 1964), 1:125.

11. John Whitefoot, *Death's Alarum* (London, 1656), dedicatory epistle.

12. *The Works of Sir Thomas Browne,* ed. Keynes, 3:134.

13. See Whitefoot, *Death's Alarum,* 28–29, and *Urne-Buriall,* 125, ll. 2–14. The overlapping ideas between the two works—the womb-tomb paradox, the allusion to Enoch and Elais in their "anomolous state of being," the emphasis on the Resurrection, and the reference to 1 Corin-

thians 15:52 ("for we shall not all sleep, but we all shall be changed"), accompanied by a recognition by both men of the textual uncertainty involving the translation of "change"—suggest, in their number and concentration, a stronger affiliation between the two works, I believe, than simply the separate, accidental replication of a few traditional, funerary sentiments.

14. *The Works of Sir Thomas Browne,* ed. Keynes, 3:123. In observing Browne's fondness for oratorical cadences, Austin Warren, "The Style of Sir Thomas Browne," *Kenyon Review* 13 (1951):680, suggests how the fifth chapter of *Urne-Buriall* relies frequently on the rhetorical figure of the *planus,* a dactyl followed by a trochee, and offers as a model the Latin *potentiam suam,* rendered in the Book of Common Prayer as "help and defend us." The connection between this rhythmic echo and reading the text in part as defensive consolation is subtle but perhaps not beyond the pale, given Browne's aural sensibilities.

15. Huntley, *Sir Thomas Browne,* (Ann Arbor, 1962), chap. 13. As several recent critics have observed, Huntley's masterful discussion of the two works can become overly schematic to the point of thoroughly subordinating *Urne-Buriall* as an artistic achievement to *The Garden of Cyrus.* They are right, but Huntley was seeking in part to restore *The Garden* to critical respectability, something that certainly needed doing given its almost complete neglect at the hands of nineteenth-century critics. A partially successful attempt at recovery had been made by Margaret Ash Heideman, "*Hydriotaphia* and *The Garden of Cyrus:* A Paradox and A Cosmic Vision," *University of Toronto Quarterly* 19 (1949):235–46.

16. Finch, "Sir Thomas Browne and the Quincunx," *Studies in Philology* 37 (1940):274–82.

17. Johnson, "Life of Browne, in *Sir Thomas Browne,* ed. Patrides, 494.

18. Dee, *The Elements . . . of Euclid* (London, 1570), preface.

19. Huntley, *"The Garden of Cyrus* as Prophecy," in *Approaches to Sir Thomas Browne,* ed. C. A. Patrides (Columbia, Mo., 1982), 141. Besides the difficulty of making a notoriously evasive term like "prophecy" apply to a work as oblique as *The Garden,* the main reservation I have about Huntley's argument is that Browne's statement that "all things began in order, so shall they end," etc., which Huntley identifies as the burden of the prophetic message, stands outside of the prophetic structure as Huntley defines it. "If one has to be wide awake in order to Prophesy," this hardly seems to be the condition of the speaker at the moment he utters his vision.

20. Stapleton, *The Elected Circle: Studies in the Art of Prose* (Princeton, 1973), 66.

21. *Coleridge on the Seventeenth Century,* ed. Roberta Florence Brinkley (Durham, 1955), 449.

22. Digby, *Observations Upon Religio Medici* (London, 1643), 2.

23. *The Works of Sir Thomas Browne,* ed. Keynes, 4:275. It should be noted that Evelyn's letter was written after, not before, the publication of *The Garden of Cyrus.* In his first edition of Browne's *Works* (1928–31), Keynes dated the letter 21 January 1657/58, a date occasionally still quoted by critics using this edition; but E. S. de Beer, "The Correspondence Between Sir Thomas Browne and John Evelyn," *Library* 4th ser., 19 (1939):103–106, argued persuasively for a date of two years later, which Keynes adopted in his revised edition of the *Works.* The issue is obviously important in any attempt to assess the traffic of ideas that flowed between the two men.

24. Cyrus the Elder had clear Royalist associations. The son of Philemon Holland had dedicated his father's translation of the *Cyropaedia* to Charles I in 1632 (the work was composed originally for Prince Henry, but with the prince's death in 1612 it was put on the shelf), and Evelyn himself continued this association in dedicating his *Sylva* (1664) to Charles II. There was even a supposed etymological link between "Cyrus" and "Sire," as Henry Peacham reports. (See *The Complete Gentleman,* ed. Virgil B. Heltzel [Ithaca, N.Y.: Cornell University Press, 1962], 25.) But during the Civil War and the Interregnum, the biblical Cyrus emerged to cast a more ambivalent light on this link. Cyrus's "annointment" by God was seen by Milton, for one, as a significant, biblically sanctioned, exception to the general Royalist assumption of the divine right of kings theory, while the special calling Cyrus received to liberate the Jews suffering captivity in Babylon was interpreted as giving authority to the whole notion of subjects rebelling against their king. See *The Complete Prose Works of John Milton* ed. Don M. Wolfe et al., 8 vols. to date (New Haven: Yale University Press, 1953–), 4:402–3, 435–37. By 1658, Cyrus the Elder could be perceived as Cromwell as well as Charles.

25. Martin, *Religio Medici and Other Works* (Oxford, 1964), 363, note to 11. 34–35, has an odd remark on the reference to the "Huntsman are up in America." "It is difficult to account for this statement save as evidence that 'the drowsy approaches of sleep' were having their effects. 'India' would be more suitable geographically, but less rhythmically pleasing." The reference is difficult only if we assume Browne is thinking in terms of daily rather than historical time. For the rise and fall of nations, see *RM,* 1.17, p. 18. Browne might also have had in mind Herbert's "Church Militant" with its westward movement of schism and destruction.

26. Edward Reynolds, *Works* (London; 1679), 931.

Chapter Eight

1. Abraham Cowley, *Poems,* ed. A. R. Waller (Cambridge: Cambridge University Press, 1905), 7 (preface to the 1656 edition of his *Poems*). Annabel Patterson, *Censorship and Interpretation: The Conditions of Writing and Reading in Early Modern England* (Madison: University of Wisconsin Press, 1984), refers, accurately, I believe, to Cowley's preface as a "a statement of literature's *temporary* neutrality" (137). Her account of Cowley's predicament during the Interregnum helps to differentiate further the kind of ambivalence Cowley felt about the relationship of imagination to history from Browne's more apparent acts of indifference (see 144–58). For Cowley, the Restoration reinspired his royalist muse; for Browne, the Restoration brought silence, as if the need to publish were no longer required.

2. C. D., "Sir Thomas Browne," *European Magazine,* 40 (1801):89–90. These and other biographical remarks published here appeared in a copy of Browne's *Work* (1686) owned by White Kennett, bishop of Peterborough. For information involving the delayed publication of *Christian Morals,* see Frank Huntley, *Sir Thomas Browne* (Ann Arbor, 1962), 224–27.

3. Stapleton, *The Elected Circle* (Princeton, 1973), 69; Huntley, *Sir Thomas Browne,* 227.

4. See *The Later Renaissance In England: Nondramatic Verse and Prose, 1600–1660,* ed. Herschel Baker (Boston: Houghton Mifflin Co., 1975), 518,719.

5. Quoted from Jeremiah S. Finch, "The Lasting Influence of Sir Thomas Browne," *Transactions and Studies of the College of Physicians of Philadelphia* 24 (1956):61.

6. See *The British Essayists,* ed. James Ferguson, 40 vols. (London: J. Richardson & Co., 1823), 38:128–29, and Saintsbury, *A History of English Prose Rhythm* (London: Macmillan, 1912), 267.

7. Finch, "The Lasting Influence of Sir Thomas Browne," 62–64.

8. Basic information on Browne and Lamb is contained in Joseph Seeman Iseman, *A Perfect Sympathy: Charles Lamb and Sir Thomas Browne* (Cambridge, Mass.: Harvard University Press, 1937); Finch, "The Lasting Influence of Sir Thomas Browne"; and Ruth M. Vande Kieft's valuable Ph.D. dissertation, "The Nineteenth Century Reputation of Sir Thomas Browne" (University of Michigan, 1957).

9. The quotations from Lamb appear, respectively, in *The Works of Charles and Mary Lamb,* ed. E. V. Lucas, 6 vols. (London: Methuen & Co., 1912), 2:195, 1:173, 2:31, 2:74.

10. Quoted from Vande Kieft, "The Nineteenth Century Reputation of Sir Thomas Browne," 91.

11. *The Works of Sir Thomas Browne,* ed. Geoffrey Keynes, 4 vols. (London, 1964), 2:xvii.

12. Matthiessen, *American Renaissance: Art and Expression in the Age of Emerson and Whitman* (London: Oxford University Press, 1941), 100–32. See also Sherman Paul, *The Shores of America: Thoreau's Inward Exploration* (Urbana: University of Illinois Press, 1958), 58–68; Herbert Childs, "Emily Dickinson and Sir Thomas Browne," *American Literature* 22 (1951):455–65; Austin Warren, "Emily Dickinson," *Sewanee Review* 65 (1957):565–86; and Jack L. Capps, *Emily Dickinson's Readings, 1836–1886* (Cambridge, Mass.: Harvard University Press, 1966), 66–68.

13. Brian Foley, "Herman Melville and the Example of Sir Thomas Browne," *Modern Philology* 81 (1984):265–77. See also Ruth M. Vande Kieft, " 'When Big Hearts Strike Together': the Concussion of Melville and Sir Thomas Browne," *Papers on Language and Literature* 5 (1969):39–50.

14. See, especially, *The Journals and Miscellaneous Notebooks of Ralph Waldo Emerson,* ed. William H. Gilman et al., 16 vols. (Cambridge, Mass.: Harvard University Press, 1960–82), 10:350: "The old writers, such as Montaigne, Milton, Browne, when they had put down their thoughts, jumped into their book bodily themselves, so that we have all that is left of them in our shelves; there is not a pinch of dust beside. The Norsemen write with a crowbar, & we with Gillot pens." Other relevant remarks found in the journals include those in 3:219–20, 255; 4:434; 5:95; 6:219; 15:12.

15. See Matthiessen, *American Renaissance,* 115–19.

16. Pater, "Sir Thomas Browne," *Macmillan's Magazine* 54 (May 1886):5–8; reprinted with minor revisions in *Appreciations* (London, 1922), 127–66.

17. Symonds, "Sir Thomas Browne," *Saturday Review* 17 (25 June 1864):794–95, and the introduction to his edition of *Religio Medici, Urn Burial, Christian Morals, and Other Writings* (London: Walter Scott, 1886); Stephen, "Sir Thomas Browne," *Cornhill Magazine* 33 (May 1871):596–611—revised version in *Hours in a Library,* 4 vols. (New York: G. P. Putnam's Sons, 1904), 2:1–41; and Strachey, "Sir Thomas Browne," *Independent Review* 8 (February 1906):158–69—reprinted in *Books and Characters,* French and English (New York, 1922), 27–38.

18. Strachey, *Books and Characters,* 36.

19. See Ronald J. Christ, *The Narrow Act: Borges' Art of Allusion* (New York: New York University Press, 1969), esp. 33, 42,n., 13,n.1, 141–47; Jorge Luis Borges, "Sir Thomas Browne," in *Inquisiciones* (Buenos Aires: Editorial Proa, 1925), 30–38.

20. T. S. Eliot, "Prose and Verse," *Chapbook* 22 (1921):3–10.

21. Willey, *The Seventeenth Century Background* (London, 1934), 49.

22. Laurence Stapleton, *The Elected Circle,* 3.

23. William Gass, *Habitations of the Word* (New York: Simon & Schuster, 1984), 113–40.

24. *The Poetry of Robert Frost,* ed. Edward Connery Lathem (New York: Holt, Rinehart, and Winston, 1969), 338–39 ("Never Again Would Birds' Song Be the Same").

Selected Bibliography

Primary Sources

1. Collected Works

Sir Thomas Browne's Works. Edited by Simon Wilkin. 4 vols. London: William Pickering, 1835–36. Contains extensive biographical material, some critical commentary. Reprints Johnson's "Life of Browne" and Digby's "Observations" on *Religio Medici.*

The Works of Sir Thomas Browne. Edited by Geoffrey Keynes. 2d ed. 4 vols. London: Faber & Faber, 1964. Brief prefaces, additional letters, and new material taken from manuscripts, but no critical commentary.

2. Selected Writings

Religio Medici and Other Works. Edited by L. C. Martin. Oxford: Clarendon Press, 1964. Other works include *UB, GC, LF* (plus manuscript version, Sloane 1862), and *CM.* Textual introduction, notes, critical commentary, index of authors cited. Reprints correspondence between Digby and Browne.

The Prose of Sir Thomas Browne. Edited by Norman Endicott. New York: New York University Press, 1968. Includes *RM, UB, GC, LF, CM;* selections from *PE, Miscellany Tracts,* notebooks (manuscript version of *LF*), and personal correspondences; chronology, introduction, textual and critical commentary, glossary, selected bibliography.

The Major Works. Edited by C. A. Patrides. Harmondsworth, England: Penguin Books, 1977. Besides containing printed works cited immediately above, it includes portions of *PE.* General introduction, critical commentary, dictionary of names, Browne's Latin translated, and Johnson's "Life of Browne" reprinted. An exemplary student edition.

3. Individual Works

Religio Medici. Edited by Jean-Jacques Denonain. Cambridge: Cambridge University Press, 1953. Introduction, extensive textual variants.

Pseudodoxia Epidemica. Edited by Robin Robbins. 2 vols. Oxford: Clarendon Press, 1981. General introduction, text thoroughly glossed, subject and source index, illustrations.

Secondary Sources

1. Bibliographies

Donovan, Dennis G. "Recent Studies in Browne." *English Literary Renaissance* 2 (1972):271–79. A convenient, topically arranged, annotated bibliography of selected scholarship and criticism from 1945 to 1969.

Donovan, Dennis G., Herman, Margaretha G. Hartley, and Imbrie, Anne E. *Sir Thomas Browne and Robert Burton: A Reference Guide*. Boston: G. K. Hall & Co., 1981. Annotated entries of writings about Browne from 1643 to 1977. Listings especially thorough from the romantics onward. Includes brief overview of author's critical reputation. A substantial supplement to, but not a substitute for, Keynes.

Keynes, Geoffrey. *A Bibliography of Sir Thomas Browne*. Rev. ed. Oxford: Clarendon Press, 1968. Detailed publishing description and history of all of Browne's writings; biographical and critical remarks about Browne listed chronologically from 1633 to 1800; from 1801 to 1966 arranged alphabetically by author; forerunners and imitators noted.

2. General

Bennett, Joan. *Sir Thomas Browne: "A Man of Achievement in Literature."* Cambridge: Cambridge University Press, 1962. Browne's life and writings are surveyed for their characteristic intelligence and good sense rather than their quaintness.

Breiner, Laurence A. "The Generation of Metaphor in Thomas Browne." *Modern Language Quarterly* 38 (1977):261–75. Argues that the "incompatability" of Browne's scientific, literary, and religious interests can be reconciled through a "covert 'master figure' " governing images of expansion and restriction in *UB, GC,* and *RM*.

Caldwell, Mark L. "The Transfigured 'I': Browne's *Religio Medici*." *Thought* 57 (1982):332–44. Pointedly distinguishing *RM* from modern autobiography, Caldwell argues for the relevance of Catholic meditative modes to Browne's particular yet universalized sense of self.

Cawley, Robert Ralston, and Yost, George. *Studies in Sir Thomas Browne*. Eugene: University of Oregon, 1965. Studies include "The Timeliness

of *Pseudodoxia Epidemica"* and "Sir Thomas Browne and His Reading,"
which originally appeared in 1933 (Cawley), and "Sir Thomas Browne
and Aristotle" (Yost). Browne's learning and research are emphasized.

Cline, James M. *"Hydriotaphia."* In *Five Studies in Literature,* edited by B.
H. Bronson. *University of California Publications in English* 8, no. 1
(1940):73–100. *UB* studied as paradox; first sustained defense of the
work's unity.

Coleridge, Samuel Taylor. "Sir Thomas Browne." In *Coleridge on the Seventeenth Century,* ed. Roberta Florence Brinkley. Durham: Duke University Press, 1955. Marginal jottings and critical meditations on the
man and his major works by one of Browne's great champions.

Croll, Morris W. *Style, Rhetoric, and Rhythm.* Edited by J. Max Patrick
et al. Princton: Princeton University Press, 1966. At least two of
Croll's studies from the 1920s reprinted here bear directly and im-
portantly on Browne but ought to be read in the context of the
forewords provided by John M. Wallace: " 'Attic Prose' in the Seventeenth Century" and "The Baroque Style in Prose."

Davis, Walter R. *"Urne Buriall:* A Descent into the Underworld." *Studies
in the Literary Imagination* 10 (1977):73–87. Sees *UB* as an imaginary
voyage of discovery.

Dunn, William P. *Sir Thomas Browne: A Study in Religious Philosophy.* Rev.
ed. Minneapolis: University of Minnesota Press, 1950. Examined in
his immediate intellectual milieu, Browne is seen as a religously
liberal antiquarian.

Endicott, N. J. "Sir Thomas Browne's *Letter to a Friend." University of
Toronto Quarterly* 36 (1967):68–86. A critically and biographically
informed discussion of the *Letter;* essay branches out to address larger
issues involving Browne's "humanism."

Finch, Jeremiah S. *A Catalogue of the Libraries of Sir Thomas Browne and
Dr. Edward Browne, his Son.* Leiden: E. J. Brill, 1986. A facsimile
reproduction of this rare but valuable document; includes commentary, notes and index.

————. *Sir Thomas Browne: A Doctor's Life of Science and Faith.* New York:
Henry Schuman, 1950. Informal but scholarly biography.

Fish, Stanley E. *Self-Consuming Artifacts: The Experience of Seventeenth-Century
Literature.* Berkeley: University of California Press, 1972. Browne is
charged with being a "bad physician" for not involving "the reader"
of *Religio Medici* in "the painful and exhausting process of self-ex-
amination and self-criticism."

Gosse, Edmund. *Sir Thomas Browne.* London: Macmillan & Co., 1905.
First book-length critical study of Browne: lively, opinionated, and
often fanciful.

Green, Peter, *Sir Thomas Browne.* British Council Pamphlet. London:

Longmans, Green & Co., 1959. A brisk, slightly over romanticized view of Browne that touches on many of the important topics.

Guibbory, Achsah. "Sir Thomas Browne's *Pseudodoxia Epidemica* and the Circle of Knowledge." *Texas Studies in Literature and Language* 18 (1976):486–99. Succinct examination of *PE,* relating it to Browne's larger epistemological concerns, which, in turn, are distinguished from Bacon's.

Hall, Anne Drury. "Epistle, Meditation, and Sir Thomas Browne's *Religio Medici.*" *PMLA* 94 (1979):234–46. Traces the work's generic affiliations to the anti-Ciceronian epistle and the religious meditation. Perhaps the best single study of *RM.*

Halley, Janet E. "Sir Thomas Browne's *The Garden of Cyrus* and the Real Character." *English Literary Renaissance* 15 (1985):100–121. Thoughtfully situates Browne's essay in a problematic relationship to the seventeenth-century universal language movement.

Houghton, Walter E. "The English Virtuoso in the Seventeenth Century." *Journal of the History of Ideas* 3, no. 1 (January 1942):51–73; no. 2 (April 1942):190–219. Charts the emergence, growth, and decline of a distinct sensibility that was, to some degree, Browne's.

Huntley, Frank L. *Sir Thomas Browne: A Biographical and Critical Study.* Ann Arbor: University of Michigan Press, 1962. Arguably the best full-length study of Browne: sympathetic to the wide range of ideas in his writings; biographical cruxes unraveled; detailed discussions of the individual works.

Johnson, Samuel. "Life of Browne." In *Christian Morals.* London, 1756. Reprinted in several editions of Browne's works (see above). The first essential critical examination of Browne's life and works.

Leroy, Olivier. *Le Chevalier Thomas Browne (1605–1682): Medecin, Styliste & Metaphysicien.* Paris: Librarie J. Gamber, 1931. A wide-angle analysis of Browne divided into four sections: life, thought, art, and criticism.

Löffler, Arno. *Sir Thomas Browne als Virtuoso.* Nuremberg: Hans Carl Verlag, 1972. Argues that Browne's later works (*UB, GC,* and *LF*) reflect the enthusiasm for collecting and observing rarities that characterized the virtuosi in the mid-seventeenth century.

Mazzeo, Joseph Anthony. "Seventeenth-Century English Prose: The Quest for a Natural Style." *Mosaic* 6 (1973):107–44. Browne escapes any simple Attic/Asian dichotomy in this wide-ranging, critically informed discussion of the major stylistic issues of the period.

Merton, Egon Stephen. *Science and Imagination in Sir Thomas Browne.* New York: King's Crown Press, 1949. Analyzes some of the major scientific and philosophical issues that fascinated Browne and his contemporaries, and attempts to define the elusive relationship in Browne between scientific and artistic modes of thinking.

Nathanson, Leonard. *The Strategy of Truth: A Study of Sir Thomas Browne.* Chicago: University of Chicago Press, 1967. A comprehensive attempt to assess the specific relevance of a Neoplatonic epistemology for understanding the thematic and structural principles of Browne's works. Individual readings of the major works exclusive of *LF* and *CM*.

Pater, Walter. "Sir Thomas Browne." In *Appreciations.* London: Macmillan & Co., 1922. Browne appears positively spectral in this memorable, fin-de-siècle assessment of his life and writings. Originally appeared in 1886.

Patrides, C. A., ed. *Approaches to Sir Thomas Browne: The Ann Arbor Tercentenary Lectures and Essays.* Columbia: University of Missouri Press, 1982. Previously unpublished essays on a wide variety of topics by notable scholars.

Raven, Charles E. *English Naturalists from Neckam to Ray.* Cambridge: Cambridge University Press, 1947. Chapter on Browne stresses his modernity.

Stapleton, Laurence. *The Elected Circle: Studies in the Art of Prose.* Princeton: Princeton University Press, 1973. Chapter on Browne ranges suggestively over the major works.

Stephen, Leslie. "Hours in a Library: No. I—Sir Thomas Browne." *Cornhill Magazine* 23 (May 1871):596–611. A Coleridgean reading of Browne as a mystic with a sense of humor.

Strachey, Lytton. "Sir Thomas Browne." In *Books and Characters, French and English.* New York: Harcourt, Brace, & Co., 1922. An appreciative defense of Browne's Latinate style; concentrates mostly on *UB*.

Warren, Austin. "The Style of Sir Thomas Browne." *Kenyon Review* 13 (Autumn 1951):674–87. Still remains the best introduction to Browne's style, or styles, as Warren makes clear.

Webber, Joan. "Sir Thomas Browne: Art as Recreation." In *The Eloquent "I": Style and Self in Seventeenth-Century Prose.* Madison: University of Wisconsin Press, 1968. Analyzes the multitextured nature of self-revelation in "Anglican" Browne's *Religio Medici*.

Whallon, William. "Hebraic Synonymy in Sir Thomas Browne. *English Literary History* 28 (1961):335–52. Counters Croll and other classically oriented studies by arguing for Scripture as an important stylistic influence on Browne.

Wiley, Margaret L. *The Subtle Knot: Creative Scepticism in Seventeenth-Century England.* London: George Allen & Unwin, 1952. Browne's double—and paradoxical—commitment to reason and faith is set in an historical tradition that includes Donne, Baxter, Taylor, and Glanvill.

Willey, Basil. *The Seventeenth Century Background: Studies in the Thought of the Age in Relation to Poetry and Religion.* London: Chatto & Windus, 1934. Browne figures prominently as a "great amphibium" inhabiting and holding in balance the divided and distinguished worlds of the seventeenth century.

Williamson, George, "The Purple of *Urn Burial.*" *Modern Philology* 62 (1964):110–17. Emphasizing the occasion of *UB,* Williamson seeks to define "the rational structure that actually informs its eloquence."

Wilson, F. P. *Seventeenth Century Prose.* Berkeley: University of California Press, 1960. The stylist, not the thinker, is the subject.

Wise, James N. *Sir Thomas Browne's "Religio Medici" and Two Seventeenth-Century Critics.* Columbia: University of Missouri Press, 1973. The two critics are Sir Kenelm Digby and Alexander Ross, whose controversial response to Browne's work are given detailed examination.

Ziegler, Dewey Kiper. *In Divided and Distinguished Worlds: Religion and Rhetoric in the Writings of Sir Thomas Browne.* Cambridge, Mass.: Harvard University Printing Office, 1943. Browne is attacked, once again, for playing with sacred truths and for reputedly reducing religion to rhetoric. Concentrates almost entirely on *Religio Medici.*

Index

Adolph, Robert, 166n15,n18
Aesop, 5
Agrippa, Cornelius, 28
Aldrovandi, Ulisse, 96
Allen, Phyllis, 161
Antipater (Macedonian general), 72, 73
Aristotle, 7, 10, 11, 31, 107, 113, 147
Arnold, Matthew, 155
Aubrey, John, 1, 9
Augustine, 76

Bacon, Edmund, 51
Bacon, Francis, 7, 11, 22, 26–39, 41, 44,
  61, 64–65, 95–97, 117–18, 163n25;
  Works cited: *Advancement of Learning,* 5,
  26, 28, 30, 32–33, 36, 95, 97; *New At-
  lantis,* 27, *New Organon,* 27, 97
Bacon, Nicholas, 12, 35, 134, 137–39, 143
Bainbridge, John, 8
Baker, Herschel, 175n4
Barrow, Isaac, 169n11
Barthes, Roland, 57
Bastwick, John, 43
Bates, Henry, 97
Baxter, Richard, 53
Bayly, Lewis, 150
Beaumont, Francis, 8
Bennett, J. A. W., 170n23
Bennett, Joan, 14, 159n1, 161n35, 162n2,
  166n21
Bible (Scripture), 5, 28, 29, 33, 40, 41, 53,
  54, 78, 85, 87, 91, 103, 110, 113–17,
  137, 143, 147, 148, 174n24; *Individual
  books:* Acts, 100; 2 Chronicles, 143; 1
  Corinthians, 78, 129; 2 Corinthians, 53;
  Ephesians, 149; Ezra, 143; Isaiah, 87,
  132, 143; John, 85, 86, 115–17; Luke,
  44, 48; Matthew, 44, 91; 1 Peter, 92;
  Psalms, 103; Romans, 84; 1 Samuel, 141
Billingsley, Henry, 141
Bodemer, Charles W., 171n13
Booty, John, 41
Borges, Jorge Luis, 156
Boswell, James, 152
Bottrall, Margaret, 168n1
Bovie, Smith Palmer, 169n13

Bowers, Fredson, 168n3
Boyle, Robert, 21, 37, 67, 117
Briggs, Henry, 8
Bradshaw, John, 52
Bredvold, Louis, 169n15
Brinkley, Roberta Florence, 162n1, 165n2,
  166n9, 168n28,n4, 171n6, 173n21
Brome, Alexander, 20
Bronson, B. H., 172n1
Browne, Dorothy (Mileham), 13–14
Browne, Edward, 2, 6, 12, 13, 15, 18,
  147–48
Browne, Elizabeth, 2, 13, 16, 18, 23
Browne, Robert, 49
Browne, Sir Thomas
WORKS:
  Christian Morals, xii, 3, 16, 23, 37, 59,
    62, 72, 147–51, 153
  Garden of Cyrus, The, xii, xiii, 22, 35–36,
    51, 60, 67, 68, 71, 95, 12, 134–47,
    155
  Hydriotaphia, or Urne-Buriall, xii, xiii, 18,
    22, 35, 37, 38, 59, 60, 62, 63, 67,
    69, 95, 115, 120–35, 139, 142, 144,
    145, 147, 148, 153, 154, 155, 157
  Letter to a Friend, A, xii, xiii, 18, 23, 68–
    75, 76, 95, 148, 154
  Miscellany Tracts, 23, 75, 155. See also: "A
    Prophecy concerning the Future State of
    Several Nations," 112; "Observations
    upon Several Plants mention'd in
    Scripture," 114; "Of Garlands and
    Coronary or Garland-plants," 22; "Of
    Languages and particularly of the Saxon
    Tongue," 6, 23
  Posthumous Works, 23
  Pseudodoxia Epidemica, xii, xiii, 4, 8, 21,
    24, 25, 28, 31–35, 58–60, 62, 63,
    67, 68, 71, 75, 95–119, 124, 145,
    147, 155
  Religio Medici, xii, xiii, 1, 3–5, 9, 11,
    12, 17–23, 28–32, 40, 41, 44–49,
    54–56, 60–63, 65, 66, 68, 76–95,
    97, 112, 121, 122, 127, 129, 145,
    147, 150, 155, 161n28
  Repertorium, 54, 134

MISCELLANEOUS WRITINGS:
"Amico Clarissimo, De Enecante Garrulo
Suo," 8; Amico Opus Arduum
Meditanti," 8; "Camdeni Insignia," 8;
"Natalitia Collegii Pembrochiani
Oxonii," 7; "Notes on the Natural
History of Norfolk," 22; "On Dreams,"
23

Browne, Thomas, Jr., 15–16, 18, 51–52
Buckle, Henry Thomas, 118
Burton, Henry, 43, 92
Burton, Robert, 64, 65, 77, 100
Bush, Douglas, 59
Butler, Samuel, 21

Caius, John, 9
Calvin, John, 86, 92, 170n30
Camden, William, 8
Capps, Jack L., 176n12
Cardano, Girolamo, 28, 34
Carlile, Joan, 14
Carlyle, Thomas, 155
Carter, John, 50, 51
Cato, the Elder (Censor), 5
Cato, the Younger (Minor), 127
Cawley, Robert Ralston, 162n5
Chalmers, Gordon Keith, 162n2, 164n32
Charles I, 9, 43, 90, 174n24
Charles V, 72, 73, 138
Charleton, Walter, 117
Childs, Herbert, 176n12
Christ, Ronald J., 176n19
Cicero, 6, 7, 61, 64–66
Clayton, Thomas, 8
Cline, James M., 172n1
Cohen, I. Bernard, 163n12
Coleridge, Samuel Taylor, 23, 24, 56–58,
    67, 75, 77, 101, 142, 154
Comenius John Amos, 5
Colie, Rosalie L., 162n5
Collinson, Patrick, 164n6
Copernicus, 10, 30, 38
Corbett, Richard, 8, 49, 170n23
Cowley, Abraham, xiv, 147
Croll, Morris, 64, 65, 166n15
Cromwell, Oliver, 52, 174n24
Crooke, Andrew, 19, 20
Crossley, James, 154
Cullender, Rose, 17
Curtis, Mark H., 161n20, 162n48
Cyrus, the Elder, 136, 143
Cyrus, the Younger, 136, 137, 143

Dante Alighieri, 115
Davis, Walter, 128, 172n1
de Beer, E. S., 159n1, 174n23
Debus, Allen G., 171n11
Dee, John, 141
Democritus, 79
Demosthenes, 6
Denonain, Jean-Jacques, 167n20
De Quincey, Thomas, 67, 127, 154
Descartes, Rene, 38, 96
Dick, Oliver Lawson, 163n7
Dickens, A. G., 42, 43
Dickinson, Emily, 154
Digby, Kenelm, 19, 20, 77, 95, 142–43
Donne, John, 1, 116, 156, 169n11
Dorset, Earl of. See Sackville, Edward
Dugdale, William, 22
Duncon, Samuel, 20, 93
Dunton, John, 76
Duny, Amy, 17
Dutton, Thomas, 3
Dryden, John, 20
Dyer, Edward, 8

Edward VI, 42
Eliot, T. S., 58, 156
Emerson, Ralph Waldo, 57, 154, 155
Endicott, Norman, 3, 72, 74, 167n21,n26
Erasmus, Desiderius, 5, 77–79
Euclid, 8, 141
Evans, John T., 165n21
Evelyn, John, 1, 18, 22, 143

Fabricius of Acquapendente, 10
Fawkes, Guy, 43
Ferguson, James, 175n6
Felltham, Owen, 83
Fielding, Henry, 77
Finch, Jeremiah S., 6, 68, 135, 153,
    159n1,n2, 160n9,n31, 162n2,
    165n18,n19, 166n21, 175n5,n8
Fish, Stanley E., 56, 57, 87–89, 159n1
Foley, Brian, 176n13
Forster, E. M., 156
Foucault, Michel, 171n3
Foxe, John, 42, 45
Frere, Daniel, 19
Frost, Robert, 157
Fuller, Thomas, 49, 88

Galen, 10, 11, 108
Galileo, 10, 27
Gass, William, 156, 157

Gesner, Konrad, 96
Gilbert, William, 36, 38, 103
Gilman, William H., 176n14
Glanville, Joseph, 117
Godwin, William, 17
Gosse, Edmund, 17, 57, 131, 160n2
Green, I. M., 165n23
Greville, Fulke, 8
Grew, Nehemiah, 38, 39
Guibbory, Achsah, 171n8, 172n17

Hakewill, George, 33
Hall, Anne Drury, 81, 168n2
Hall, Joseph, 49, 54, 133, 134
Hall, Marie Boas, 37
Hartlib, Samuel, 5
Harvey, William, 9, 10, 26, 38
Hattaway, Michael, 163n17
Hazlitt, William, 17, 23
Heideman, Margaret Ash, 173n15
Heinemann, Margot, 170n27
Heltzel, Virgil B., 161n43
Henry VIII, 42
Heraclitus, 79
Herbert, George, 25, 29, 108, 109, 116
Hermes Trismegistus, 30
Herrick, Robert, 1
Heylyn, Peter, 53, 92, 93
Heywood, John, 8
Hill, Christopher, 25, 171n5
Hill, W. Speed, 164n2
Hobbes, Thomas, 39, 98, 117
Holtgen, Karl Joseph, 167n22
Homer, 136
Hooke, Robert, 37
Hooker, Richard, 40, 41, 58
Horace, 7, 8, 77, 83, 84, 122
Howell, A. C., 168n7
Howell, James, 20
Hues, Robert, 8
Huizinga, Johan, 90
Hunter, Michael, 162n3,n6, 163n12
Huntley, Frank L., 8, 35, 50, 69, 102,
    134, 142, 145, 148, 159n1,
    160n2,n10,n11,n16, 161n24,
    161n26,n42, 162n2, 163n26,
    167n22,n26, 170n29, 175n2
Hutchinson, F. E., 162n4, 171n10
Hutchinson, Francis, 17
Hutchinson, Sara, 24

Ireton, Henry, 52
Iseman, Joseph Seeman, 175n8

Isham, Gyles, 161n34
Isocrates, 6

Jackson, Holbrook, 171n4
James I, 42–44
Johnson, Samuel, 3, 23, 35, 57–59, 86, 94,
    127, 135, 136, 145, 152, 153, 159n1
Jones, R. F., 33, 161n27, 166n15
Jonson, Ben, 1, 8
Jordan, W. K., 54
Joubert, Laurent, 33, 95
Joyce, James, 58, 67
Juliana of Norwich, 76

Keck, Thomas, 20, 168n2
Kennett, Dr. White, 159n1, 175n2
Ketton-Cremer, R. W., 164n13, 165n20,
    172n10
Keynes, Geoffrey, xiii, 154, 160n11,
    161n40,n42, 162n44,n46,
    172n10,n12,n14, 174n23
Kierkegaard, S., 80, 84
Kippis, Andrew, 3
Knox, Vicesimus, 152

Lactantius, 118
Lamb, Charles, 23, 74, 153, 154
Landor, Walter Savage, 169n19
Lathem, Edward Connery, 177n24
Laud, William, 43, 44, 48, 49, 54, 90, 93
Leach, Arthur F., 160n19
Le Gros, Charles, 132
Le Gros, Thomas, 22, 51, 121, 122, 128,
    132, 133
Leiden, 4
Le Strange, Hamon, 165n21
Letts, Malcolm, 17
Lewyn, Justinian, 12, 51
Lily, William, 5
Linacre, Thomas, 8, 9
Linnell, C. L. S., 172n7
Löffler, Arno, 159n1
Loveday, Robert, 68
Low, Anthony, 163n27
Lucan, 77
Lucas, E. V., 175n9
Luyendijk-Elshout, A. M., 168n6
Lushington, Thomas, 8, 9, 12
Lyttleton, George, 16
Lytton, Edward G. E. Bulwer, 58

Mantuan, (Baptista Mantuanus), 5
Marlowe, Christopher, 29

Marvell, Andrew, xii, 54, 137
Martin, L. C., xiii, 174n25
Mary Tudor, 42
Matthiessen, F. O., 154, 176n15
Mazzeo, J. A., 166n15
McGee, J. Sears, 170n25
Melville, Herman, 23, 154, 155
Mercurio, Scipio, 95
Meredith, George, 79, 169n19
Merrett, Christopher, 22
Merton, Egon Stephen, 159n1, 162n2, 164n29
Merton, Robert K., 162n6
Michelangelo, 110, 111
Milton, John, xii, 1, 2, 4, 5, 7, 38, 54, 91, 111, 118, 156
Montaigne, Michel de, 20, 64, 65, 75, 145, 168n2
Montpellier, 4, 8, 9–11
More, Henry, 38
More, Sir Thomas, 42
Morris, G. C. R., 160n2

Nardo, Anna K., 89
Nathanson, Leonard, 47, 162n2, 163n18, 172n1
Newton, Isaac, 27, 38
Nieremberg, Juan Eusebius, 104
Norwich, 1, 12, 13, 18, 22, 49–55, 132–34

Olney, James, 168n1
Origen, 46, 48
Osborne, Francis, 21
Osler, William, 17
Ovid, 5
Oxford, 4, 12

Padua, 4, 9, 10
Paracelsus, 11, 28–30
Parks, George B., 161n27
Pascal, Blaise, 65
Paston, Robert, 22
Pater, Walter, 23, 69, 74, 155
Patrick, J. Max, 166n15
Patrides, C. A., 86, 160n6, 163n23, 164n28, 165n28, 165n4, 166n7, 168n7, 167n18, 170n24, 171n7, 172n2, 173n17,n19
Patterson, Annabel, 175n1
Paul, St., 25, 78, 79, 84, 86, 100, 129, 141, 149
Paul, Sherman, 176n12

Peacham, Henry, 161n43, 174n24
Pebworth, Ted-Larry, 166n15
Peele, George, 8
Pembroke College (Broadgates Hall), 6–9
Pepys, Samuel, 20
Perkins, William, 88
Persius, 70
Pettus, Sir John, 69
Pharmacopoei Londoniensis, 13
Philosophical Transactions (Royal Society), 12, 69
Plato, 30, 38, 109
Pliny (Caius Plinius Secundus), 96, 104, 108
Plutarch, 15
Popkin, Richard H., 163n9
Porta, Giambattista della, 28, 34, 36, 135
Post, Jonathan F. S., 166n21
Potter, George R., 169n11
Power, Henry, 10
Primerose, James, 33, 95
Pritchard, Allan, 168n2
Proclus, 9
Prynne, William, 43, 90, 91, 93
Puttenham, George, 86
Pythagoras, 30, 35, 79, 148

Rabelais, François, 11, 77, 79
Raphael of Urbino, 110, 111
Ray, John, 18
Reynolds, Edward, 52–54, 144
Ridley, Nicholas, 42
Riviere, Lazare, 10
Robbins, Robin, xiii, 24, 113, 160n14, 162n47,n49, 163n21, 171n2,n9, 171n15
Rogers, John, 42
Ross, Alexander, 20, 21, 56, 57
Rossi, Paolo, 28, 163n18
Royal College of Physicians, 9, 13, 15
Royal Society, 7, 8, 27, 117, 142
Ruskin, John, 155
Russell, Conrad, 164n6
Rye, Walter, 165n21

Sackville, Edward (fourth Earl of Dorset), 19
Saintsbury, George, 128, 175n6
Savile, Sir Henry, 7
Scaliger, Julius, 6, 72, 74, 96
Schoeck, R. J., 169n14
Scott, Sir Walter, 17
Seneca, 6, 65, 94
Sennertus, Daniel, 11
Serapion (the Moor), 104
Shakespeare, William, 77–79, 99, 113

Shapiro, Barbara J., 163n12, 163n4, 164n32
Shaw, A. Batty, 161n31
Sidney, Sir Philip, 79, 136
Simpson, Evelyn, 169n11
Sinclair, H. M., 161n21
Socrates, 45, 127
Solomon, 29, 91, 148
Spedding, James, 163n8, 164n4, 166n32
Spenser, Edmund, 136
Spratt, Thomas, 27
Stapleton, Laurence, 142, 148
Stephen, Leslie, 77, 155
Strachey, Lytton, 57, 61, 155, 156, 159n1
Symonds, J. A., 69, 127, 155
Sypher, Wylie, 169n9,n10, 170n19

Tave, Stuart M., 169n11
Tennyson, Alfred, 156
Tertullian, 31, 85
Theophrastus, 10
Thomas, Keith, 12, 117, 161n32, 171n12
Thoreau, Henry David, 154
Tillotson, John, 46
Tillyard, E. M. W., 168n27
Tomlins, Richard, 7
Toynbee, Margaret, 161n34
Traugott, John, 93
Trevor-Roper, H. R., 170n23
Trumbull, William, 15
Tuke, Samuel, 15
Tyacke, Nicholas, 164n27
Tyler, Dorothy, 17, 161n38

Vande Kieft, Ruth M., 175n8,n10, 176n13
Van Dorsten, J. A., 168n6
Varro, Marcus Terentius, 140
Vaughan, Henry, xii, 1

Vesalius, Andreas, 10, 168n6
Virgil, 6, 7, 136, 140
Vos, Alvin, 166n15

Waddington, Raymond B., 170n24,n30
Walker, Alice, 169n17
Walker, D. P., 46
Waller, A. R., 174n1
Walton, Isaac, 5
Warnke, Frank J., 165n4
Warren, Austin, 56, 173n14, 176n12
Webber, Joan, 87, 88, 159n1, 168n5
Weber, Max, 162n6
Webster, Charles, 27
Westfall, Richard S., 162n6
Whicher, Stephen E., 166n6
Whitefoot, John, 3–5, 13–14, 18, 51, 68, 133–34, 159n1, 172n13
Wilding, Michael, 165n28
Wiley, Margaret L., 159n1
Wilkin, Simon, 15, 159n1, 160n5, 162n45, 170n32
Willcock, Gladys Doidge, 169n17
Willey, Basil, 118, 156
Williams, Charles, 160n2
Williamson, George, 59, 129
Wilmot, John, Earl of Rochester, 15
Winchester School, The, 4–7
Wolfe, Don M., 160n12, 170n28, 171n35, 174n24
Wood, Anthony a, 4
Wotton, Henry, 5
Wren, Christopher, Sr., 25
Wren, Christopher, 15
Wren, Matthew, 49, 54

Xenophon, 136, 143

Yost, George, 162n2